Italian Aviation Units
in the
First World War
Volume 3
Roberto Gentilli

ISBN: 978-1-953201-92-8
Text © 2024 Roberto Gentilli
Text edited by: Colin Owers
Cover Painting: Thomasz Sadzinica
Color Profiles: Bob Pearson
Design and layout: Jack Herris
Cover design: Aaron Weaver
Digital photo editing: Jack Herris

Books for Enthusiasts by Enthusiasts
www.aeronautbooks.com

Table of Contents

Cover Painting: In one of the most legendary aviation feats of the war, Italian SVAs drop leaflets on Vienna on 9 August 1918. SVA Number 12736 in the foreground carried d'Annunzio in the front cockpit. It is missing its Lion of St. Mark emblem, which was applied *after* the flight.

Above: Italian aircraft were exhibited in New York in 1919; an Ansaldo Balilla, an SVA, and a Caproni Ca.4 triplane can be seen.

Above: Paola Ruffo di Calabria, queen of the Belgians until 2013, visiting the Spad of her father in the Italian Air Force Museum.

Part 7: The Fighter Squadrons from April 1916 (continued)

73ª Squadriglia

Above: An Aviatik of the Sezione Aviatik of Aviano. The first pilot on the left is Pier Ruggero Piccio.

This unit was born as Sezione Aviatik of Aviano, with commander cap. Ferruccio Coppini. It was equipped with four Aviatik with Salmson Canton-Unné 125 hp motor, and with cap. Coppini there were the pilots s.tenenti Guido Keller (an extravagant artist, one of the most eccentric figures of Italian aviation) Gustavo Hermann and Vittorio Bergonzi, soldati Gino Capasso and baron Gastone Della Noce, a pioneer of aviation, born in 1875. Its equipment included Aviatiks 463, 467, 472, 473, 474 with Salmson Canton Unné 125 hp motors and Farmans 557, 561, 562, 807 and 810 all with Fiat 100 hp engine. More pilots appeared in its rolls: *sold*. Giovanni Girardini and Alessandro Borgato. On 22 November it moved to Verona from where it began flying constant patrol flights with the Aviatiks carrying gunners and on 1 December it became 4ª Squadriglia Caccia.

In December the unit joined the new III Gruppo, flying very little on account of the weather. On 11 January 1916 *cap*. Fernando Sanità, coming from the 3ª Caccia, became commander. In February the unit got new Aviatiks with Canton Unné 140 hp engine 680, 691, 692, 693 and 696. On 19 February 1916 test pilot Francesco Brach Papa flew with the squadron, testing Lloyd C.II 42.11 of Flik 7 which had landed behind Italian lines on 21 December 1915, many pilots of the 4ª then frequently flew this plane.

In March 1916 three new pilots flew with this unit, *soldati* Luigi Lucchini, Antonio Nava and Gustavo Rizzoli, who immediately raised to the rank of *caporale*.

"*On 20 March while a thick fog covered the sky, alarm announced the arrival of enemy aircraft* – so wrote Carlo Monzù – *Ignoring the bad weather conditions, our airmen climbed above 800 meters where they found a clear sky; they attacked the Austrians and drove them away, then landing on high mountains in harsh places where only their bravery could challenge and win.*" *S.ten.* Keller landed at S. Anna di Alfaredo, *cap.* Coppini at Rivoli Veronese and Dalla Noce, now a *sottotenente*, at Ferrara di Montebaldo, wrecking Aviatik 682.

Above: Aviatik 472 of the 4ª Squadriglia at Aviano. (Archive Centro Culturale Polivalente)

On 27 March the unit sent up no less than eight aircraft to contrast a strong Austrian attack against Verona, using together with the Aviatiks also Lloyd 42.11. In Early April it got Aviatiks 140 hp 1423 and 1424. The 4ª Caccia, with eight pilots and eight Aviatik Salmson became 73ª Aviatik on 15 April 1916, part of III Gruppo.

On 1 May 1916 *soldato* G. Battista Chesta was killed by the propeller of Aviatik 472 as he was trying to put off a fire. On 10 May the unit moved to S. Anna d'Alfaedo, some 10 miles north, where it remained until September, and then it returned to Verona.

On 1 January 1917 the 73ª Squadriglia da difesa with its commander *cap.* Sanità had pilots *cap.* Arnaldo Bevagna, *s.ten.* Gino Tonietti and *serg.* Giuseppe Pascoli. It was re-equipped with SAMLs 1569, 1570, 1571, 1575, 1590 and after the winter lull it resumed standing patrol flights in March 1917. On 10 April it was assigned to the new IX Gruppo.

On 16 April 1917 *cpr.* Eugenio Beria d'Argentine attacked an enemy aircraft during a standing patrol above Riva. On 24 April 1917 *s.ten.* Leopoldo Eleuteri with gunner *sold.* Gresino dueled with an enemy aircraft over the Pasubio and saw it going away in a dive. Another duel, with possibly a victory for Guido Keller took place on that same day. This pilot also on 26 May had a combat with an enemy. On 29 May (23, according to other sources) SAML 1586 crashed on landing returning from an alarm flight. Its pilot *cpr.* Carlo Brambilla was killed, the gunner Arturo Marzari

was wounded. On 8 June *serg.* Alfredo Tagliapietra had another inconclusive air combat against two enemies above Nogaredo. On 19 June the 73ª sent up six SAMLs to escort a mission of Caproni bombers, with pilots *cap.* Sanità, *ten.* Flaminio Avet, *ten.* Clemente Giorelli, *serg.* Giuseppe Pascoli, *serg.* Tagliapietra and *cpr.* Beria, the observers *ten.* Pasquale De Anseris, Raoul Simonini and Ernesto Udine and three gunners, repeatedly engaging the enemy.

On 7 July 1917 *cap.* Sanità was shifted and *cap.* Mario Van Axel Castelli became the new commander. In August 1917 the 73ª Squadriglia had pilots *capitani* Van Axel and Giorelli, *tenenti* Avet and Fernando Armati, *s.ten.* Eleuteri, *aspiranti* Beria d'Argentine and Pascoli, *serg.* Giuseppe Negri, *caporali* Pasquale Ceccarelli and Rinaldo Bulgheroni, the observers *tenenti* De Anseris, Udine, Lorenzo Bellei, Corrado Cortese, Ugo Fischetti, and *s.tenenti* Raoul Simonini and Tullio Tagliabue, and the gunners (many of them later becoming pilots) Boccafoglia, Bottero, Corti, Gresino, Lanza, Marrocchi and Marzari.

On 20 September 1917 the 73ª Squadriglia, still at Verona in the IX Gruppo, was re-numbered as 121ª Squadriglia SAML. Guido Keller received a *Medaglia d'Argento* for his combat on 24 April.

A new 73ª Squadriglia was formed in Macedonia on 10 November 1917 from the 1ª Sezione of the 83ª Squadriglia, operating from Thessaloniki supporting the Italian 35ª Divisione in Macedonia. Its commander was *ten.* Ernesto Bonavoglia, with *ten.* Giovanni Righi, *aiut. batt.* Giovanni

Above: At Aviano, Aviatik 474 armed with a Fiat and a Villar Perosa gun. The Salmson Canton-Unné was a radial water-cooled engine.

Miracca and *serg.* Giovanni Contò. It was equipped with Nieuport 17 and 11, and it also had one Spad. It was based at "quota 619" (Hill 619) 20 km south of Monastir.

On 1 January 1918, *ten.* Bonavoglia was badly wounded in an accident with a Nieuport 17, and *ten.* Righi took up command. On 29 January Righi also returned to base wounded in the face by an explosive bullet, and he crash landed. Therefore, on early February the unit got a new commander, *ten. pil.* Vittorino De Biasi. In the early spring of 1918, the 73ª received some Nieuport 27: in March it had on strength *ten.* De Biasi, *s.ten.* Eugenio Beria d'Argentine, *aiutante di battaglia* Contò and *soldato* (later *cpr.*) Guerrino Randi.

On 4 April De Biasi damaged a Nieuport 27 on account of bad weather, and he smashed one more on 11 April due to an engine failure. In that same mission Contò chased and attacked an enemy aircraft, firing 150 bullets, but he was forced to land with his airplane damaged.

On 25 May 1918 the 73ª Squadriglia joined the new XXI Gruppo. It also used one Spad. On 26 June *cpr.* Randi force

landed a Nieuport 27 with a stopped engine and smashed it. The next day the rudder pedals of a Nieuport broke under Randi's feet, but the pilot nursed his fighter back to base.

In the summer of 1918, the 73ª Squadriglia was completely re-equipped with Hanriots, receiving no less than 26 of them, for its four pilots. In September, reinforced both in pilots and aircraft, it formed a second flight, while its 1st flight was deployed at Uskub. The unit suffered from the bad condition of many engines, but in the month, it put up 80 combat missions, deploying also to advanced landing fields. In September, as the Bulgarian front collapsed, the war in that theatre was to all effects finished.

Globally the 73ª Squadriglia was not much engaged, suffering from bad equipment, lack of spares, particularly for the Nieuport 27 and bad weather, but it flew many escort and patrol sorties. It flew a total of 384 combat missions, engaged in 27 air combats and claimed no victory. Two of its pilots were decorated: *ten.* Righi with the *Medaglia d'Argento*, *s.ten.* Beria d'Argentine with the *Medaglia di Bronzo*. The unit returned to Italy in August 1919 and was disbanded.

Above: Captured Lloyd 42.11 was used on operations in the 73ª Squadriglia. It was probably the first instance of roundels appearing on an Italian airplane.

Above: SAML S.1 1569 of the 73ª Squadriglia.

Identified Victory Claims of the 73ª Squadriglia

Date	Place	Pilots	Victim
24.4.1917	Savogna	*S.ten*. Keller	Hansa Br. C.I 129.34 ? FLG 1? FTL

Casualties and Combat Losses of the 73ª Squadriglia

Date	Place	Aircraft	Crew	Cause
29.5.1917	Verona	SAML 1586	*Cpr*. Brambilla KIC, sold. Marzari WIC	Accident
1.1.1918	Macedonia	Nieuport 17	*Ten*. Bonavoglia WIC	Accident
29.1.1918	Macedonia	Nieuport 17	*Ten*. Righi WIA	Combat

Above: The observer *ten*. Raoul Simonini was from Argentina; he died in a crash on 27 February 1918 with the 120[a] Squadriglia.

Above: SAML 2887, adorned with the head of a Native American chief, is believed to be the personal mount of the future ace Leopoldo Eleuteri.

Above: A beautifully decorated Nieuport 27, "*Jane*" of the 73ᵃ Squadriglia in Macedonia.

Above: Pilots of the 73ª Squadriglia, from the left, Contò, De Biasi, Randi (?), and Beria d'Argentine.

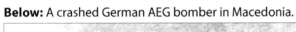

Below: A crashed German AEG bomber in Macedonia.

Above: A crashed Nieuport 27 in Macedonia. Its serial number, 5863, confirms that it is an airplane of the 73ª Squadriglia.

Above: Hanriot Hd.1 7510 with its pilot, *s.ten*. Beria d'Argentine.

Above: A mixed line of Spads and Nieuports of different models in Macedonia.

Above: Spad "*Paquita*" of the 73ª Squadriglia had as emblem a prancing lion with his paw over a German spiked helmet.

74ª Squadriglia

Above: An Aviatik of the 5ª Squadriglia Caccia at Taliedo.

The 5ª Squadriglia Caccia equipped with Aviatiks and Farmans was activated on 16 January 1916 for the defense of Milan and was based at Taliedo airport, where there was also a factory of Caproni. With commander *cap. pil.* Vincenzo Lombard the 5ª Squadriglia Caccia had pilots *sergenti* Mario Canova, Finelli and Emilio Stillio, *caporali* Damiano Miari Fulcis and Rachele Mori, *soldati* Paolucci and Tito Ragnelli. On 13 February 1916 during a test flight Aviatik 681 went into a spin and crashed at Taliedo airport killing *cpr.* Francesco Apolloni and Giovanni Romanoni, volunteer gunner.

It was then equipped with Farmans 515, 516, 520, and Aviatiks 685. 686. 688. 689, 690.

On 14 February it failed to intercept a raid by Austrian airplanes over Brescia and its commander was asked to justify this failure. In March the 5ª Caccia had *s.ten.* Damiano Collacchini, *sergenti* Stillio and Canova, *caporali* Beniamino Giussani, Miari Fulcis, Mori and Bruno Valenti, *soldato* Ragnelli, and was equipped with a dozen Aviatik Salmson 140 hp.

It became 74ª Squadriglia Aviatik on 15 April 1916,

commander was still *cap.* Lombard. It reported to the *Gruppo Settentrionale per la Difesa Aerea* (Northern Air Defence Group). On 21 October 1916 *cap.* Ferdinando Giorgi became the new commander.

In November the unit received Farman Colombo pushers, and at the end of the month it moved to Trenno, near Milan. Its equipment now consisted of Farmans 1505, 1942, 1988 and 1989, Farman Colombo 1991, 2000, 2629, 2648, 2650, 2655, 2659, and Aviatiks 688, 694 and 701. During 1916 this unit flew about 300 uneventful standing patrol flights.

On 1 January 1917 the 74ª Squadriglia at Trenno had *cap.* Giorgi, *ten.* Antonio Dominici, *m.llo* Pagano, *sergenti* Francesco Leccese, Miari Fulcis, Mario Orsi, Emilio Stillio, Mario Strina, *sold.* Paolucci and ten gunners. In March the unit started to get new equipment, SAML and the SP.2's serials 2668, 2765 and 2770. On 9 April one of the new aircraft, 2765, crashed wounding the pilot *serg.* Frigerio and the gunner *sold.* Arquati.

On 10 April 1917 the 74ª became part of the new IX Gruppo. On 16 April Savoia Pomilio 2770 had an engine back-fire and crashed, killing *soldato* Arturo Biasoli, while the

Aviatik 686 of the 5ª Squadriglia Caccia. There was a wide variety of armament and gun mounts among the Aviatiks of the defense units.

Above: Aviatik 1599 of the 74ª Squadriglia; its serial number is very high, indicating that it was built after the production of SAMLs had already begun.

pilot *ten*. Nino Bartoli was wounded. On 6 May *cap*. Ercole Ercole (back from Albania, where he had earned a *Medaglia d'Oro* in the 11ª Squadriglia) became commander. There was another accident on 13 May, Farman Colombo 1999 fell but its pilot, *v.brig*. Mario Facciocchi and his gunner survived. On 31 May the unit dismissed its last Aviatiks. On 7 June 1917 *cap*. Alessandro Chiarenza was killed at Trenno, in a take-off accident with SAML 2886.

On 16 June 1917 also the Farman Colombo were retired, and the unit flew just SAMLs and SP.2's. In this period with *cap*. Ercole there were the pilots *tenenti* Bartoli, Emilio Botturi, Francesco Petrosemolo, Antonino Serra and Eriberto Torello, *s.tenenti* Corradino Raineri, Carlo Tacchi Venturi and Ruggero Tarantelli, *serg.m*. Romeo Massagli, *v.brig*. Mario Facciocchi and *serg*. Onorato Bianchi, ten gunners and one observer, *ten*. Luigi Premoli. *Ten*. Torello was killed on 10 July 1917 in an accident with SAML 2975 at Trenno.

On 11 August 1917, as the large Italian offensive began, the unit sent two *sezioni* of SAMLs to Campoformido, with pilots *tenenti* Petrosemolo, Serra, Tacchi Venturi and Tarantelli, *sergenti* Angelo Lucchini and Alfredo Tagliapietra, with *cap*. Ercole, *ten*. Premoli and ten gunners. Their SAMLs had serials 2445, 2478, 2869, 2871, 4467 and 2878, the last one received from the 73ª Squadriglia. They immediately

started patrols over the lines, and on 17 August the SAML of Tagliapietra returned with battle damage. On 19, 21 and 25 August flights of four aircraft struck at the Hermada, on the 26th some planes dropped leaflets while two more bombed Panovizza, on the 28th the unit flew two bombing raids. On 4 September flights of four SAMLs twice attacked the enemy, and this rate of operations continued the whole month. On the 4th *s.ten*. Raineri was wounded in his shoulder, his gunner, *sold*. Daniele Damelli, stopped the bleeding and they returned over the Hermada to strafe. Raineri was killed in combat on 9 November, now flying with 122ª Squadriglia. On 3 October the 74ª still flew five sorties of patrol and leaflet dropping, then on the 12th its detached flights returned to base.

The two flights that had remained at Trenno were at the command of *cap*. Clemente Giorelli. On August 18 *serg*. Bianchi had done an unauthorized flight with two mechanics on SP.2 2766 and crashed, but luckily the three of them were just lightly wounded. On 24 August a Caproni flight was formed, with aircraft 1132 and 1164 and pilot *ten*. Ariboldo Soliani. On 12 September 1917, recognizing its state of a SAML unit, the 74ª was renamed 122ª Squadriglia. *S.ten*. Raineri and *sold*. Damelli had earned the *Medaglia d'Argento* for their action on 4 September.

Above: Pilots of the 74ª Squadriglia with a SAML.

A new 74ª Squadriglia was formed on 20 May 1918 at Castenedolo airfield, near Brescia, with personnel and equipment of the 2ª Sezione (flight) of the 83ª Squadriglia, already based there, and it was assigned to the IX Gruppo. Its first temporary commander was *cap.* Bruno Lodolo, then came the regular commander, *cap.* Marinello Nelli (later of fame for his record flights on the D'Ascanio helicopter).

One flight of this squadron was immediately sent to Cividate Camuno, north-east of the Garda Lake, for the defence of the Tonale zone, providing escort flights for the 113ª Squadriglia, and remained there until the end of the war with the pilots *cap.* Pietro Marchesini and *sergenti* Cesare Giordano and Francesco Sodani. In the last ten days of May 1918 there were actions in the Sella di Tonale, and the fighters of the 74ª gave their support.

On 1 June 1918 the 74ª Squadriglia had *cap.* Nelli, *cap.* Nilo Tibaldi (who married the daughter of Eugenio Chiesa, chief of the *Commissariato d'Aeronautica*), *ten.* Pierfausto Barelli, *serg.m.* Guido Branca, *sergenti* Carlo Campana, Eligio Cruciani, Cesare Giordano, Giovanni Riva, Francesco Sodani, *cpr.* Raffaele Tarducci, *soldati* Giosuè Lombardi, Stefano Borla and Guido Roncuzzi. It was equipped with Nieuport 27s and Hanriots.

On 1 June *sold.* Roncuzzi got lost and landed in

Switzerland: he was interned and remained in the Confederation until the end of the war. On 8 June *cap.* Serafino Battaini became the new commander, and on the 24th he forced an Austrian airplane to land at Breguzzo, this claim was not confirmed.

On 7 July 1918 the 74ª Squadriglia left the IX Gruppo and joined the XXIV. On 14 July *ten.* Ottorino Frazzi with *serg.* Campana and *cpr.* Tarducci escorting a Caproni attacked an enemy airplane over the frontline and shot it down. On 19 July *sold.* Lombardi landed in an emergency his Hanriot on the glacier of Adamello, at an altitude of over 2,000 metres, earning the praise of the Comando Aeronautica of the 7ª Armata.

On 20 July the 74ª Squadriglia at Castenedolo had three Nieuport 27, 13 Hanriots, one SP.2, 3501, and three Farman MFCs, 2660, 2674, and 2711 of a night defense flight received from the 72ª Squadriglia. With *cap.* Battaini were the pilots *capitani* Lodolo and Nelli, *tenenti* Barelli and Frazzi, *s.ten.* Gino Baldi, *serg.m.* Branca, *sergenti* Campana, Raffaele Capo (an Argentinian), Angelo Comolli, Cruciani, Teresio Marcellino, Riva, Alberto Sacco, Bruno Scaruggi, Attilio Simonetta, *caporali* Tarducci and Giovanni Vercelli, *soldati* Borla and Lombardi. At Cividate Camuno there were four Hanriots with pilots *sergenti maggiori* Giordano

Above: The Hanriot Hd.1 572 of *sold*. Roncuzzi who got lost and landed in Switzerland. (Archive Hans-Heiri Stapfer)

and Sodani and *serg.* Amedeo Poggiali. The Farman flight had been attached to the 72ᵃ Squadriglia for the defence of Brescia.

On 29 July *cap.* Battaini with Nieuport 5820 and *serg.* Riva with Hanriot 13276 escorted a Pomilio tasked to bomb Breguzzo. Riva was forced back by engine troubles, but *cap.* Battaini alone managed to shoot down an Austrian airplane, *Magg.* Chiaperotti, commander of the XXIV Gruppo, occasionally flew with them, their operations rate was very high all through the summer. The other claims for this squadron, all from the Sezione at Cividate Camuno, were: on 11 August, when *serg.* Giordano shot down an enemy in Val Camonica, (possibly BR C.1 369.124 of Flik 27, shared with two SVAs of the 6ᵃ Sezione), on 20 August *serg.* Giordano again, in Val di Genova, *serg.* Raffaele Capo at Tonale on 28 October, and on 2 November *cap.* Nelli in Val di Genova, this being the only Allied claim on that day. On 24 August sold. Lombardi was wounded, crashing his Hanriot 13332 during

a standing patrol over the Garda Lake.

On 25 September 1918 the XXIV Gruppo was disbanded and the 74ᵃ Squadriglia briefly returned to the IX and then on 4 October it was assigned to the XX Gruppo, and it moved to Ponte S. Marco airfield, near Brescia, where it remained until the end of the war, returning to Castenedolo on 11 November. On 28 October it got a new pilot, *serg.* Battista Bottalla, later a test pilot with Fiat. The Sezione at Cividate Camuno had *cap.* Nelli, *serg.m.* Giordano and Sodani, *serg.* Capo and Angelo Lucchini and *soldato* Adolfo Novarese. On 2 November cap. Nelli claimed a victory over Carisolo, in the Adamello front, which was accepted, this was the last Italian victory claim of the war.

During the war this unit had flown about 800 combat missions, with 14 air combats, claiming eight victories, of which six were accepted. Its decorations consisted of a *Medaglia d'Argento* to *cap.* Battaini, *cap.* Nelli and *serg.* Riva. The 74ᵃ Squadriglia was disbanded on 6 February 1919.

Above: Hanriot Hd.1 of *sold*. Lombardi force landed on the Adamello glacier on 19 July 1918. (Archive Ragni)

Identified Victory Claims of the 74ª Squadriglia

Date	Place	Pilots	Victim
24.6.1918	Breguzzo	*Ten*. Barelli	Enemy aircraft FTL
24.6.1918	Breguzzo	*Cap*. Battaini	Enemy aircraft FTL
14.7.1918	Riva	*Serg*. Campana, ten. Frazzi, cpr. Tarducci	Fighter
29.7.1918	Corno Lomar	*Cap*. Battaini	Enemy aircraft
11.8.1918	Nadro	*Serg*. Giordano	Hansa Br. C.1 369.124 Flik 27/F?
20.8.1918	Val di Genova	*Serg*. Giordano	Enemy aircraft
28.10.1918	Tonale	*Serg*. Capo	Enemy aircraft
2.11.1918	Val di Genova	*Cap*. Nelli	Enemy aircraft

Casualties and Combat Losses of the 74ª Squadriglia

Date	Place	Aircraft	Crew	Cause
13.2.1916	Taliedo	Aviatik 681	*Cpr*. Apolloni KIC, *sold*. Romanoni KIC	Accident
16.4.1917	Trenno	SP.2 2770	*Ten*. Bartoli WIC, *sold*. Biasoli KIC	Accident
7.6.1917	Trenno	SAML 2886	*Cap*. Chiarenza KIC	Accident
10.7.1917	Trenno	SAML 2975	*Ten*. Torello KIC	Accident
4.9.1917	Hermada	SAML	*Ten*. Raineri WIA, *sold*. Damelli UNH	?
1.6.1918	Switzerland	Hd.1 572	*Sold*. Roncuzzi POW	?
24.8.1918	Garda Lake	Hd.1 13332	*Sold*. Lombardi WIA	?

Above: Farman Colombo 2650 of the 74ª Squadiglia.

Right: Hd.1 13261 crash-landed in the harsh terrain of the Alps.

Above: Nieuport 27 5820 of the 74ª Squadriglia. Its insignia was a white circle with the initials of the king, VE, and the royal emblem, the "knot of Savoy".

Below: Hanriot Hd1 19253 of the 74ª Squadriglia at Castenedolo airfield, which at the end of the war was renamed Montichiari.

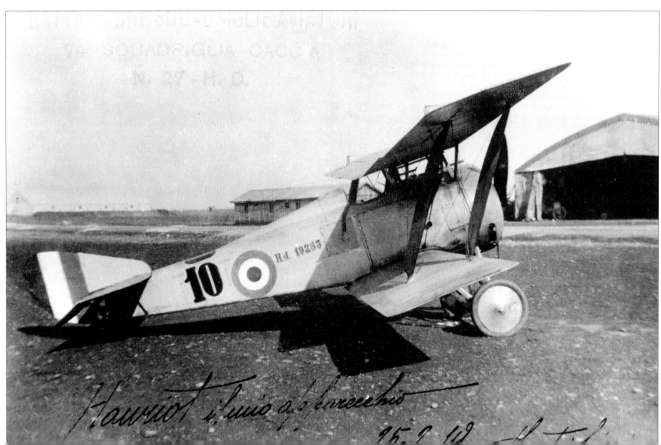

Above: Three Hanriots and three Nieuport 27s of the 74ª Squadriglia.

Above: Hanriot HD.1 19253 was assigned to the 74ª Squadriglia. Behind it, two Ansaldo Balilla.

SAML S.1 S.1569
73ª Squadriglia
Spring 1917

SAML S.1 S.2887
73ª / 121ª Squadriglia
Autumn 1917

Hanriot HD.1 #7510
S.Ten. Beria d'Argentine
73ª Squadriglia
Macedonia 1918

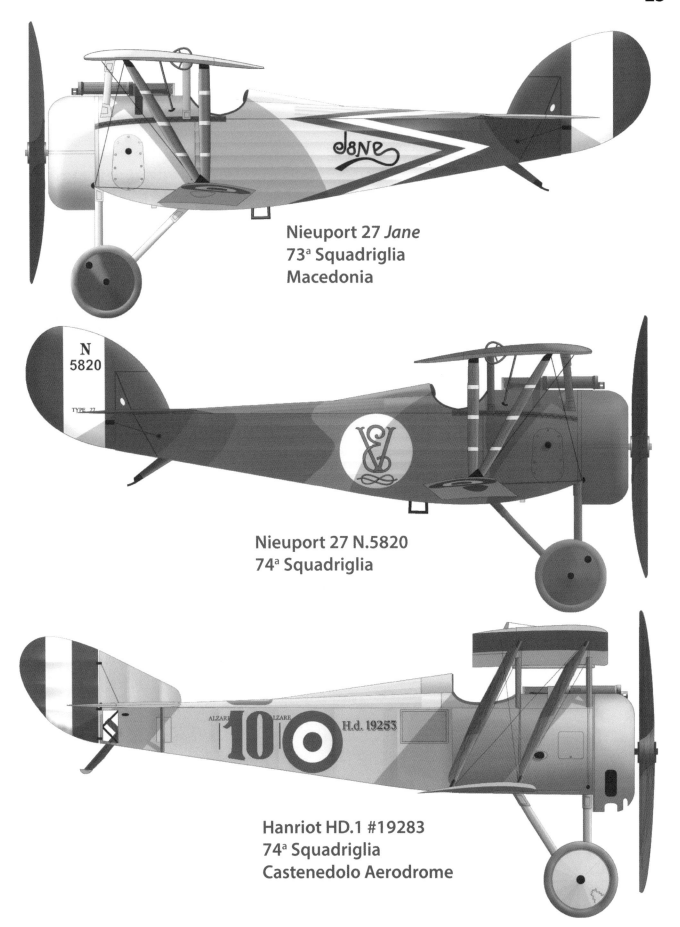

Nieuport 27 *Jane*
73ª Squadriglia
Macedonia

Nieuport 27 N.5820
74ª Squadriglia

Hanriot HD.1 #19283
74ª Squadriglia
Castenedolo Aerodrome

75ª Squadriglia

Above: Nieuport 11 1649 and 1624 of the 75ª Squadriglia at Verona.

The 75ª Squadriglia was formed on 1 May 1916 at Tombetta, Verona, assigned to the III Gruppo and tasked with the defence of Verona, home to many high commands and depots. Its commander was *cap.* Maffeo Scarpis with pilots *s.ten.* Alessandro Buzio, *s.ten.* Mario De Bernardi and *cpr.* Elia Liut, joined within the month by *cap.* Ettore Croce, *s.ten.* Paolo Michetti, *cpr.* Guido Consonni and volunteer *soldato* Guido Nardini. The unit was equipped with Nieuport 11 serials 1455, 1456, 1457, 1458 and 1459.

On 3 May the unit detached a flight to Villaverla, with pilots *s.ten.* Michetti, *cap.* Croce and cpr. Liut. On 10 May De Bernardi and Buzio flew the first operative alarm flights. The same two pilots first met the enemy in the air the next day. On 16 May *s.ten.* Buzio, *cpr.* Consonni and *sold.* Nardini intercepted a raider and drove it away: the Austrian crew dropped the camera, which was recovered.

On 20 June an Austrian airplane bombed Tombetta airfield, causing no damage. On 27 June *s.ten.* De Bernardi, Buzio, Consonni and Nardini intercepted and forced down near Arpignano Brandenburg C.1 26.11 of Flik 21, whose crew was captured. This event was a sensation in the city of Verona, the four pilots received a large money prize, which they delivered to humanitarian organizations. On 18 August *cap.* Scarpis was assigned to the Direzione Tecnica of the air service, and *cap.* Mario Gordesco replaced him.

The 75ª Squadriglia was also tasked with escort flights for bombers and two-seaters, and its actions during the Pasubio operations in October were praised, On 28 December its fighters escorted an airship cruising between Verona and the Garda Lake. *Cap.* Salvatore Calori became the new commander, replacing Gordesco in December.

At the end of 1916 the 75ª Squadriglia had pilots *cap.* Calori, *ten.* Giovanni De Briganti (the future test pilot of Fiat), *s.ten.* Buzio, De Bernardi, Pietro Bergonzi, *cpr.* Consonni and Liut, *soldati* Carlo Iannace and Dante Nannini, flying Nieuport 11 serials 1646, 1647, 1649, 1654, 1688, 1690 and 1695. During the year the unit flew 361 combat missions, with 24 air combats and one victory, for which Buzio, De Bernardi, Consonni and Nardini each had the *Medaglia di Bronzo*.

The first four months of 1917 were marked by bad weather conditions, and flying activity was curtailed. On 8 April 1917 *cap.* Antonio Bosio, coming from the 81ª Squadriglia, became the new commander, replacing Calori, who went to the 81ª. On 10 April the 75ª left its III Gruppo and was assigned to the new IX Gruppo.

On 24 April 1917 *serg.* Fermo Macchi attacked three enemy aircraft near Levico and saw one driven down, hit by his bullets. His victim possibly was Br.C.1 192.27 of Flik 21, which made an emergency landing at Levico. *S.ten.* Aldo Anesini also briefly served with the 75ª Squadriglia, and on 20 May, protecting an airplane spotting for the artillery, he drew off an attacking Austrian fighter. On 11 July *asp.* Alfredo Ghidotti crashed on take-off with Ni 2148 but was

Above: The Nieuports of the 75ᵃ Squadriglia at Verona were used for a series of propaganda pictures.

unhurt. By this time, the squadron had been receiving some Spads, one of which *serg*. Macchi wrecked on 25 June and another one, 5414, was lost on 21 August for engine failure, its pilot, *cap*. Bosio, lightly wounded.

Through the spring and summer of 1917, the 75ᵃ Squadriglia provided escort and standing patrol flights, frequently forcing Austrian airplanes to turn back. On 31 August 1917 its 3ᵃ Sezione was re-equipped with Spads and deployed at Castenedolo airfield. *Serg*. Fermo Macchi crashed another Spad, 4692, on 5 September, due to an engine failure, while *serg*. Francesco Pomponi smashed two Nieuports, Ni.11 2292 on 22 September and Ni.17 3289 on the 25ᵗʰ.

On 22 October two Sezioni of the 75ᵃ were removed and gave birth to the new 72ᵃ Squadriglia. On 24 October the 75ᵃ was re-assigned to the III Gruppo. On 30 October the 1ᵃ Sezione SVA was attached to the 75ᵃ Squadriglia: the new unit originally had just *ten*. Natale Palli and *serg*. Giovanni Bartolomeo Arrigoni, with SVAs 6789 and 6781. These pilots flew long-range misssions to Trento and Bolzano, but also some Ni.17s were fitted with cameras and they flew 21 photo-recce missions from October 1917 to January 1918. In the same period, they flew 148 interception missions and 59 air patrols.

Above: In this well-posed picture, a pilot points at the incoming enemy raiders, mechanics are ready to spin the propellers, and an officer is watching with a telescope.

Dante Nannini Sandoval was the first licensed pilot of Guatemala. He died of the Spanish flu in New York in early 1919.

S.ten. Alessandro Buzio with French-built
Nieuport 11 1763 in original camouflage finish.

Above: The same Nieuport 1763 now appears in natural fabric with a band in the Italian colors of green, white, and red.

In the morning of 3 November *serg.* Andrea Mancini flying Nieuport 17 3685 over the Caldonazzo Lake attacked an enemy aircraft and saw it going down apparently out of control. On the way back Mancini attacked two more airplanes, until his gun jammed. On 7 December 1917, during the Battle of the Melette, the squadron was tasked to escort a mass air attack of Italian two-seaters but failed the rendez-vous, *ten.* Pietro Danieli had an engine failure, made an emergency landing and was wounded. On 16 December *ten.* Pietro Campanaro had an air duel over Val d'Assa but his gun jammed, and the Italian pilot escaped with a spin. On 30 December *m.llo* Antonio Palpacelli crashed on landing with Nieuport 3567.

At the end of 1917 the 75ª Squadriglia had *cap.* Bosio commander, with pilots *tenenti* Campanaro, Danieli, Argiro Mele, Giuseppe Vanasco and *s.ten.* Carlo Rovedati, *m.llo* Palpacelli, *serg.* Consonni and Mancini. The unit, besides its Nieuports and SVAs, also had a flight of two Farmans MFC (one was 1978) coming from the 50ª Squadriglia, with pilots *sergenti* Antonio Coda and Luigi Recchioni, the observer *s.ten.* Raffaele Marini and gunners Arturo Marzari and Randalli for the night defence of Verona. The obsolete Farmans did manage to scare some Austrian raider with their unexpected gunfire. During 1917 this unit had flown 803 combat missions with 35 combats and one victory claim, without losses. For feats during 1917 there was a *Medaglia d'Argento* for *cpr.* Consonni and a Bronze for Nannini (who was a volunteer from Guatemala) now *sottotenente.*

In the night of 31 December/1 January three bombers attacked Verona, the airplane of *serg.* Coda and gunner Marzari took off and one enemy was attacked and the other two were chased until Vicenza, another night mission was flown the next night, but the returning two Farmans got lost in the fog and landed in the countryside, one turning over and badly wounding *serg.* Coda and Marzari. At the end of January 1918, the 75ª Squadriglia started receiving French Nieuport 27s. Cold was a problem, over the Alps: on 25 January *ten.* Argiro Mele, returning from a long escort flight, collapsed and on landing smashed his Nieuport 17 3698.

In February the 75ª Squadriglia had nine Nieuport 27s, one Ni 17 and one Farman. The first combat of 1918 arrived on 27 February, when *serg.* Consonni and *m.llo* Palpacelli drove away an enemy that threatened a two-seater under their escort. Consonni again in the morning of 18 March spotted two enemies over Mount Baldo, attacked one of them and saw it going down out of control. On that day, and in the same area, Franzi of the 72ª Squadriglia shot down *Zgsf.* Brunner and *Lt.* Crobath of Flik 10/F on 269.06, and the victim could be the same, claimed by two pilots.

On 18 March 1918 the 75ª Squadriglia moved to the new San Luca di Paese airfield, close to the front, where it began receiving Hanriots: by 1 April the unit had Hanriots serials 545, 6199, 6220 and 6223, one Ni.17 and ten Ni.27s. Its Farman flight, now equipped also with two SP.4s, was training the observers of the 61ª Squadriglia. On 1 May the unit got new pilots: *cap.* Raffaele Lioce, *serg.* Francesco Cutropia, *cpr.* Carlo Novelli and *sold.* Manlio Manzolini.

On 14 May the unit moved back to Ganfardine airfield,

Above: Buzio, De Bernardi, Consonni, and Nardini being decorated for their victory on 27 June 1916.

Above: De Bernardi, in the cockpit, with other pilots of the 75ª Squadriglia.

Above: French-built Neuport 17 2618 of the 75ª Squadriglia.

east of Verona. On 18 May *serg.* Augusto Levrero fought alone against three enemies, and escaped them by throwing his Ni 11326 in a spin. In the morning of 20 May *ten.* Campanaro flying Nieuport 27 11372 escorting a Pomilio two-seater spotted over Mori three Austrian fighters, and he attacked one of them and saw the fighter spinning with its propeller stopped and crashing at Lenzina. For this action, *ten.* Campanaro received the *Medaglia d'Argento*.

On 1 June 1918 the 75ª Squadriglia had *capitani* Bosio, Lioce and Vanasco, *tenenti* Campanaro, Danieli, Mele, Rovedati, *s.ten.* Benedetto Claris Appiani, *s.ten.* Remo Segala, *asp.* Arnaldo Brandolini, *serg.* Nazzareno Natalini, *cpr.* Rolando Spuri and Novelli and *soldati* Michele Gresino and Manzolini, flying eight Ni.27s and one Ni.17. On 15 June the unit moved to Busiago, closer to the frontline, assigned to the *Massa di Manovra* under the command of the *Ispettorato Squadriglie da Caccia*.

On 16 June *s.ten.* Claris Appiani, during a strafing mission over the Montello, got a bullet in his hand, but managed to return safely to base. On 17 June *ten.* Danieli twice tangled with a flight of five enemy fighters, both times holding his ground. On 19 June *cap.* Bosio, *cap.* Vanasco, *ten.* Danieli and *cpr.* Spuri cruising between Fonzaso and the Grappa spotted five enemies and engaged combat. Spuri stalled and dropped out of the fight, but Vanasco, Bosio and Danieli shot down one of the enemies, that crashed over Mount Cismon. This victory was assigned to *cap.* Vanasco alone. On 26 June

a formation of six Hanriots flew to Quinto di Treviso to participate in the funeral of Francesco Baracca.

On 29 June 1918 the unit returned to Ganfardine. *Cap.* Lioce was acting commander since 4 July, then on 20 July *cap.* Arturo Oddo arrived as effective commander. The 75ª Squadriglia was the last unit still equipped with the old Nieuport 17: on 14 July it still had 3696, together with eight Ni.27s and nine Hanriots.

On 14 July *ten.* Danieli flying Nieuport 27 11289 attacked an Austrian plane over Coni Zugna firing 250 rounds and drove it away in a fast dive. The squadron was much active during the summer, escorting the Pomilios of the 61ª and 134ª Squadriglia of the III Gruppo. On 12 August, it flew a formation of 12 fighters scorting a raid of Capronis, in which *ten.* Campanaro also dropped six bombs. That same day, five more sorties were flown, and *ten.* Campanaro dropped six more bombs over the enemy trenches.

On 22 August, during a patrol, three pilots, *ten.* Campanaro, *serg.* Bellino and *sold.* Manzolini met enemy aircraft, and *sold.* Manzolini, flying Ni.27 11318, claimed an enemy out of control over Coni Zugna, which ground observers confirmed. On August 23, a patrol of four pilots, Bellino, Ferrari, Manzolini and Spuri attacked an enemy, which was last seen diving toward Val Terragnolo.

On 28 August 1918 the unit detached a Hanriot flight to reinforce the 71ª Squadriglia with pilots *ten.* Danielli, *cpr.* Gresino, *serg.* Natalini, *cpr.* Novelli, *cpr.* Spuri, *s.ten.* Pietro

Above: Pilots with a French-built Nieuport 17. The Vickers machine gun is not fitted, there is a Lewis gun on the top wing.

Above: Mario De Bernardi in the cockpit of a brand new French-built Nieuport 17 carrying the Vickers machine gun. (Archive Fiorenzo Longhi)

S.ten. Aldo Anesini with Nieuport 17 3132 with both a Vickers and a Lewis gun, and a roundel over the deck of the fuselage.

Cascina and *serg.* Francesco Bellino. In mid-October it detached also pilots Campanaro, Berti, Bellino, Novelli, Aime and Gresino with their Nieuport 27s.

On 29 October, during the final offensive, the 75ᵃ Squadriglia suffered its only casualty, when *serg.* Bellino flying Nieuport 27 19763 with the 71ᵃ Squadriglia failed to return from a strafing mission. At the end of the war the unit, based at Ganfardine, had Nieuport 27s serials 11318, 11327, 19748, 19758, 19762, 19769, 19778, 19785, 19812, 19815, and Hanriots 6156, 13248, 13269, 13298, 13347, 19215, 19248, 19264, 19333 and 19339. *Cap.* Oddo was commander, with pilots *cap.* Lioce, *ten.* Campanaro, *s.tenenti* Calcina, Giovambattista Berti, Remo Segala, *sergenti* Enrico

Ferrari, Carlo Novelli, Fortunato Sicco, *caporali* Attilio Aime, Gresino, Manzolini, *soldati* Ferruccio De Paoli, Raffaele Garicone, Nunziato Greco, Leonello Rizzotto and Viapiana.

In the last year of the war, the 75ᵃ Squadriglia had flown 946 war sorties with 30 air combats and two confirmed victories. Its decorations consisted of three *Medaglie d'Argento*, to *cap.* Bosio, *ten.* Campanaro and *asp.* Claris Appiani, and six Bronzes, to *cpr.* Aime, *ten.* Campanaro, *ten.* Danieli, *cpr.* Gresino and *cap.* Vanasco (two) bringing its total for the war to eight Silvers and eight Bronzes. Totally during the war, the 75ᵃ Squadriglia had flown 2,110 missions with 89 air combats and four confirmed victories. The unit was disbanded at Ganfardine in March 1919.

Identified Victory Claims of the 75ᵃ Squadriglia

Date	Place	Pilots	Victim	Unit
27.6.1916	Verona	*S.ten.* De Bernardi, s.t. Buzio, Consonni, Nardini	Hansa Br. C.1 26.11	Flik 21
24.4.1917	Levico	*Serg.* Macchi	Hansa Br. C.1 129.27 FTL?	Flik 21?
3.11.1917	Caldonazzo	*Serg.* Mancini	Enemy a/c OOC	
18.3.1918	Mount Baldo	*Serg.* Consonni (& *sold.* Franzi, 72ᵃ)	Hansa Br. C.1 269.06	Flik 10/F?
20.5.1918	Lenzina - Mori	*Ten.* Campanaro	Fighter OOC	
19.6.1918	Mount Cismon	*Cap.* Vanasco	Fighter	
22.8.1918	Val Terragnolo	*Sold.* Manzolini	Enemy a/c OOC	
23.8.1918	Val Terragnolo	*Serg.* Bellino, *cpr.* Spuri	Enemy a/c OOC	

Casualties and Combat Losses of the 75ᵃ Squadriglia

Date	Place	Aircraft	Crew	Cause
1.1 1918	Verona	Farman MFC	*Serg.* Coda WIA, *sold.* Marzari WIA	?
29.10.1918	Piave	Ni.27 19763	*Serg.* Bellino KIA	?

Above: A Nieuport 27, 11320, of the 75ª Squadriglia at Ganfardine, July 1918. (Archive Achille Vigna)
Below: Nieuport 27 at Ganfardine; the individual number 6 is in the style of Escadrille N 82 that operated in Italy, possibly given to the Italians after their return to France. (Archive Achille Vigna)

76ª Squadriglia

Above: Nieuport 10 and 11 aircraft of the 76ª Squadriglia at Santa Maria la Longa airfield. (Archive Caliaro)

The 76ª Squadriglia was formed at La Comina on 25 May 1916, equipped with Nieuport 10 and 11 serials 1042, 1043, 1805 and 1806. Its commander was *cap.* Ettore De Carolis with pilots *s.ten.* Giuseppe Rigoni, *serg.* Mario Stoppani and volunteers *soldati* Giovanni Menegoni and Otello Venchiarutti. On 29 May the squadron moved to S. Maria la Longa, assigned to the I Gruppo, and the next day it flew its first combat mission. On 1 June it had the first contact with the enemy: Stoppani, escorting two Voisins in a reconnaissance, spotted an enemy seaplane, attacked it but was forced to give up when his gun jammed. In the following days the 76ª, deployed in the busiest part of the front, launched many flights against Austrian intruders, with Stoppani and Venchiarutti chasing off enemy aircraft with many alarm flights almost every day. A new pilot joined the unit on June 5, *caporale* Carlo Gambotti. On 12 June Gambotti on landing wrecked Nieuport 10 1462 and two days later Venchiarutti crashed with Ni.11 1806. The unit got a new *pilot,* sold. Carlo Iannace. On 14 June Stoppani mets an enemy Aviatik, fired a whole drum of his Lewis and forced it to land behind its lines. On June 15 Rigoni over Pravcina found an Aviatik that was pursuing a Voisin, he forced the Austrian to land at Aisovizza, and Stoppani made a similar claim in the evening. On 22 June another pilot flew his first mission, *s.ten.* Giuseppe Grassa, who claimed an enemy forced to land on 30 June.

At the end of June 1916, the 76ª Squadriglia had a mix of Nieuport 10, 1042, 1464, 1806, and 11, 1606, 2182 and 2206. The unit directly faced Aisovizza, the main Austian airfield, home to Flik 2, 4, 12 and 19, and Italian observers could even spot the take-offs. On 9 July three Nieuports engaged a formation of six aircraft together with other Italian fighters, one of the enemies was badly hit and was seen going down. On 18 July seven Austrian aircraft took off, and four Nieuports got ready for the interception, among them was *cap.* Mario Gordesco, who for one month flew with this squadron. Stoppani engaged an enemy, fired but then lost his quarry.

On 28 July *s.ten.* Grassa had a combat defending Voisins under attack, and reported an enemy airplane falling vertically over Gorizia. The fighters also escorted bombers and two-seaters: on 6 August, flying along the Caproni bombers attacking Opcina station, Stoppani saw two Austrian seaplanes, pursued them all the way to Muggia forcing them to alight. On 24 August 1916 *cpr.* Guido Iori, with Ni 1615 in a mission to strike at a kite balloon at Mavinje, failed to return. Having run out of gas, he landed behind enemy lines and was captured. His intact Nieuport was tested by the Austrians, who gave it serial 00.27.

On 29 September 1916 the 76ª Squadriglia became part of the II Gruppo, still based at Santa Maria la Longa. At this time, it had on force *cap.* De Carolis, *ten.* Luigi Olivi, *s.ten.* Grassa, *s.ten.* Rigoni, *serg.* Stoppani and *caporali* Menegoni and Venchiarutti. For its support to the offensives of Autumn 1916 the Command of the 2ª Armata praised it. On 3 October *ten.* Olivi shot down an enemy aircraft, earning fame and the *Medaglia d'Argento.* On 1 November *ten.* Ernesto Bonavoglia returned from a combat with his Nieuport badly shot up. *Ten.* Olivi scored more victories in the fall, becoming an ace, and so did serg. Stoppani, while *ten.* Grassa had to leave for medical reasons (he was an enthusiastic pilot, he died in 1920 with cap. Gordesco flying from Rome to Tokyo), but all pilots of 76ª Squadriglia had flown intensively.

By the end of 1916, the 76ª Squadriglia, having lost in different accidents its Nieuports 1650, 1683, 1699, 2111, 3128 and 3133, had flown 624 combat missions with 39 air combats and claiming many victories, five of them confirmed. Besides Olivi, there had been a *Medaglia d'Argento* for Stoppani and a Bronze for *s.ten.* Rigoni.

At the start of the new year the pilots were *cap.* De Carolis, *ten.* Olivi, *s.tenenti* Rigoni and Ernesto Bonavoglia, *sergenti* Virginio Appiani, Giovanni Bartolomeo Arrigoni, Edoardo Olivero, Stoppani, *caporali* Giovanni Menegoni and Venchiarutti, and the first Nieuport 17 110 hp had arrived. On 1 January 1917 the pilots of the 76ª had no less than eight

Above: Visiting officers in front of Nieuport 10 1464 of the 76ª Squadriglia.

Left: Officers examining a brand new Nieuport 11 1615 at Santa Maria la Longa.

duels, with *serg.* Appiani first having an inconclusive duel with a two-seater, and then driving down an enemy seaplane. On 26 January all pilots had different fights with enemy aircraft, none was claimed, but an observer of Austrian Flik 2 was killed in one of these encounters. There were many combat flights, but the unreliability of alarms, gun stoppages and the higher speed of enemy airplanes made most of them fruitless. *Serg.* Arrigoni on 13 February first drove away a two-seater that attacked a Farman, then engaged combat with two more enemies. His gun jammed but he remained over the lines, to keep the Austrians at bay just by his presence. On 16 February Arrigoni had his Ni.17 wrecked by an anti-aircraft shell, so he force-landed close to the frontline, near Merna, under enemy fire, during the night with the help of two soldiers from the squadron, the plane was disassembled, loaded on a truck and brought back to base.

In mid-February 1917 Stoppani was assigned to the *Direzione Tecnica dell'Aeronautica Militare* to start his great

career as a test pilot, and *ten.* Giuseppe Retinò arrived. On 25 February 1917 the 76ª Squadriglia moved to Borgnano field, also called Langoris, close to the most contested part of the front. On 28 February Arrigoni and Bonavoglia had a hard combat with a Brandenburg, which they claimed as damaged.

In the afternoon of 13 April Arrigoni scored a double victory, first, together with Retinò, he drove down an enemy airplane over Ranziano, then alone, half an hour later, he attacked another plane, Brandenburg 29.55 of Flik 4, with crew of *Hptm.* Veljacic and *Lt.* Barkasz, and forced it to land near Schonpass. Three days later, on 16 April, Arrigoni scored his fourth confirmed victory forcing Brandenburg 129.13 of Flik 34, of *Fw.* Renner and *Oblt.* von Szebenyi to land with a seriously wounded observer.

On 22 April De Carolis, promoted to Major, left command of the squadron to *ten.* Luigi Olivi. On that same day Arrigoni had another combat and claimed an enemy forced to flee, possibly Brandenburg 27.16 of Flik 32,

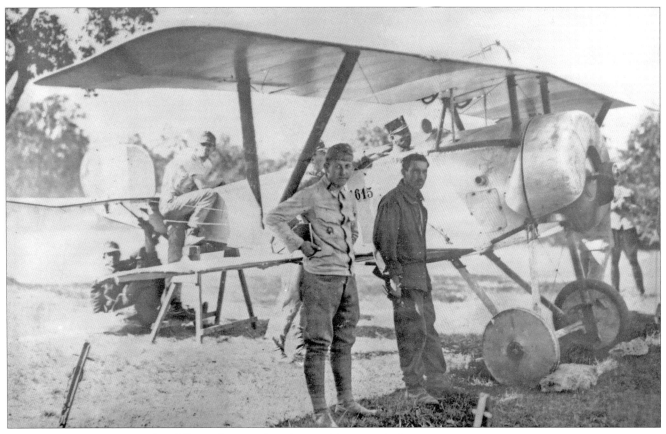

Above: Nieuport 11 1615 that fell into Austrian hands on 24 August 1916.

with *Korp*. Schmidt and *Lt*. von Weinmann, who made an emergency landing at Aidussina with a wounded pilot and a shot-up plane after a combat over Castagnevizza. On 8 May Austrian artillery targeted the airfield, without causing much damage. On 13 May *serg*. Luigi Fanti claimed participation in a victory of Baracca.

On 14 May 1917 the unit had its first combat casualty, as *ten*. Francesco Broili battled an Austrian airplane near Gorizia and was shot down at Ciprianisca, most likely victim of *Zgsf*. Stefan Fejes and *Lt*. Alexander Tahy of Flik 19. As the 10th Battle of the Isonzo was raging, the pilots were engaged in many missions, including the escort of Caproni bombers.

In June the 76ª Squadriglia had a mixed complement of Nieuport 11s and 17s and a few Spads, and new pilots, *ten*. Giuseppe Vanasco, *sergenti* Giuseppe Bovio, Antonio Pellanda and Vittorio Aquilino and the gallant Argentinian *serg*. Edoardo Olivero. On 17 June the unit scored twice: first *ten*. Bonavoglia shot down an enemy near Ranziano, and then *ten*. Olivi hit another one that went down near Merna. Olivi returned to base and took off again on Spad 5403 to take pictures of his downed opponents but his engine failed him, the Spad stalled and crashed, killing the commander. *Ten*. Olivi had six confirmed victories.

On 1 July 1917 *cap*. Salvatore Calori, coming from the 81ª Squadriglia, became the new commander. On 9 July the 76ª Squadriglia passed under the VI Gruppo, reporting to the Comando d'Aeronautica of the 2ª Armata. On 15 July

ten. Flavio Torello Baracchini, a rising ace, arrived from the 81ª Squadriglia, and just two days later he scored his tenth confirmed victory, shooting down over Lom Brandenburg C.1 129.57. He shot down four aircraft in his period with the 76ª, but on 8 August he was badly wounded in combat: on 30 August Baracchini was awarded Italy's highest decoration, the *Medaglia d'Oro*.

The 76ª Squadriglia was heavily engaged during the 11th Battle of the Isonzo in August 1917. On 11 August three fighter squadrons, 76ª, 78ª and 81ª, formed the *Sottogruppo Aeroplani di Borgnano*, *cap*. Calori took command of this new unit and young *ten*. Gastone Novelli received command of the 76ª. The unit started receiving the new Hanriot Hd.1 fighter, and on 13 August it had six Hanriots, six Nieuports and three Spads.

On 28 September 1917 the unit got another acting commander, coming from the 91ª, *ten*. Francesco Di Rudinì, the son of a former Prime Minister, who was killed just five days later, on 3 October, shot down in an air combat over Mount Fleme, probably the victim of *Lt*. Schroeder of Jasta 1. On 24 October the Germans and Austrians broke through the Italian lines at Caporetto. The front collapsed and the 76ª Squadriglia retreated, leaving at Borgnano four burned fighters. The last one to leave, on 25 October, was *ten*. Alessandro Veronesi, but he failed to return, crashing against a hill in the clouds. Italians attributed his death to an accident, but he was probably the victim of *Vzfw*. Hippert of Jasta 39. On 27 October the unit was at Campoformido,

Above: Nieuport 11 1651 with a diagonal band in the three colors of Italy.

the next day it moved to La Comina and on 1 November it retreated to Arcade, just behind the Piave River, the new line of defense.

On that date commander of the 76ª Squadriglia became *cap.* Alberto De Bernardi, and the pilots were *tenenti* Alessandro Buzio, Mario Fucini, *s.ten.* Giorgio Michetti and Silvio Scaroni, *asp.* Renato Donati, *sergenti* Fernando Armati, Raimondo Di Loreto, Luigi Fanti and Gastone Razzi. On 10 November the unit, having just four Hanriots, moved to Istrana airfield, near Treviso.

On 14 November 1917 *s.ten.* Scaroni scored his first victory, shooting down an Austrian two-seater at Colbertaldo. Scaroni scored again on 18 November at S. Donà and on the 19th at Vidor, his vicitim likely being a German Albatros D.III. On the other hand, on 18 November *cap.* Ernesto Sequi, of the Reali Carabinieri, was wounded in combat and hospitalized. On 10 December Scaroni became an ace, shooting down an Austrian two-seater near Noventa di Piave. More victories followed, the 76ª Squadriglia taking a heavy toll of German airplanes.

On 26 December 1917 there was the "air battle of Istrana" when, in retaliation for a strafing attack by Maj. Barker, RFC on Christmas Day, forty German bombers attacked that important Italian air base. The Hanriots of the 70ª, 76ª, 78ª and 82ª Squadriglia and three British Camels took off under the falling bombs and faced the bombers, while the escorting Albatros fighters did not intervene. A second later attack, at noon, met a similar fate, and a total of eleven bombers were claimed shot down, three of them by Scaroni, including an A.E.G. heavy bomber.

During 1917 the 76ª Squadriglia had flown about 2,000

combat missions, with 300 air duels and 30 enemy aircraft shot down. Besides the Gold Medal to Baracchini, the *Medaglia d'Argento* went to *ten.* Appiani, *serg.* Arrigoni (two), *ten.* Baracchini, *s.ten.* Bonavoglia, *ten.* Di Rudinì, *serg.* Donati, *s.ten.* Michetti, *ten.* Olivero, *ten.* Olivi, *serg.* Razzi, *s.ten.* Scaroni, *cpr.* Venchiarutti and *ten.* Veronesi.

At the beginning of 1918 the 76ª Squadriglia at Istrana had *capitani* De Bernardi and Sequi, *tenenti* Buzio, Fucini, Lodovico Censi, Retinò, Michetti and Scaroni, *asp.* Donati, *sergenti* Razzi, Di Loreto, Fanti and Romolo Ticconi. On 14 January Scaroni scored another victory forcing down KD 28.71 of Flik 21, its pilot *Fw.* Karl Cislaghi was captured, later on Scaroni met him.

On 24 January Nieuport 27 serial 5846 was wrecked in landing, this fact showing that the 76ª had received at least one example of that French fighter. Profiting from the snow, which made hangars and barracks more prominent, the German and Austrians repeatedly bombed Istrana by night. In the night of 31 January two bombs damaged seven fighters, three of them seriously, and the next night another attack caused serious damages to infrastructures. The 76ª Squadriglia was forced to move from Istrana to Isola di Carturo (nowadays Isola Mantegna) on 2 February 1918 and then, on 17 February, it moved to Casoni, 3 miles south of the Grappa Mountain that was the keystone of Italian defense. After two and a half years being deployed in the hottest part of the Isonzo front, the 76ª Squadriglia was now deployed in the hottest part of the Piave front.

On 5 February a new pilot arrived, *cap.* Giulio Lega, a doctor. On 11 February the ever more aggressive pilots of the 76ª Squadriglia claimed two victories that were not

Above: *Serg*. Venchiarutti in a French-built Nieuport 11; 1806 is its Italian serial number. (Archive Caliaro)

Right: Macchi-built Nieuport 11 2137 with the name *"Terribile"* written in its roundel. It has been identified as the airplane of the ace Baracchini.

confirmed, although Austrian data seem to confirm their claims.

Night attacks by German bombers continued also on the new base, and in the night of 27 February a soldier was killed.

On 24 March 1918 *ten*. Baracchini returned to service after his bad wound in August 1917. The squadron, which now had some twenty Hanriots and one Nieuport, regularly flew leaflet dropping missions and it operated in flights of three to five fighters.

In mid-May 1918 the 76ᵃ Squadriglia, now with commander *cap*. De Bernardi included *cap*. Giulio Lega, *tenenti* Baracchini, Buzio, Michetti, Scaroni, Ludovico Censi, Giuseppe Retinò, *s.ten*. Donati, Dante Nannini, *brig*. Pacifico Malfranci, *sergenti* Di Loreto, Fanti, Razzi, Piero Mondini

and *cpr*. Umberto Baggini and Luigi Boccasavia. They were flying Hanriots 519, 524, 541, 546, 558, 6182, 6206, 6216, 6222, 6239, 6254, 6269, 6270, 6274, 6280, 6558, 7458 and 7460. In March *serg*. Fanti was jailed for simulating an illness, and in May he was removed, assigned to the Airplanes Depot at Poggio Renatico, an unfair lot for a gallant pilot, who was simply worn out, after many combat flights, in which he was credited with three victories.

On 25 May the engine of Hanriot 7458 caught fire in flight, and *serg*. Ticconi made an emergency landing near S. Martin di Fonte, suffering serious burns on his legs. On 26 May *ten*. Baracchini had a hectic duel against six Austrian fighters, together with other Italian and British pilots, and he claimed a victory, possibly this was the combat in which the Austrian ace *Zgsf*. Udvardy of Flik 42/J was forcced to land.

Above: Nieuports 11s of the 76ᵃ Squadriglia: the first one, 1623, carries the name "*Fringuello*" (finch), the second one, 1700, with Bonavoglia, shows a Happy Hooligan, the third one, 2161 of Olivero, another comic character.

Left: A close-up of Nieuport 11 2161 of Olivero with its comic character.

In the 76ᵃ Squadriglia, however, the national hero Baracchini did not go along well with the reserved and determined Scaroni, so on 31 May he moved on to the 81ᵃ Squadriglia, the sister unit within the VI Gruppo.

On 15 June 1918 the Austrians launched a huge offensive, from the Grappa to the sea, and all fighters took off at dawn, first to preclude any Austrian activity in the air, and then to strafe and attack enemy troops, particularly boats, bridges and gangways across the Piave River. The most contested area was the Montello hill, where the enemy had gained a foothold. These low-level attacks were very dangerous, and fighters often returned having been hit by enemy ground fire. In the morning of 7 July Scaroni and Ticconi cruising over Asiago spotted a formation crossing the lines, Hansa-Brandenburg C.1 169.68 of Flik 45/D and its escort, Albatros 153.240 and 153.98, of *Zgsf.* Oswald Bierlotter and *Korp.* Franz Pensl, of Flik 9/J and another aircraft. Scaroni shot down first the two-seater and then the fighter, Ticconi claimed the other fighter but did not get confirmation, although Pensl had made an emergency landing, wounded

Above: The fighters of the 76ª Squadriglia. The second Ni.11 carries Le Prieur rockets, the ninth airplane is a French-built Nieuport 17.

in his arm. One hour later Scaroni scored his third victory in the day, shooting down over his own airfield Phönix 128.19 of Flik 14/J, its pilot, Zgsf. Josef Laczko was captured unhurt. On 30 June *ten.* Camillo Sivori was assigned, while in the same days *ten.* Baracchini was shifted to 81ª Squadriglia.

On 12 July 1918 luck changed for the Italian ace. Scaroni, tasked with the escort of a Pomilio of the 36ª Squadriglia with cap. Lega, *ten.* Michetti and *ten.* Carlo Fornasari strayed, and joined a dogfight between two Camels of No. 45 Squadron and six Austrian fighters. He joined the fray, claiming two victories and then, as he was about to attack another fighter, he was bounced and an enemy, probably Josif Vratil, targeted his Hanriot 7517 and put an explosive bullet in Scaroni's back. The ace crashed in a brook near the Grappa. He was not able to return to service before the end of the war, nor to reach the victory toll of Francesco Baracca. In July the 76ª Squadriglia had Hanriots 558, 541, 546, 6206, 6239, 6254, 6269, 6274, 6280, 7523, 7524, 7529, 11406, 13309.

In the summer the unit flew many missions of leaflet dropping, besides its usual tasks of interdiction and escort. The pilots on force on 1 September were *capitani* De Bernardi and Lega, *tenenti* Buzio, Fornasari, Sivori, *s.ten.* Michetti, *serg.m.* Alberto Pasta, *brigadieri* Balandi and Malfranci, *sergenti* Baggini, Di Loreto, Mondini, Razzi, Ticconi, *cpr.* Ramberti.

On 9 September cap. Amerigo Notari became its new commander. The fighters of the 76ª Squadriglia were very active during the final phase of the conflict, supporting the Italian advance to Vittorio Veneto. A Silver Medal motivation credited *s.ten.* Donati with a victory over a fighter

with pilot *"Carlo Schuller, who had shot down 17 Italian airplanes"* but Donati was no longer with the squadron, and no such event is reported.

At the time of the armistice the 76ª Squadriglia was based at Casoni, with 21 efficient fighters. With commander *cap.* Calori there were the pilots cap. Lega, *tenenti* Roberto Carrara, Carlo Fornasari, Camillo Sivori, *asp.* Di Loreto, *serg.m.* Alberto Pasta, *sergenti* Umberto Baggini, Giuseppe Magnetti, Pietro Mondini, Romolo Ticconi, *brig.* Roberto Balandi and Pacifico Malfranci, *cpr.* Armando Ramberti, *cpr.* Carlo Neri, *soldati* Vasco Giovanardi, Giovanni Randali and Renato Silvi.

During 1918 the 76ª had flown 2.464 combat sorties, engaging in 101 air combats and shooting down 34 enemy aircraft.

Its pilots were highly decorated: *Medaglia d'Oro* and *Medaglia d'Argento* to Scaroni, *Medaglia d'Argento* to *cap.* Lega, *tenenti* Buzio, Censi, Donati (three), Fucini, Michetti, Nannini, Retinò, Sivori, *sergenti* Baggini, Di Loreto (who, according to his citations, was credited with six victories), Mondini, Razzi (also virtually an ace, as he was credited with five victories), Ticconi, *cpr.* Ramberti, *Medaglia di Bronzo* to *cap.* De Bernardi, *ten.* Fornasari, *brigadieri* Balandi and Malfranci, *sergenti* Di Loreto, Fanti, Porta and Ticconi. Overall during the war the 76ª Squadriglia flew 5,088 missions, had 340 air duels shooting down 69 confirmed enemy aircraft, (but claiming 99) and its roll included no less than eight Aces: Scaroni, Fucini, Olivi, Stoppani, Ticconi, Buzio, Lega and Michetti. After the end of the war, it received most of the personnel of the 81ª Squadriglia, and was not disbanded.

Above: A French Nieuport 17 with both a Vickers and a Lewis gun.

Identified Victory Claims of the 76ᵃ Squadriglia

Date	Place	Pilots	Victim
14.6.1916	Medea	*Serg.* Stoppani	Enemy aircraft FTL
15.6.1916	Aisovizza	*S.ten.* Rigoni	Enemy aircraft FTL
15.6.1916	Aisovizza	*Serg.* Stoppani	Enemy aircraft FTL
30.6.1916	Gorizia	*S.ten.* Grassa	Enemy aircraft FTL
9.7.1916	Salcano	*Serg.* Stoppani, *s.ten.* Rigoni (& Olivari, 70ᵃ)	Lloyd C.III 43.67? Flik 12?
18.7.1916	S. Marco	*Serg.* Stoppani	Lloyd 43.83 Flik 4
28.7.1916	Merna	*S.ten.* Grassa	Fokker A.3 03.51 FTL
3.10.1916	Aisovizza	*Ten.* Olivi	Hansa Br. C.I 68.01 Flik 2
11.10.1916	Aisovizza	*Ten.* Olivi, *serg.* Stoppani	Hansa Br. C.I 61.72 Flik 19
23.10.1916	Biglia	*Ten.* Olivi	Hansa Br. C.I 26.28 Flik 2
31.10.1916	Nad Logem	*Serg.* Stoppani (& Tesei 77ᵃ, Caselli, Rossi 70ᵃ)	Hansa Br. C.I 68.25 Flik 12
23.11.1916	Gorizia	*Ten.* Olivi, *serg.* Stoppani	Hansa Br. C.I 68.10 Flik 4
25.11.1916	Schoenpass	*Ten.* Olivi (& Ranza 77ᵃ)	Hansa Br. C.I 29.54 Flik 23
1.12.1916	S. Marco	*Serg.* Stoppani	Enemy aircraft
1.1.1917	Porte di Ferro	*Serg.* Appiani	Seaplane FTL
26.1.1917	?	?	Flik 2
28.2.1917	Isonzo	*Serg.* Arrigoni, *ten.* Bonavoglia (& Ruffo 70ᵃ)	Hansa Br. C.I 27.56? Flik 34?
10.3.1917	Ranziano	*Serg.* Venchiarutti	Enemy aircraft FTL
13.4.1917	Mount Stol	*Ten.* Retinò, *serg.* Arrigoni	Enemy aircraft OOC
13.4.1917	Mount Stol	*Serg.* Arrigoni	Hansa Br. C. 29.55 Flik 4
16.4.1917	Ternova	*Serg.* Arrigoni	Hansa Br. C.I 129.13 Flik 34
24.4.1917	Mt. S. Michele	*Serg.* Arrigoni, *s.ten.* Appiani	Hansa Br. C.I 129.04 Flik 12

Above: All the pilots of 76ᵃ Squadiglia in front of French-built Ni.17 3130. From the left, Fanti, Olivero, Appiani, Retinò, Venchiarutti, De Carolis, Olivi, Bonavoglia, Arrigoni.

12.5.1917	Vertoiba	*Serg*. Fanti	Enemy aircraft OOC
13.5.1917	Mt. Corada	*Serg*. Fanti (& Baracca, 91ᵃ)	Hansa Br. C.I 129.20 FLG 1
23.5.1917	San Daniele	*Serg*. Arrigoni	Hansa Br. C.I FTL
28.5.1917	Peuma	*Ten*. Olivi (& Piccio, 91ᵃ)	Hansa Br. C.I 229.01 Flik 32
1.6.1917	Chiapovano	*S.ten*. Appiani, *serg*. Aquilino	Hansa Br. C.I 69.04? Flik 23?
17.6.1917	Ranziano	*S.ten*. Bonavoglia	Enemy aircraft FTL
17.6.1917	Vertoiba	*Ten*. Olivi	Brandenburg Flik 35?
17.7.1917	San Daniele	*Ten*. Baracchini (& *ser*. Poli, 70ᵃ)	Hansa Br. C.I 69.81 Flik 19
17.7.1917	Lom	*Ten*. Baracchini	Hansa Br. C.I 129.57 Flik 12
29.7.1917	Kneza	*Ten*. Baracchini	Hansa Brandenburg C.I Flik 2
3.8.1917	Val di Sava	*Ten*. Baracchini (& Baracca 91ᵃ)	Two-seater
7.8.1917	Aisovizza	*Ten*. Baracchini	Small balloon
8.8.1917	S.Lucia Tolmino	*Ten*. Baracchini	Brandenburg
12.8.1917	Fratta	*Ten*. Retinò	Enemy aircraft OOC
12.11.1917	Susegana	*Ten*. Fucini, *asp*. Donati	Enemy aircraft
13.11.1917	Arcade	*Ten*. Fucini, *serg*. Razzi (& Masiero, Chiri 78ᵃ)	DFW C.V FA 232
14.11.1917	Colbertaldo	*S.ten*. Scaroni	Flik 28/D?
18.11.1917	San Donà	*S.ten*. Scaroni	Albatros D Jasta 39 or Jasta 1?
19.11.1917	Vidor	*S.ten*. Scaroni (& *Ten*. Masiero?)	Albatros D Jasta 31
19.11.1917	Valdobbiadene	*Ten*. Fucini	Albatros D.III?
30.11.1917	Vidor	*Ten*. Fucini	DFW? FA 14?
5.12.1917	Cornuda	*S.ten*. Scaroni	Aviatik C.I 114.12 Flik 53/D
10.12.1917	Noventa di P.	*S.ten*. Scaroni (& Masiero, Chiri 78ᵃ)	Aviatik C.I 37.24 Flik 58?
16.12.1917	Mount Tomba	*Asp*. Donati	Albatros D.III?
19.12.1917	Conegliano	*S.ten*. Scaroni	Two-seater FA 204?
19.12.1917	Mount Grappa	*Ten*. Buzio, *asp*. Donati, *serg*. Avenati	Two-seater

Above: In 1917 the 76ª Squadriglia also received a few early production Spad 7s.

26.12.1917	Musano	*S.ten.* Scaroni, *ten.* Fucini	DFW FA 2
26.12.1917	Camalò	*S.ten.* Scaroni, *s.ten.* Michetti (& Riva 78ª)	DFW FA(A) 219
26.12.1917	Biadene	*S.ten.* Scaroni (& Brenta 78ª)	AEG G.IV BG.IV/19
11.1.1918	Fontanasecca	*Serg.* Di Loreto	Hansa Br. C.I 369.26 Flik 2/D
12.1.1918	Valstagna	*S.ten.* Scaroni, *s.ten.* Michetti, *serg.* Razzi	Aviatik C.I 114.04 Flik 16/D
14.1.1918	Valbella	*S.ten.* Scaroni	KD 28.71 Flik 21
28.1.1918	Biadene	*S.ten.* Scaroni, *ten.* Fucini	DFW C.V FA(A) 219
28.1.1918	M. Cismon	*Serg.* Razzi	Fighter
1.2.1918	Col S. Martino	*S.ten.* Scaroni	Two-seater
11.2.1918	Fontanasecca	*S.ten.* Scaroni, *serg.* Razzi	Aviatik C.I 137.20? Flik 101/G?
11.2.1918	Cismon	*S.ten.* Scaroni, *serg.* Razzi, *cap.* Sequi, Di Loreto	Phönix D.I 328.18 Flik 8/D
18.2.1918	Pederobba	*S.ten.* Scaroni	Two-seater
22.2.1918	Alano - Brenta	*S.ten.* Nannini	Two-seater
11.3.1918	Fontanasecca	*S.ten.* Scaroni, *cap.* Sequi, *serg.* Razzi, Di Loreto	Av. Berg C.I 137.13 Flik 13
17.3.1918	Val Seren	*Ten.* Retinò, *s.ten.* Nannini, *serg.* Fanti	Two-seater
17.3.1918	Col d'Astico	*S.ten.* Donati	Fighter
21.3.1918	Asiago	*S.ten.* Scaroni, *s.ten.* Michetti	Albatros D.III 153.100 Flik 55/J
25.3.1918	Biadene	*Cap.* Lega, *serg.* Fanti, *ten.* Retinò	Fighter
25.3.1918	S. Pietro di Fel.	*Ten.* Retinò	Fighter
3.4.1918	Premador	*S.ten.* Scaroni, *ten.* Baracchini, *s.ten.* Nannini	Drachen BK 20
23.4.1918	Soprapiana	*Serg.* Razzi	Enemy aircraft
2.5.1918	Cimadolmo	*Ten.* Baracchini	Av. Berg C.I 137.06? Flik 50?
3.5.1918	Sernaglia	*Ten.* Baracchini, *ten.* Michetti	Enemy aircraft
3.5.1918	Col Moschin	*S.ten.* Nannini, *serg.* Ticconi	Two-seater
3.5.1918	Monfenera	*S.ten.* Donati	Hansa Br. CI 169.78? Flik 16?
11.5.1918	Conegliano	*Ten.* Baracchini	Kite Balloon
13.5.1918	Arcade	*Ten.* Baracchini	Albatros D.III 153.189 Flik 68/J
18.5.1918	Conegliano	*Ten.* Baracchini, *serg.* Di Loreto	Kite Balloon
20.5.1918	Sernaglia	*Ten.* Baracchini, serg. Di Loreto, *cpr.* Baggini	Albatros D.III 153.163? Flik 42/J?
22.5.1918	Quero	*Ten.* Scaroni, *s.ten.* Michetti	Two-seater
26.5.1918	Cornadella	*Ten.* Baracchini	Albatros D.III? Flik 42/J?

Above: Pilots of the 76ª Squadriglia with a Spad 7: from the left, Retinò, unknown, De Carolis, Olivi, Bonavoglia. The serial is either 4690 or 4696. (Archive Caliaro)

Right: Baracchini with a Spad; the photo is dated 16 June 1917.

Above: Three Hanriots of the 76ª Squadriglia with a Nieuport 11 showing the heart insignia of the 77ª Squadriglia.

8.6.1918	Mt. Cismon	*Ten.* Scaroni	Hansa Br. C.I 369.40 Flik 11
15.6.1918	Piave River	*Ten.* Scaroni, *s.ten.* Michetti	Two-seater
21.6.1918	Montello	*Ten.* Scaroni, *ten.* Buzio	Av. Berg D.I 115.31 Flik 68/J
24.6.1918	Possagno	*Ten.* Scaroni, *s.ten.* Michetti, *cap.* Lega	Hansa Br. C.I 369.112 Flik 2/D
25.6.1918	Mareno di Piave	*Ten.* Scaroni, *serg.* Ticconi	Albatros D.III 153.202? Flik 42/J?
25.6.1918	Mareno di Piave	*Ten.* Scaroni, *serg.* Ticconi, *serg.* Mondini	Phönix D.II 222.02? Flik 43/J?
7.7.1918	Cima Eckar	*Ten.* Scaroni	Hansa Br. C.I 169.68 Flik 45/D
7.7.1918	Valbella	*Ten.* Scaroni, *serg.* Ticconi	Albatros D.III 153.240 Flik 9/J
7.7.1918	Foza	*Serg.* Ticconi	Albatros D.III 153.98 Flik 55/J
7.7.1918	Casoni	*Ten.* Scaroni, *ten.* Sivori, *serg.* Di Loreto	Phönix D.I 128.19 Flik 14
12.7.1918	Mt. Tomatico	*Ten.* Scaroni (& Magistrini, Keller, 91ª)	Albatros D.III 153.259? Flik 30/J?
14.8.1918	Rasai	*Serg.* Ticconi, *ten.* Michetti, *serg.* Baggini	Fighter
15.8.1918	Colbertaldo	*Serg.* Ticconi	Phönix D.I 328.04 Flik 37/P
20.8.1918	S. Polo di Tezze	*Serg.* Razzi	Fighter OOC
15.9.1918	Bessica	*Serg.* Mordini	Enemy aircraft OOC
16.9.1918	Val Stizzone	*Serg.* Baggini, *serg.* Mondini	Enemy aircraft
17.9.1918	Mt. Cismon	*Serg.* Baggini, *serg.* Mondini	Enemy aircraft
27.10.1918	S.Pietro Barboz.	*Ten.* Sivori, *serg.* Baggini	Fighter
28.10.1918	Asolone	*Ten.* Sivori, *sold.* Magnetti, *sold.* Giovanardi	Hansa Br. C.I 369.146 Flik 48

Casualties and Combat Losses of the 76ª Squadriglia

Date	Place	A/c	Pilot	Cause
21.8.1916		Ni 1615	*Serg.* Iori POW	Accident
16.2.1917	Merna	Nieuport 17	*Serg.* Arrigoni UNH	Ground fire
14.5.1917	Ciprianisca	Nieuport	*Ten.* Broili KIA	Enemy aircraft
17.6.1917	Merna	Spad 4703	*Ten.* Olivi KIC	Accident
8.8.1917	Vocheiner	Spad	*Ten.* Baracchini WIA	Fighter
3.10.1917	M. Fleme	Hanriot?	*Ten.* Di Rudinì KIA	Fighters
25.10.1917	Jdersko	Hanriot	*Ten.* Veronesi KIA	Fighters?
18.11.1917		Hanriot?	*Cap.* Sequi WIA	Fighters
6.2.1918		Hd 6191	*Serg.* Ticconi UNH	Ground fire
12.7.1918		Hd 7517	*Ten.* Scaroni WIA	Fighters

Above: Hanriot Hd.1 c/n 50 abandoned at Borgnano during the retreat.

Above: Hanriot Hd.1 6647 of *ten*. Mario Fucini at Istrana, December 1917.

Above: Baracchini with his Hanriot 515 marked with the four aces.

Above: The Hanriot of Renato Donati had an old shoe as insignia. (Archive Franz Selinger)

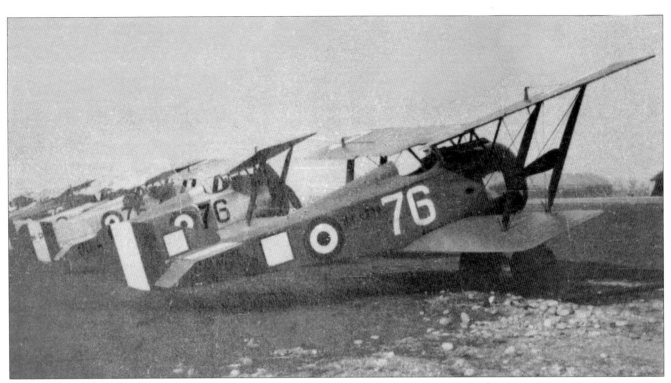

Above: The Hanriot of Silvio Scaroni, with his square insignia on its fuselage and tail. (Archive Achille Vigna)

Above: *Cap*. Lega, a doctor, in front of his Hanriot, missing its tail. (Archive Franz Selinger).

Above: The Hanriot, French c/n 519, of *tenente* Giuseppe Retinò: during the war he flew 135 combat missions, consisting of 57 offensive patrols, 45 patrols, and 32 escort flights. In 1919 he was an instructor in Poland.

Above: Silvio Scaroni with his Hanriot 7517 modified to carry two Vickers guns.

Above: The Hanriot 6206 of *aspirante* Raimondo Di Loreto. (Archive Franz Selinger)

Magg. Vincenzo Lombard with his Hanriot with the insigna of Group commander. On the fuselage, where the 6 is, there is a fairing with holes, to drop bombs.

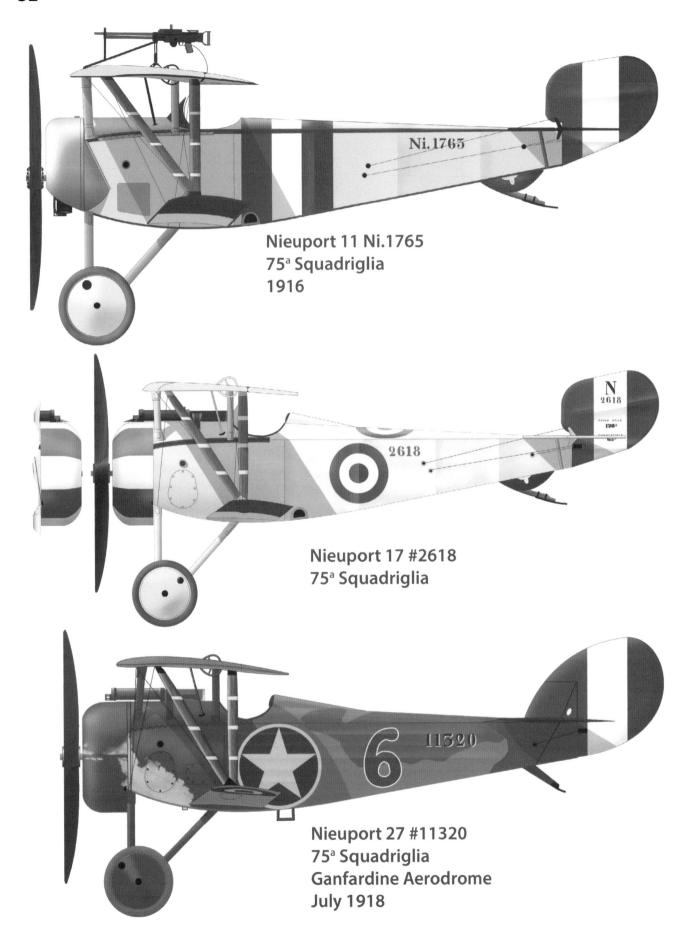

Nieuport 11 Ni.1765
75ª Squadriglia
1916

Nieuport 17 #2618
75ª Squadriglia

Nieuport 27 #11320
75ª Squadriglia
Ganfardine Aerodrome
July 1918

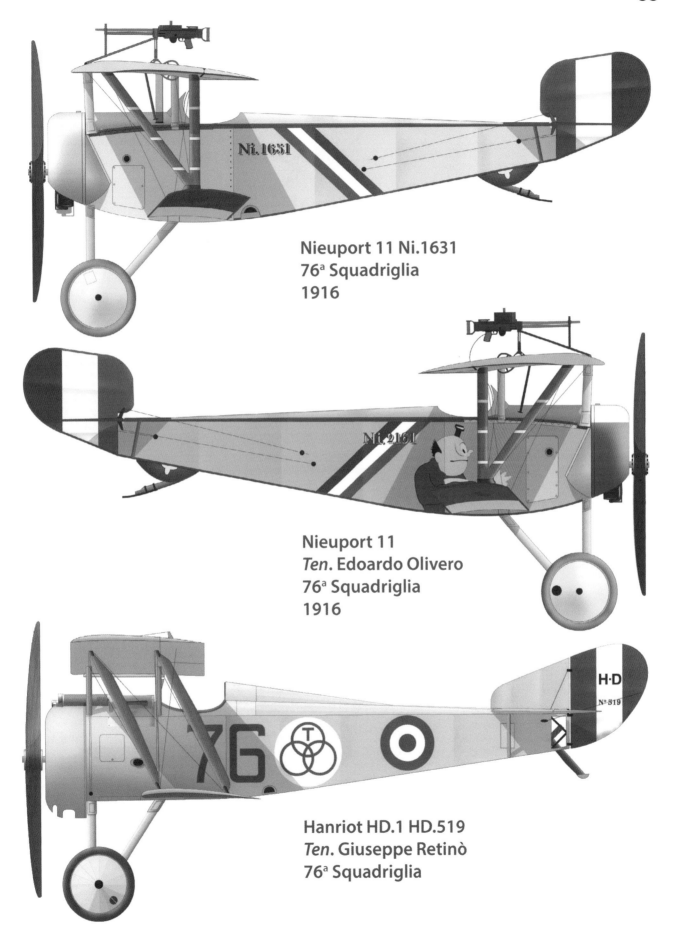

Nieuport 11 Ni.1631
76ª Squadriglia
1916

Nieuport 11
Ten. Edoardo Olivero
76ª Squadriglia
1916

Hanriot HD.1 HD.519
Ten. Giuseppe Retinò
76ª Squadriglia

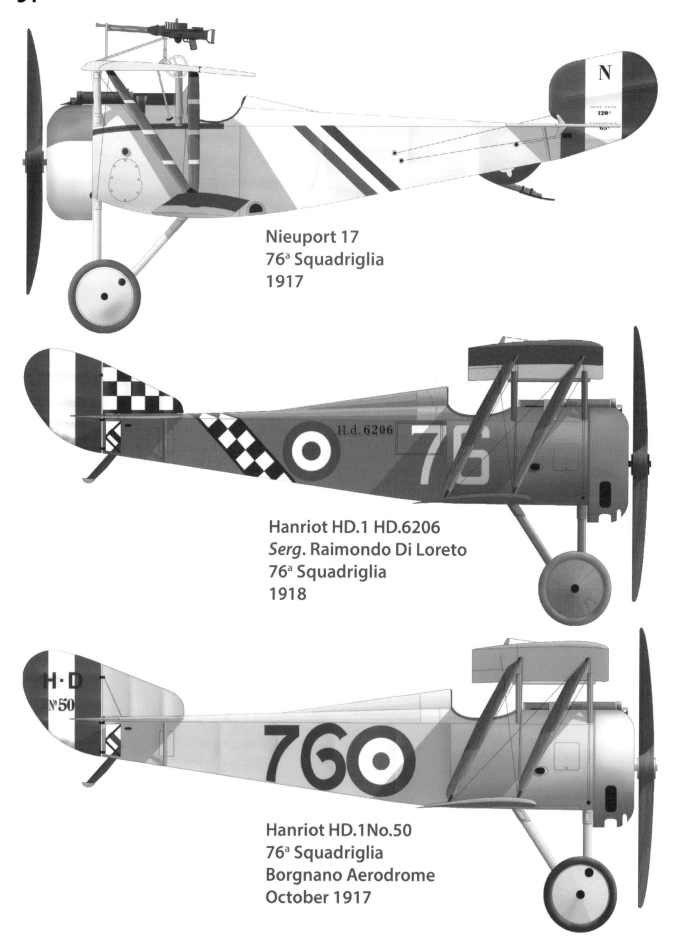

Nieuport 17
76ª Squadriglia
1917

Hanriot HD.1 HD.6206
Serg. Raimondo Di Loreto
76ª Squadriglia
1918

Hanriot HD.1No.50
76ª Squadriglia
Borgnano Aerodrome
October 1917

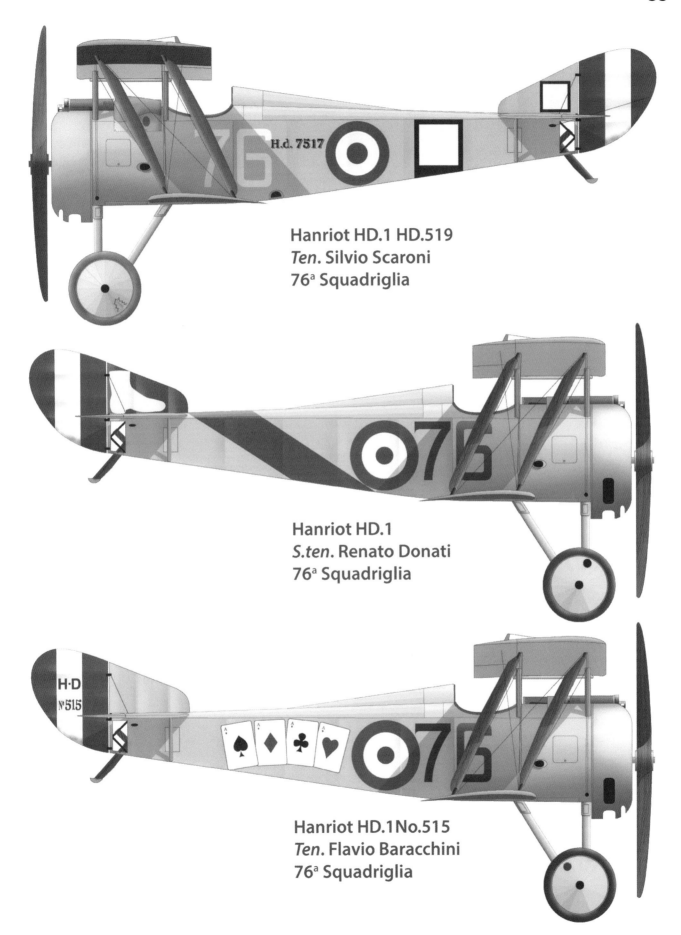

Hanriot HD.1 HD.519
Ten. Silvio Scaroni
76ª Squadriglia

Hanriot HD.1
S.ten. Renato Donati
76ª Squadriglia

Hanriot HD.1 No.515
Ten. Flavio Baracchini
76ª Squadriglia

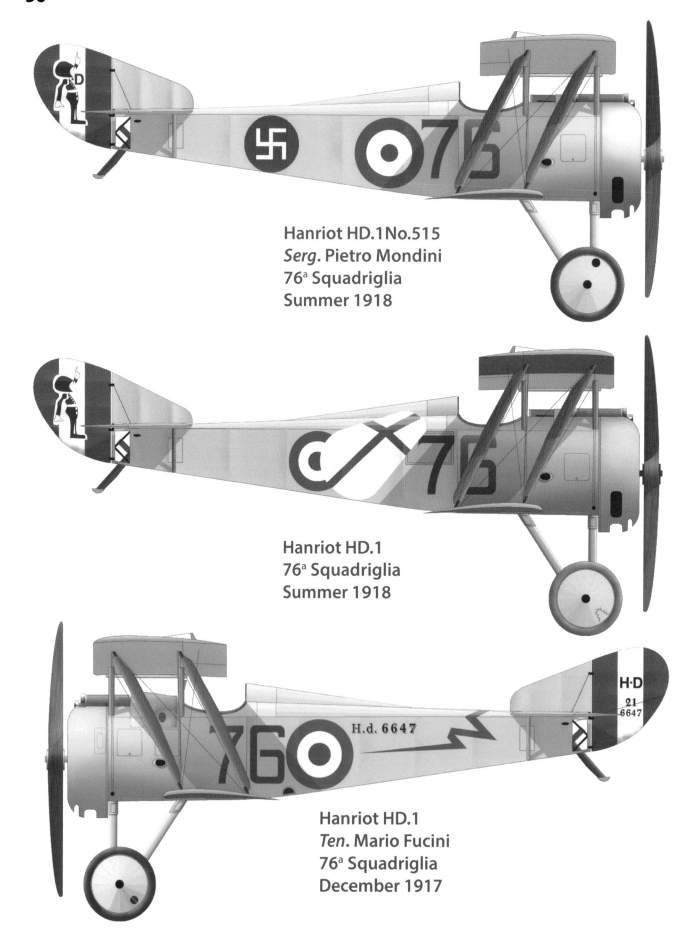

Hanriot HD.1 No.515
Serg. Pietro Mondini
76ª Squadriglia
Summer 1918

Hanriot HD.1
76ª Squadriglia
Summer 1918

Hanriot HD.1
Ten. Mario Fucini
76ª Squadriglia
December 1917

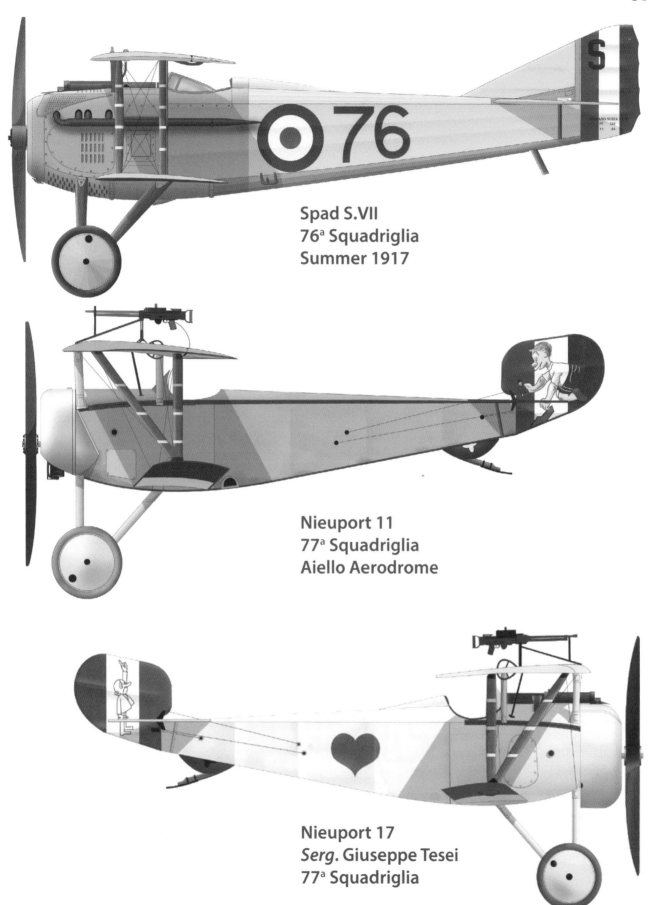

Spad S.VII
76ª Squadriglia
Summer 1917

Nieuport 11
77ª Squadriglia
Aiello Aerodrome

Nieuport 17
Serg. Giuseppe Tesei
77ª Squadriglia

Above: Near the end of the war, each Hanriot of the 76ᵃ Squadriglia had a personal insignia, but some shared a cartoon character on the rudder, also from the book "*Come ti erudisco il pupo*". The first one, with a white swastika, is the one of Mondini, the second one, a white owl, Pasta, the third one, cross on a shield, Sivori, the fifth one, checkerboard, Di Loreto.

Above: Near the end of the war, supply of Macchi-built Hanriots with dark camouflage was plentiful.

77ª Squadriglia

Above: *Sergente* Tesei with Nieuport 11 1611 of the 77ª Squadriglia.

The 77ª Squadriglia Nieuport was formed on 31 May 1916 at La Comina airfield. It was assigned to the Supreme Command and based at Istrana, and it became operative on Nieuport 10s on 18 June 1916, with as commander *cap.* Pier Ruggero Piccio, and with the pilots *ten.* Carlo Savio, *s.tenenti* Ferruccio Ranza and Giovanni Fasoli, *sergenti* Giuseppe Tesei, Domenico Piaggio and Cosimo Rizzotto, *cpr.* Giovanni Bozzetto. It began its combat missions in July 1916, meanwhile re-equipping with the Nieuport 11, flying 22 missions in the month, with two air duels, one on the 26th, with *s.ten.* Fasoli and Ranza, and one on the 27th, Ranza and *ten.* Savio against a Brandenburg that was hit, dropping its machine gun and camera. This event was recognized as a confirmed victory for Ranza, although the pilot himself reported that the airplane "*visibly hit, has crossed the lines at low altitude*" and in effect Br. C.1 61.23 of Flik 24 with the crew of *Zgsf.* Jezek and *Oblt.* Kenzian von Kenzianhausen crashed, with its occupants wounded.

In August 1916 the 77ª Squadriglia moved to the field of Cascina Farello, Aquileia, close to the Adriatic Sea, with the mission of giving protection to the seaplanes of the Navy, and in that month, it flew 38 sorties. On 5 September it was assigned to the I Gruppo. In September the unit flew 124 sorties, and had 11 air combats. On 13 September there was a large combined operation against Trieste, with formations of Caproni bombers and the escort of 16 seaplanes, from

Venice and Grado, 14 Italian and French fighters of the Escadrille de Venise. On the next day the Austrians retaliated and three flying boats attacked the Italian positions, during a visit of King Victor Emmanuel and of the King of Serbia. The 77ª Squadriglia rose up to the challenge and Ranza, flying Nieuport 17 2613 armed with a Vickers gun, and Savio claimed victories against two seaplanes, that alighted in the Gulf of Panzano, one of them listing, as the observers of the Navy reported. In the second half of the month there were several encounters with enemy Brandenburg C.1 with two of them facing the guns of *serg.* Tesei and *cap.* Piccio.

In October 1916 the 77ª Squadriglia flew 109 sorties with many air combats. *Cap.* Piccio using Le Prieur rockets obtained from the French fighters in Venice shot down a Drachen on 18 October, while on the 23rd and 31st Piaggio and Tesei claimed a victory each. In November the unit flew 156 missions, and on the 25th there were a series of air combats during which Ranza forced down two enemy two-seaters, both confirmed, in two separate flights. The events of that day are confused, the Austrians lost several airplanes and the identity of victims cannot be positively assigned.

On 14 November 1916 the airfield of Cascina Farello was bombed, and *serg. pil.* Adelmondo Nardi and motorist Gustavo Madon were killed.

In December the 77ª Squadriglia flew 77 war missions, leading to five air combats for Savio, Rizzotto, Piccio, Ranza

Above: Giuseppe Tesei in the cockpit of Nieuport 1625, showing camouflage applied in the field.

Above: This Nieuport 11 at Aiello airfield, with an ugly kid playing with a Kaiser doll and a submarine, could be either of the 77ª or the 80ª Squadriglia, behind it there is another Ni.11 with a red heart and the shield of Savoy.

and Bozzetto, all of them inconclusive. During 1916 the 77ª Squadriglia flew 526 combat flights, had 30 air combats and shot down two airplanes and one balloon – according to the official report, that ignores several reliable victory claims. *Cap.* Piccio received a *Medaglia d'Argento* while there was a Bronze Medal for Ranza and two for Piaggio and Savio.

On 1 January 1917 the 77ª Squadriglia was still at Cascina Farello in I Gruppo for the 3ª Armata, with the same commander and pilots, plus *cap.* Ettore Croce, equipped with Nieuports 80 and 110 hp. On 26 January *cap.* Croce became commander, but *ten.* Feruccio Ranza very soon replaced him. In February the 77ª put up 103 sorties and scored two victories, Brandenburg 29.63 shot down by Piaggio on the 16th, and 27.60 shot down by Rizzotto on the 28th, while Tesei claimed a probable victory on the 17th. In March 1917 the unit moved to the airfield of Aiello, in the same area, and received its first Spad 7 fighters. A new pilot joined its ranks, *ten.* Giovanni De Briganti, of later fame as Schneider Trophy racer and Fiat test pilot.

In May 1917 the 77ª Squadriglia had on strength Nieuport 11s serials 1627, 1680, 2113 and 2132, Nieuport 17s serials 2613, 3135, 3136, 3137, and Spads 3121, 4695 and 4696.

Its pilots were *tenenti* Pier Carlo Bergonzi, Giovani Fasoli, Alberto Marazzani, Carlo Molinari, Ranza, Savio, *asp.* Piaggio, *sergenti* Tesei and Rizzotto, *cpr.* Giovanni Bozzetto.

In that month, as the 10th Offensive took place, there

were many air combats, but the pilots could claim only one victory, by *ten.* Alberto Marazzani on the 27th. On 25 May there was a tragic accident, as motorist Edoardo Cucchetti was killed by the propeller as he was starting the engine of Nieuport 2117 of Marazzani. In June again there were frequent encounters with Austrian aircraft, and on 22 June *asp.* Piaggio together with Baracchini of the 81ª Squadriglia forced down Brandenburg 229.05 at Aisovizza (the Command however rejected his claim).

On 7 July Cosimo Rizzotto with the help of *ten.* Giulio Sambonet shot down an airplane over Mount Stol, soldiers recovered parts of the burned wreck, showing serial 112.2, but Austrian sources provide no identification for this event. Four days later, on the 11th, Rizzotto claimed another victory over a fighter, after a tough dogfight, near Voiscizza. The unit received *ten.* Guido Keller and *serg.* Ambrogio Viganò from the 80ª while *ten.* Marazzani became the commander on 9 July.

During the period of the big August 1917 offensive, the 77ª Squadriglia flew no less than 398 sorties, had three air combats and shot down two airplanes. On 19 August an air battle developed as Marazzani and De Briganti were in an escort mission for a SP.2, both pilots each claimed to have shot down a fighter. Their opponents were fighters of Flik 42/J. The intense air activity during the 11th Offensive also caused losses, and on 20 August *s.ten.* Mario Leggiadri was shot down and killed at Vizovlia (Visaglie) in his Nieuport

Above: French-built Nieuport 17 2613 of the 77ᵃ Squadriglia.

3623. The winner was the Austrian Sabeditsch flying on Berg D.1 38.01, it was the first victory for this new type of fighter.

In September 1917 there were other duels, with only a possible victory reported by Rizzotto near Gorizia. On 29 September the 77ᵃ Squadriglia lost *serg. pil.* Giuseppe Tesio, three fighters of Flik 55/J shot him down at Medana, near Ternova. On that day Rizzotto shared in the destruction of a Brandenburg C.1 at Pietrarossa together with fighters of the 91ᵃ Squadriglia. On 9 October Rizzotto attacked an all-red enemy fighter over Punta Sdobba: it may have been the enemy top ace, Godwin Brumowski, who had just shot down a kite balloon in that area. Rizzotto went after him at low level, but then his engine malfunctioned, so the tables turned and when the engine failed the Italian pilot crash landed in a swamp at Matarussi. Austrian records don't report this event as a victory for Brumowski.

At the time of the Caporetto breakthrough, the 77ᵃ Squadriglia began an orderly retreat, while taking part in many strafing and ground attack missions. Its pilots scored several victories, at the expense of Austrian flying boats and aircraft, and some of its pilots reached acedom: *s.ten.* Carlo Lombardi, *s.ten.* Giannino Ancillotto, *brig.* Ernesto Cabruna. The squadron moved to La Comina, then to Arcade and finally it settled at Marcon, near Venice, again in the lowest part of the front of the 3ᵃ Armata, and there on 8 November it became part of the new XIII Gruppo of *cap.* Gordesco. Meanwhile it received some pilots from its sister unit, the 80ᵃ, those who were better suited for its Spad fighters. Its force now included *cap.* Gordesco, *ten.* Marazzani, commander, *ten.* De Briganti, *s.tenenti* Ancillotto, Bozzetto, Lombardi, *asp.* Degli Esposti, *brig.* Cabruna, *sergenti* Allasia, Avon and Rizzotto.

On 6 November *serg.* Rizzotto shot down Brandenburg 229.24 of Flik 12 at San Michele di Conegliano, in collaboration with *s.ten.* Contardini of the 82ᵃ and *serg.* Leonardi of the 80ᵃ Squadriglia, and the next day *serg.* Felice Avon and Allasia shot down another aircraft near the Livenza River.

Ancillotto could see his house, across the Piave River, now occupied by the Austrians, and used as a command post. He managed to obtain an old Nieuport 11 equipped with Le Prieur rockets and flew it against the kite balloons floating over his land. He shot down the first one on 30 November, another one on 3 December. On 5 December he attacked so aggressively that he flew his Nieuport through the burning balloon, and returned to base with big pieces of cloth wrapped around the wing struts. The *Medaglia d'Oro*, Italy's highest award, crowned his daring. Also, on 5 December Cabruna with *asp.* Amleto Degli Esposti of the 80ᵃ and Carabelli of the 83ᵃ shot down Brandenburg 69.13 of Flik 32 at Salgareda.

The decorations assigned to the pilots of the 77ᵃ Squadriglia for service in 1917 included the *Medaglia d'Oro*, to Ancillotto, Silver Medals to *tenenti* De Briganti, Marazzani (two) *s.ten.* Lombardi (two), *sergenti* Allasia, Rizzotto (two), Tesei, Tesio, and Bronzes to *cap.* Croce, *tenenti* Fasoli and Savio, *serg.* Allasia and Piaggio.

On 1 January 1918 the 77ᵃ Squadriglia Spad based at Marcon was part of the XIII Gruppo, with *cap.* Gordesco who was also the Group commander, and the pilots *ten.* Alberto Marazzani, acting squadron commander, *s.tenenti* Ancillotto, Lombardi, Bozzetto, *brig.* Cabruna, *asp.* Degli Esposti, *sergenti* Rizzotto, Avon and Allasia.

In February the 77ᵃ Squadriglia attacked the enemy

Above: A Nieuport tail with the cartoon *"Come ti erudisco il pupo"*, and behind it, again the Ni.11 with the heart and the shield of Savoy.

airfield at Falzè with pilots Marazzani, Ancillotto and Lombardi. On 29 March Cabruna alone attacked a formation of ten enemy fighters that were escorting a two-seater, and he downed the formation leader over Conegliano. This feat was much commended, and the pilot received the highest award, the *Medaglia d'Oro al Valor Militare* although no source from Austrian archives confirms this event.

By mid-May, the pilots of the 77ª Squadriglia were its commander Marazzani, *tenenti* Sambonet and Vincenzo Arone, *s.tenenti* Carabelli, Lombardi, Ancillotto and Bozzetto, *brig.* Cabruna, *sergenti* Rizzotto, Elia Liut and Albino Giannotti. Exchanges with the other fighter unit of the XIII Gruppo, the 80ª Squadriglia, however were very common. During the month of May 1918, the 77ª Squadriglia flew 216 combat missions, engaged in 12 air combats but didn't claim any victory.

During the large air combats accompanying the Austrian offensive in mid-June, victories were frequent, no less than 22 on the single first day of the battle, 15 June, although overclaiming is possible in the hectic activities of that day, so the eight claims of the 77ª Squadriglia cannot be connected to known Austrian losses. On 16 June *s.ten.* Carabelli fought against an Albatros D.3 at Negrisia and claimed it shot down near the Piave River. He was then assigned to 108ª Squadriglia. *Cap.* Filippo Serafini, a gallant pilot who had been a Caproni pilot, was sent to the 77ª Squadriglia, and

on 19 June, together with another Spad of his squadron, of *ten.* Sambonet, and with a Hanriot of the 80ª, with pilot Gelmetti, shot down a Brandenburg near Monastir. On 20 June Cabruna scored another victory with Piermattei and Sottani of the 80ª. On 21 June *s.ten.* Pietro Molino attacked a kite balloon at Ceggia, shooting no less than 300 machine gun rounds at close range without any result, until Cabruna also joined the attack, finally setting it on fire. On 21 June *cap.* Serafini assumed command of the 77ª on 21 June, relieving Marazzani

New pilots arrived: *cap.* Umberto Gelmetti, *ten.* Carlo Alberto Conelli de Prosperi and *serg.* Luigi Corti, all coming from the 80ª Squadriglia. In this period the 77ª had on strength Spads with serials 164, 238, 248, 272, 389, 1077, 1184, 1666, 1689, 1690, 2361, 2475, 2476, 6294, 6302, 6361, 6334, 14208. Its emblem was a red heart, which used to be the personal insignia of Piccio.

On 16 July Serafini, *ten.* Conelli and *serg.* Corti attacked a lonely enemy fighter above Zenson, but they couldn't ascertain the result of this combat. This victory however later on was credited to Conelli de Prosperi. On 24 July the 77ª Squadriglia got credit for a remarkable feat, the first night victory (and a double one, too) by Italian fighters. The author of this accomplishment was Ancillotto, who shot down two Brandenburg C.1s engaged in a night bombing raid against Treviso. Despite this outstanding victory, all that

Above: The Nieuport 17 of Tesei. The caption says: "It raised the wrath of the Supreme Command for the innocent good luck charm painted on the rudder."

the squadron papers in the archives present is a letter by the (Gold Medal holder) pilot, who had to justify himself to the Command of the XIII Gruppo for having dared collect a machine gun and two rudders as souvenir. The rudders now are in the Museum of Vicenza.

On 11 August *ten.* Conelli de Prosperi, with his wingman *serg.* Corti, shot down a reconnaissance Berg in the sky of Pralongo. On 14 (or 15?) September *ten.* Carlo Lamperti, who had joined the 77ᵃ just the day before, shot down a fighter together with *serg.* Bruno Albertazzi. Many new pilots arrived in the last weeks of the war from the 5ᵃ Sezione Caccia at Padua.

On 26 September Cabruna, had an accident landing at Castenedolo on Ansaldo A.1 serial 16548, he was hospitalized with a broken clavicle, but the next day, against the doctors advise, he returned to the squadron, flying since the 29ᵗʰ with an almost useless right arm.

On 23 October 1918 the 77ᵃ Squadriglia was assigned to the *Massa da Caccia*, the Fighter Mass assembled for the final offensive. During the Battle of Vittorio Veneto this unit flew 243 sorties, with pilots flying three missions a day, was engaged in seven combats and shot down nine enemy aircraft, according to the official reports, but less according to detailed analysis of the data. On 28 October there were many

combats, in one of them *ten.* Nicola Corbo attacked at close range an enemy fighter and saw it going down steeply toward Mansuè, but he couldn't ascertain its fate as six more fighters attacked him. Also, on that day Serafini and Ancillotto went in an offensive patrol over San Fior airfield, had a dogfight with enemy fighters, which they mis-identified as Pfalz, that were already dueling with some Sopwith Camels. The Italians shot down two enemies, one certain and one probable, while the British pilots claimed a third one, while losing one of their number. On 2 November *serg.* Carlo Ferrario made an emergency landing with his Spad 1673 hit by enemy ground fire, but he rejoined the lines on Armistice Day.

On 4 November 1918 the 77ᵃ Squadriglia, directly reporting to the Comando Superiore d'Aeronautica, had 13 serviceable Spads and its pilots were *cap.* Serafini, *tenenti* Giovanni Amendolito, Nicola Corbo, Antonio Morganti, Bartolomeo Cussino, *s.tenenti* Alessandro Ballesio, Lamperti, Cabruna, Molino, Alberto Ortali, *sergenti* Inardo Avandino, Nicola Malaspina, Bruno Albertazzi, Corti, Carlo Ferrario, *caporali* Domenico Padovan, Antonio Abba, Raul Oladini, *soldato* Luigi Capitani.

Overall, from 1 November 1917 (the papers for all preceding periods were lost during the retreat) to 4 November 1918 the 77ᵃ Squadriglia flew 372 offensive

Above: Three different types, Spad, Nieuport 11, and Nieuport 17, of the 77ª Squadriglia at Aiello.

patrol sorties, 667 escort flights, 1,466 standing patrols, 44 photographic reconnaissance flights, for a total of 2,549 combat missions and 2,374 hours of flight, plus 47 sorties against kite balloons and 34 night sorties. It was engaged in 108 air combats, shooting down 25 enemy aircraft (10 within Italian lines and 15 in enemy territory) and 5 kite balloons; it dropped 188 spherical bombs and 335 small bombs. Five of its pilots were officially credited as aces: Ancillotto with 11 victories, Lombardi with 8, Cabruna with 8, Rizzotto with 6 and Allasia with 5.

During 1918 the decorations awarded to its personnel were: the Gold Medal to brig. Cabruna, the *Medaglia d'Argento* to Ancillotto, Allasia, Bozzetto, Conelli de Prosperi, Luigi Corti, *cap*. Gelmetti (for a different feat, a night mission carrying behind the lines the secret agents of the "Giovane Italia" operation), to Lombardi, (three), Marazzani, (three), *ten*. Pietro Molino (for his previous service as a bomber pilot), Rizzotto and Sambonet (two each). Albertazzi, Carabelli, Ferrario, Pascoli and Serafini received a Bronze Medal.

The complex of the war activities of this unit is over 5,000

Above: A pilot of the 77ª Squadriglia in the cockpit of Nieuport 17 3656.

combat sorties, about 250 air combats, 50 credited victories, two fallen on the field of honour, two *Medaglie d'Oro*, nineteen *Medaglie d'Argento*, ten *Medaglie di Bronzo*.

After the armistice the 77ª Squadriglia was posted at Zaule airfield, Trieste, under the command of *cap*. Raoul Da Barberino, and it was disbanded in May 1919, to be re-formed in 1923.

Identified Victory Claims of the 77ª Squadriglia

Date	Place	Pilots	Victim
27.7.1916	?	*S.ten*. Ranza, *ten*. Savio	Hansa Br. C.I 61.23 Flik 24
14.9.1916	Gulf of Panzano	*S.ten*. Ranza, *ten*. Savio	Seaplane
17.9.1916	Isonzo	*Serg*. Tesei	Hansa Br. C.I 64.06? Flik 28?
25.9.1916	Doberdò	*Cap*. Piccio	Hansa Br. C.I 64.47? Flik 12?
18.10.1916	Mauhinie	*Cap*. Piccio	Kite Balloon
23.10.1916	Schoenpass	*Serg*. Piaggio	Hansa Br. C.I 26.28 Flik 2
31.10.1916	Nad Logem	*Serg*. Tesei (& Stoppani 76ª, Caselli 70ª)	Hansa Br. C.I 68.25 Flik 12
25.11.1916	Schoenpass	*Ten*. Ranza (& Olivi 76ª)	Hansa Br. C.I 29.54 Flik 23
25.11.1916	Hermada	*Ten*. Ranza	Hansa Br. C.I 27.53 Flik 28
17.1.1917	Vermegliano	*Asp*. Piaggio	Hansa Br. C.I 27.67 FTL? Flik 23?

Above: The fighters of the 77ᵃ Squadriglia at Aiello.

Left: Carlo "Francis" Lombardi in a Spad of the 77ᵃ Squadriglia.

16.2.1917		*Asp.* Piaggio	Hansa Br. C.I 29.63? Flik 19?
17.2.1917	Hermada	*Serg.* Tesei	Enemy aircraft
28.2.1917	Monfalcone	*Serg.* Rizzotto	Hansa Br. C.I 27.60 Flik 34
4.4.1917	Oppachiasella	*Ten.* Ranza	Enemy aircraft FTL
27.5.1917	Sistiana	*Ten.* Marazzani	Enemy aircraft
22.6.1917	San Marco	*Asp.* Piaggio (& Baracchini, Novelli, 81ᵃ)	Hansa Br. C.I 229.05 Flik 35
7.7.1917	Mt. Stol	*Serg.* Rizzotto (& Sambonet, 80ᵃ)	112.2??
11.7.1917	Voiscizza	*Serg.* Rizzotto	Fighter
19.8.1917	Voiscizza	*Ten.* De Briganti, *ten.* Marazzani	Albatros D.III 153.14 Flik 42/J
19.8.1917	Voiscizza	*Ten.* De Briganti, *ten.* Marazzani	Albatros D.III 153? Flik 42/J
29.9.1917	Pietrarossa	*Serg.* Rizzotto (& Sabelli, Parvis, 91ᵃ)	Hansa Br. C.I 329.16 Flik 28
26.10.1917	Lake Doberdò	*S.ten.* Lombardi (& Leonardi, Ancillotto, 80ᵃ)	K212
27.10.1917	Lake Doberdò	*S.ten.* Lombardi (& Leonardi, Ancillotto, 80ᵃ)	Hansa Br. C.I 329.23 Flik 101/G
27.10.1017	Ranziano	*S.ten.* Lombardi	Hansa Br. C.I 329.02 Flik 101/G
27.10.1917	Lake Doberdò	*Ten.* Sambonet	Albatros D.III Flik 42/J?
3.11.1917	Oderzo	*S.ten.* Lombardi (& Ancillotto, 80ᵃ)	DFW FA 14
4.11.1917	Cividale	*S.ten.* Lombardi	Albatros D? Jasta 39?
6.11.1917	Conegliano	*Serg.* Rizzotto (& Leonardi, 80ᵃ)	Hansa Br. C.I 229.24 Flik 12
7.11.1917	Livenza River	*Serg.* Avon (& Allasia, 80ᵃ)	? FA 204 (A)?
30.11.1917	Fossalta	*S.ten.* Ancillotto	Kite balloon BK 13

Above: Carlo "Francis" Lombardi had a full and rewarding life. After the war he volunteered with d'Annunzio in the revolt of Fiume, in 1930 he flew with a tourist plane to Somalia, then to Japan and finally he toured all of Africa; in 1934 he flew a SIAI S.71 direct to Somalia, then he tried a flight to Argentina that was stopped on the coast of Brazil. He then founded the AVIA company that produced the much-loved FL-3 tourist plane and then sport cars until the '70s. He wrote books about his memories, one, "*Gli amici di Marcon*", recalling his times at 77ª Squadriglia. Here he is (second from left) with the SIAI S.71 I-ALPI in Natal, Brazil.

3.12.1917	S. Polo	*S.ten*. Ancillotto	Kite balloon BK 10
5.12.1917	Rustignè	*S.ten*. Ancillotto	Kite balloon BK 2
5.12.1917	Salgareda	*Brig*. Cabruna (Degli Esposti, 80ª Carabelli, 83ª)	Hansa Br. C.I 69.17 Flik 32/B
12.3.1918	San Donà	*Brig*. Cabruna (& Rossi, Riva, 83ª)	Aviatik Berg C.I 214.04? Flik 49/D?
16.3.1918	San Donà	*Serg*. Liut	Berg D.I Flik 69?
29.3.1918	Piave	*Brig*. Cabruna	Fighter?
15.6.1918	Grave di P.	*Cap*. Serafini	Hansa Br.C.I 369.69? Flik 19/D?
15.6.1918	Roncadelle	*Ten*. Sambonet	Albatros 153.211 Flik 51/J?
15.6.1918	San Biagio	*Ten*. Lombardi	Albatros Flik 41/J?
15.6.1918	Tezze	*M.llo* Cabruna	Albatros D.III 153.211 Flik 51/J?
15.6.1918	Candelù	*Ten*. Marazzani	Hansa Br. C.I 169.111 Flik 69
15.6.1918	Ponte di Piave	*Serg*. Rizzotto	Enemy aircraft OOC
15.6.1918	S. Bartolomeo	*S.ten*. Carabelli	Enemy aircraft
16.6.1918	Vascon	*Ten*. Lombardi	Hansa Br. C.I 29.32?
16.6.1918	Fontana	*S.ten*. Carabelli	Alb.? Flik 42/J?
19.6.1918	Monastir	*Cap*. Serafini, *ten*. Sambonet (& Gelmetti, 80ª)	Aviatik C.I 137.40 Flik 5/F
20.6.1918	San Donà	*M.llo* Cabruna (& Piermattei, Sottani, 80ª)	Hansa Br. C.I 329.39 Flik 22/D
21.6.1918	Ceggia	*M.llo* Cabruna (& Piermattei, 80ª)	Kite balloon
16.7.1918	Piave	*Cap*. Serafini, *ten*. Conelli, *serg*. Corti	Fighter OOC
24.7.1918	Treviso	*Ten*. Ancillotto	Hansa Br. C.I 169.121 Flik 101/G
24.7.1918	Treviso	*Ten*. Ancillotto	Hansa Br. C.I 129.38 Flik 101/G

Above: Pilots of the 77ª Squadriglia; third from left is Serafini, fifth Lombardi.

11.8.1918	Pralongo	*Ten*. Conelli de Prosperi	Aviatik Berg C.I 37.56 Flik 22/D
21.8.1918	Salgareda	*Ten*. Conelli de Prosperi, *ten*. Ancillotto	Brandenburg
14.9.1918	Roncade	*Ten*. Lamperti, *serg*. Albertazzi (& Corti, 80ª)	Phönix D.I 228.08? Flik 46/P?
25.10.1918	Aiello?	*M.llo* Cabruna	Fighter?
25.10.1918	Aiello?	*M.llo* Cabruna	Fighter?
28.10.1918	San Fior	*Ten*. Ancillotto, *cap*. Serafini	Fighter

Casualties and Combat Losses of the 77ª Squadriglia

Date	Place	Aircraft	Pilot	Cause
20.8.1917	Vizovlie	Ni.17 3623	*S.ten*. Leggiadri KIA	Fighters
29.9.1917	Medana	?	*Serg*. Tesio KIA	Fighters
9.10.1917	Matarussi	?	*Serg*. Rizzotto UNH	Fighters
2.11.1918		Spad 1673	*Serg*. Ferrario UNH	Ground fire?

Left: *Cap*. Gelmetti with a Spad of the 77ª Squadriglia.

Above & Below: Giannino Ancillotto with the Nieuport 11 carrying the cloth from the kite balloon he destroyed on 5 December 1917.

Above: The Spads of the 77ª squadriglia ai Marcon. (Collection Lancellotti)

Above: The Spad of Cabruna, showing his emblem, the shield of the city of Cortona, and little iron crosses on the fuselage deck, marking his victories.

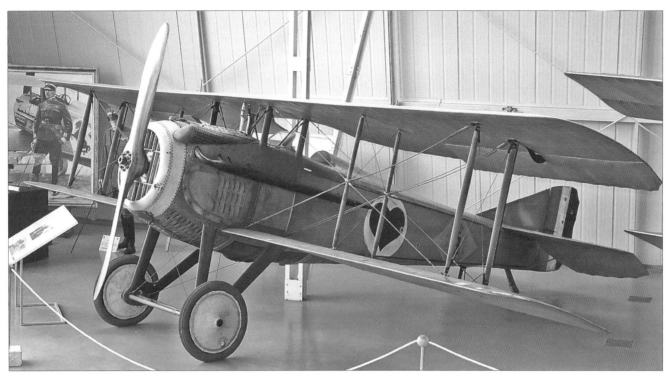

Above: Cabruna's original Spad is now preserved in the Italian Air Force Museum at Vigna di Valle.

Above: Two Spads survive in Italy with the colors of Cabruna: his original one, in the Italian Air Force Museum in Vigna di Valle, and another original Spad, in the Officers School of the Carabineri in Rome.

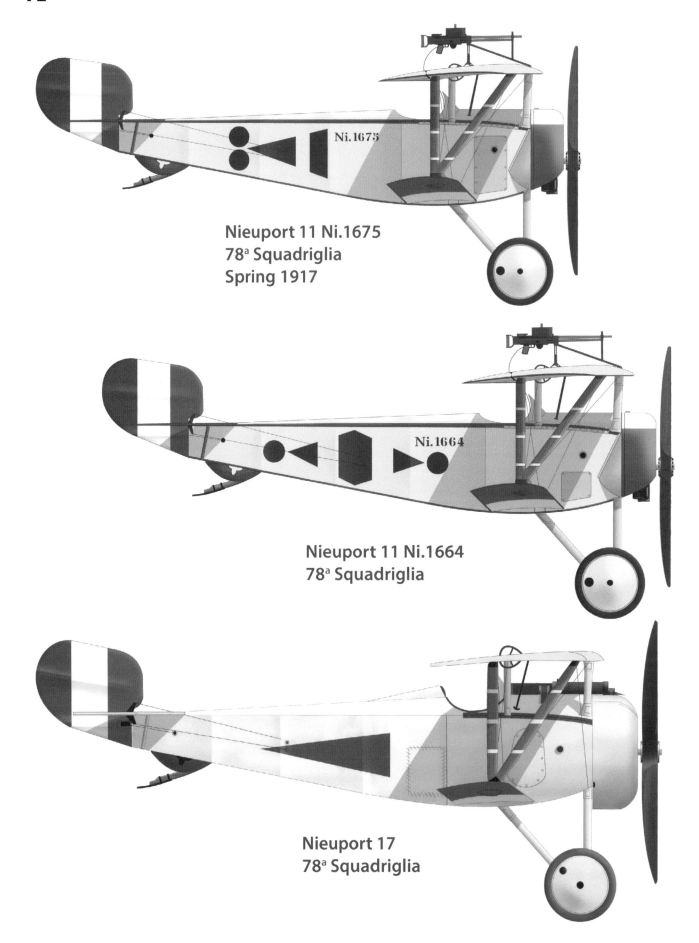

Nieuport 11 Ni.1675
78ª Squadriglia
Spring 1917

Nieuport 11 Ni.1664
78ª Squadriglia

Nieuport 17
78ª Squadriglia

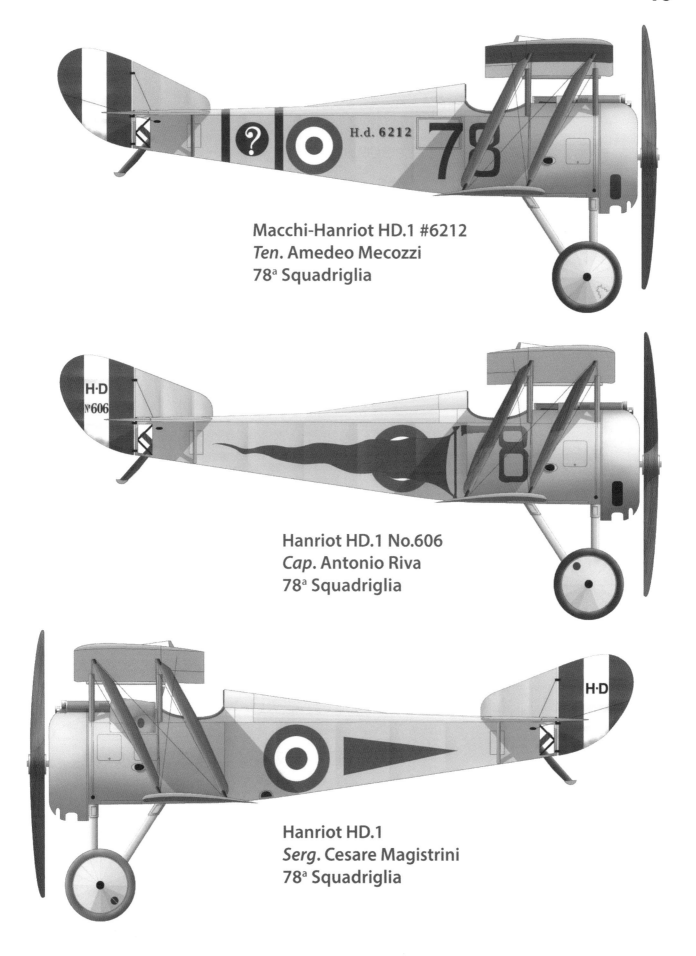

Macchi-Hanriot HD.1 #6212
Ten. Amedeo Mecozzi
78ᵃ Squadriglia

Hanriot HD.1 No.606
Cap. Antonio Riva
78ᵃ Squadriglia

Hanriot HD.1
Serg. Cesare Magistrini
78ᵃ Squadriglia

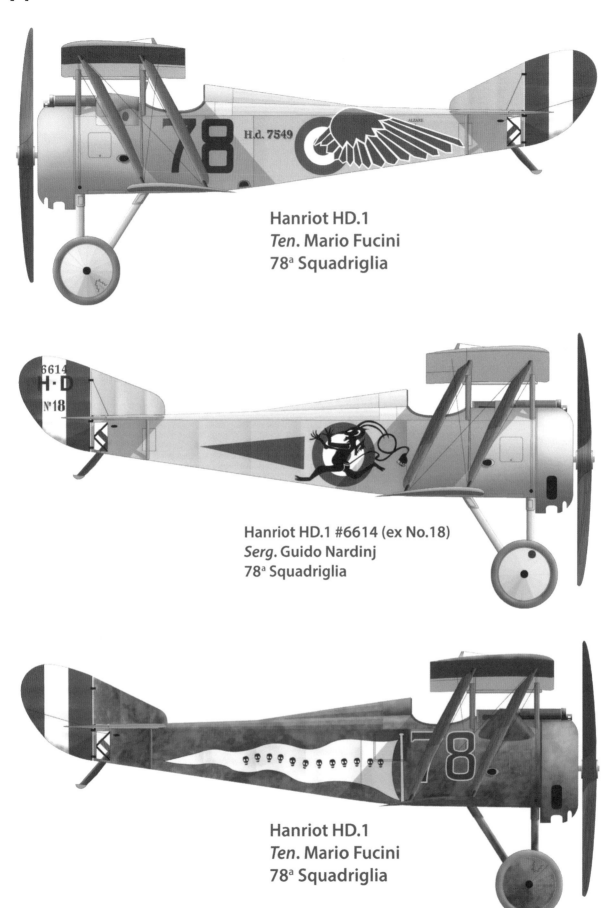

Hanriot HD.1
Ten. Mario Fucini
78ª Squadriglia

Hanriot HD.1 #6614 (ex No.18)
Serg. Guido Nardinj
78ª Squadriglia

Hanriot HD.1
Ten. Mario Fucini
78ª Squadriglia

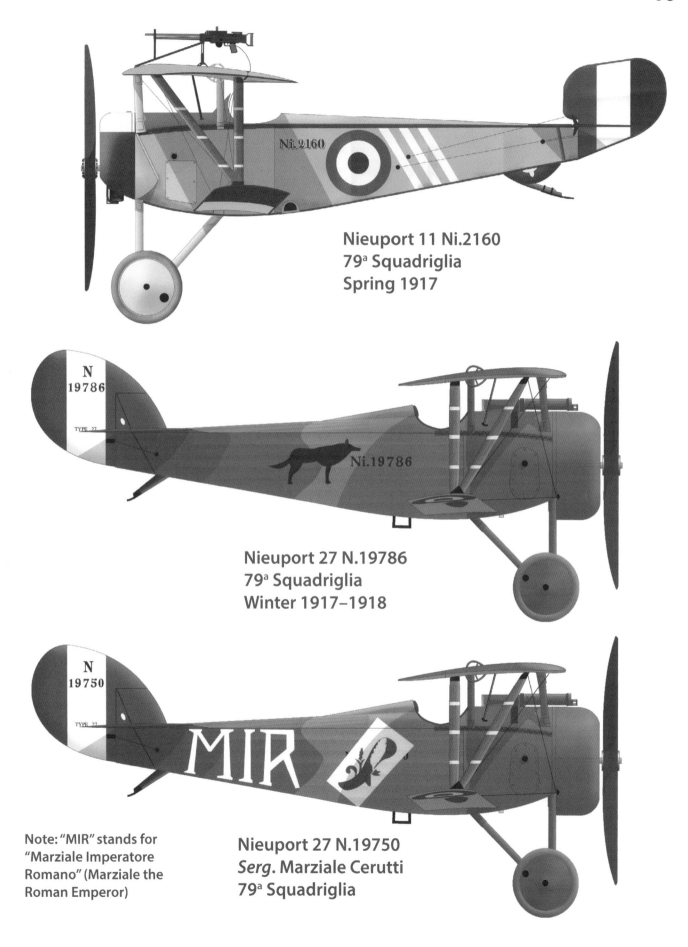

Nieuport 11 Ni.2160
79ª Squadriglia
Spring 1917

Nieuport 27 N.19786
79ª Squadriglia
Winter 1917–1918

Note: "MIR" stands for
"Marziale Imperatore
Romano" (Marziale the
Roman Emperor)

Nieuport 27 N.19750
Serg. Marziale Cerutti
79ª Squadriglia

78ª Squadriglia

Above: Nieuport 11 2303 of the 78ª Squadriglia, with a Lewis with a 97 round magazine.

The 78ª Squadriglia Caccia was activated at La Comina airfield on 15 August 1916. On 3 September it moved to Istrana airfield, being equipped with seven Nieuport 11s and one Nieuport 10. From Istrana, their field of action was the northern part of the front, close to the Alps. It was an autonomous unit, that is, not assigned to any Group, reporting directly to the Comando Supremo. Its commander was *cap.* Domenico Bolognesi, with pilots *ten.* Bortolo Costantini, *s.ten.* Giacomo Brenta and Francesco di Rudinì, *sergenti* Vittorio Aquilino, Antonio Chiri, Teresio Marcellino, *caporali* Agusto Vola and Cesare Magistrini. It began its active service on 9 September 1916.

On 1 November it flew a formation mission escorting Caproni bombers in a raid over Schoenpass and Ovcia Draga, and pilots Bolognesi, Costantini, Aquilino and Vola engaged combats with the enemy, without scoring any victory. Other combats took place in November with the participation of Bolognesi, Di Rudinì, Chiri and Vola. Di Rudinì on 12 November attacked an enemy airplane over the Asiago Plateau and forced it to dive and escape across the lines. On 14 November enemy gunners hit the Nieuport of *serg.* Chiri, who with a still engine made a forced landing at Nove di Bassano. On 25 November Di Rudinì attacked twice an enemy airplane over Castel Tesino. On 29 November there were three air combats, engaging Vola, Chiri and Di Rudinì, each time their adversaries running away to a quick landing. Totally during 1916 the 78ª Squadriglia had flown 211 combat sorties, and was engaged in 11 air combats. Ten. Di Rudinì received a *Medaglia di Bronzo*.

On 1 January 1917 the 78ª Squadriglia at Istrana had the same pilots, *cap.* Bolognesi, *ten.* Costantini, *s.ten.* Brenta and Di Rudinì, *sergenti* Aquilino, Marcellino, *caporali* Magistrini and Vola, plus *serg.* Guglielmo Fornagiari and *cpr.* Guido Nardini, with Nieuport 11 serials 1655, 1658, 1666, 1667, 1669, 2109, 2153, 2156, 2158, 2184, 2619, and French-built Nieuport 17s 3122 and 3126. The year began with Di Rudinì engaging an enemy airplane on 6 January and two more on the 7th, forcing them to run away. On 8 January the Capronis flew to bomb the area of San Daniele del Carso enjoying the escort of Bolognesi, Costantini, Brenta, Fornagiari, Marcellino and Nardini; the Italian fighters had several encounters with Austrian airplanes, that were kept safely away from the bombers. *Cap.* Bolognesi near Aidussina found himself with a jammed gun under the attack of two fighters, but escaped. On 22 January 1917 *serg.* Vola crashed to his death when the wings of his Nieuport 2158 broke.

In March 1917, supporting an attack on Mount Santo, the 78ª Squadriglia deployed a flight under the command of *ten.* Di Rudinì to Borgnano. On 19 March *serg.* Chiri shot down Brandenburg 27.55 of Flik 21, its crew was captured. Still based at Istrana, the 78ª Squadriglia on 10 April became part of the new X Gruppo. On 3 May *serg.* Chiri claimed an enemy shot down near Gorizia. On 19 May *cap.* Bolognesi, flying Ni.17 2619, shot down near Feltre Brandenburg 29.70, its pilot was taken, the observer was killed.

In June 1917 the 78ª Squadriglia was in action supporting the attack on Mount Ortigara. On 3 June Bolognesi claimed a victory over Mont Zebio, fighting together with a Sopwith ½ Strutter of French Escadrille Espinasse, pilot Louis Weiller and observer Olphe Galliard, but it was not

Above: Fornagiari, Brenta, and Magistrini with Nieuport 11 1675. The 78ª Squadriglia seems to have used a combination of triangles and circles for identification.

Above: Nieuport 11 1664 with a different combination of circles and triangles.

Above: A Sopwith 1A2 of the French Escadrille Espinasse in June 1917. Second from the left is Louis Weiller, an outstanding pilot and later creator of the Gnome et Rhône aircraft engine factory. The fourth one is cap. Bolognesi, commander of the 78ᵃ Squadriglia.

confirmed. 14 June *serg.* Nardini, on Nieuport 17 3213, forced down an enemy and flamed another one. The next day ground fire wounded serg, Giovanni Riva. On 17 June Magistrini, on Nieuport 17 3126, damaged and maybe forced down an airplane over Fort Luserna. On 27 June tragedy stuck: *serg.* Guglielmo Fornagiari had to land at Fossalunga his Ni.11 1664. Once fixed the problem, he took off again but civilians had entered the strip, trying to avoid them the pilot stalled, the plane fell in a vineyard killing two boys who were watching the airplanes.

In July 1917 the 78ᵃ Squadriglia had pilots *cap.* Bolognesi, *ten.* Giuliano Parvis, *s.tenenti* Brenta and Giuseppe Buffa, *sergenti* Aquilino, Chiri, Fornagiari, Magistrini, Marcellino, Nardini and Riva. On 9 July this unit was assigned to VI Gruppo, but it was given back to X Gruppo on l8 August. On 18 July, *serg.* Nardini and *serg.* Magistrini shot down a Brandenburg and damaged the two fighters escorting it, that were forced to land at Pergine.

In early August 1917 the 78ᵃ Squadriglia was deployed at Borgnano (Cormons) close to the part of the front where the large offensive toward Bainsizza was about to begin. In the ferry flight a Nieuport stalled, and *s.ten.* Giuseppe Buffa was killed. This unit was suffering for the age of its fighters, as it still used some old Ni.11s.

The intensive combats brought new victory claims: on 22 August *serg.* Fornagiari, on the 26ᵗʰ *serg.* Chiri at Loque, on 30 August *serg.* Aquilino had his fighter badly shot up, and he barely managed to return.

Serg. Nardini claimed a victory on 6 September against

aircraft attacking Gorizia. A new pilot entered action, *serg.* Cosimo (Cosme) Rennella, a volunteer from Ecuador who scored his first victory on 24 September. On 2 October Fornagiari had a long duel and shot down an enemy, probably a German at Podmelec, in the area where German troops were concentrating for a surprise attack. The next day together with *magg.* Piccio of 91ᵃ Squadriglia he shot down a Brandenburg, its two airmen were taken prisoners. *Serg.* Giovanni Riva went to 77ᵃ Squadriglia and *ten.* Antonio Riva arrived, coming from 71ᵃ, together with *serg.* Alessandro Borgato. On 10 October command passed from *cap.* Bolognesi to *ten.* Antonio Riva. On 16 October Magistrini shot down another German two-seater.

The enemy breakthrough at Caporetto forced the unit to retreat, saving some fighters but destroying twelve Hanriots. The 78ᵃ Squadriglia moved to La Comina, then to Aviano, Arcade and finally Istrana on 9 November. Up to that time, it had flown 512 fighter sorties, 456 cruise flights and 106 escort sorties, engaging in 106 combats with 18 confirmed victories.

It was assigned to the new VI Gruppo, operating in the sector of 4ᵃ Armata, which had retreated from the Cadore region to Mount Grappa, now the linchpin of Italian defense. On 10 November it had on strength just two Hanriots for pilots *tenenti* Riva and Brenta, *s.tenenti* Amedeo Mecozzi, and Guido Masiero, *asp.* Aquilino, *serg.m.* Fornagiari, Giustino Germino and Schiona, *sergenti* Rennella and Chiri. New Hanriots arrived, and 78ᵃ Squadriglia in many combats scored several victories agains German and Austrian planes,

Right: The daring pilot Guglielmo Fornagiari with Nieuport 11 1666. (Archive Fiorenzo Longhi)

Above: *Sergente* Giovanni Riva in a Nieuport 17 showing the simple markings of the 78ª Squadriglia, a pennant.

Above: *Sergente* Cesare Magistrini; after the war he was an airline pilot, reaching 20,000 flight hours.

but losing on 14 November *asp.* Vittorio Aquilino, shot down on Hanriot 6120 at Maser by a German two-seater. *S.ten.* Masiero, later of fame for his Rome to Tokyo flight, was particularly successful in this period.

The 78ª Squadriglia was in full action in the battle of Istrana, on 26 December, and Brenta, Riva, Mecozzi, Masiero, Fornagiari and Chiri claimed victories. Riva made two claims: a DFW shot down at Camalò, its pilot Pallasch a prisoner, and another one at Signoressa. Decorations were awarded to its pilots in 1917: the Silver Medal to *cap.* Bolognesi, *tenenti* Brenta, Costantini, *s.tenenti* Buffa, Masiero and Nardini, sergenti Aquilino (two), Chiri (two), Fornagiari, Magistrini, Giovanni Riva and Vola, and the Bronze to *cap.* Bolognesi and *ten.* Brenta.

On 15 January 1918 *serg.* Rennella in an escort mission for Caproni bombers shot down a fighter at Arsié. On 24 January the 78ª Squadriglia passed from the VI to the XV Gruppo. In January 1918 the unit had ten combats and claimed five victories, while *serg.* Germino was badly wounded on the 27th in a combat in which *cap.* Riva shot down a fighter, possibly the Austrian ace Joszef Kiss, who was wounded in a dogfight on that day. On 31 January Istrana was bombed again, Hanriots 6121 and 6238 were destroyed and five more were damaged.

On 3 February *s.ten.* Mecozzi and *soldato* Fortunato Celio

had a dogfight with an enemy squadron, their guns jammed but *serg.* Oreste Codeghini on Hanriot 6113 joined the fray and shot down an enemy in Val Brenta. The Austrian Flik 60/J actually didn't suffer any loss, but claimed two Hanriots shot down.

On 16 February the 78ª Squadriglia moved from Istrana to Nove di Bassano, from where it supported the action on Mount Valbella. On the 21st, Fornagiari and Chiri shot down a fighter, a victory assigned also to the crew they were escorting, *cap.* Fusco and *ten.* Calì, 33ª Squadriglia, also a fighter was seen going down to land in its territory.

On 15 March 1918 the unit moved from Nove to San Luca, two miles away from Nove, and on 1 June it was assigned to the 8ª Armata when this was formed. On 17 April Rennella took part in the combat in which the pilots of the 70ª Squadriglia shot down two enemies in the area of Valdobbiadene. On 17 May there was a confused action to which pilots from four squadrons, 78ª, 79ª, 70ª and 91ª took part, and a two-seater and two fighters were shot down: Rennella claimed a fighter at Greve di Piave, then with Fucini and Avet of the 70ª he downed a two-seater at Maserada and Chiri on Hanriot 556 shot down a fighter at San Biagio with Nardini, now flying with the 91ª Squadriglia.

At this time, based at San Luca, the 78ª Squadriglia had

Above: Two Hanriots and two Ni.17s of the 78ª Squadriglia at Borgnano.

cap. Riva, *tenenti* Brenta, Mecozzi and Fucini, *s.ten.* Attilio Businelli, *serg.m* Fornagiari and Schiona, *sergenti* Rennella, Chiri, Codeghini, Luigi Capparucci and Ermenegildo Bocca (both volunteers from Argentina) and Francesco Gritti, *caporali* Rinaldo Bulgheroni and Lino Gandini and *sold.* Celio. On 26 May there was another confused action with overlapping claims, a fighter fell at Casa Postiona, assigned to Piccio, 91ª, a two-seater at Maserada and another fighter at San Michele, claimed by Mecozzi, on Hanriot 11435 with the help of Capparucci on Hanriot 6278. The Albatros of Zgsf. Udvvardy, of Flik 42/J, forced to land, was claimed by

pilots of the 78ª Squadriglia, by Baracchini of the 76ª and by four pilots of RAF No.28 Squadron. On 30 May Rennella claimed a fighter that the British pilots of RAF No. 66 Squadron also claimed. On 11 June *serg.* Emanuele Morfino crashed on take-off with Hanriot 7555 and was wounded.

During the Austrian offensive in June, the 78ª was intensively in action from the Mount Grappa to the Piave, flying 42 sorties on the 15ᵗʰ, engaging in seven combats and claiming two victories, forcing two kite balloons to be winched down, strafing troops and dropping hand grenades. *Cpr.* Bulgheroni was wounded and ground fire disabled

Above: The elegant markings of Hanriot Hd.1 7549 of *ten.* Mario Fucini (first from the right).

Above: Hanriots of the 78ª Squadriglia at San Luca. The second one, 6212, sporting a question mark, is believed to be the airplane of *ten.* Amedeo Mecozzi.

his fighter that made an emergency landing at Cusignana. On 16 June Riva, Fucini and *sold.* Severino Venier scored a victory between Malborghetto and Fontigo. There were 29 more sorties in that day, with three more victories in the afternoon, five bullets wounded *serg.* Bocca, he returned and was hospitalized, expressing his regret for being out of the fight. On 17 June bad weather curtailed flights, still there were 17 sorties, one combat and strafing attacks with 2,500 rounds fired. On June 18, with better weather, 27 sorties were flown, two Hanriots were damaged by ground fire, *serg.* Fornagiari scored a victory. 45 sorties were flown on the 19ᵗʰ, with two victories and a Drachen balloon flamed, more intense action on June 20, with four victories. It is likely that in these intense combats some claims were duplicated, but Austrian losses were very serious and on June 21 the pilots of 78ª Squadriglia flew 40 sorties without finding any enemy aircraft. There were ten more flights on June 22, and one claim for *serg.* Codeghini, on the 23ʳᵈ the pilots spotted the removal of the floating bridge at Villa Jacur, the proof that the enemy offensive had failed. There were still 45 sorties on that day and one more victory for Rennella.

On 8 July the 78ª Squadriglia became part of the XXIII Gruppo, formed at San Luca with the 79ª Squadriglia. It had the same pilots plus *serg.m.* Mario Mey, and was then equipped with Hanriots 57, 510, 525, 550, 554, 556, 6109, 6154, 6185, 6212, 6218, 6240, 6261, 6278, 6282 and 7454.

On 16 July there was a freak drama: *ten.* Moresco met an unusual airplane, blinded by the sun, he though it had black crosses, and fired just five bullets, enough to kill Maj. A. M. Vaucour, commander of No. 45 Squadron of the RAF, whose Sopwith Camel crashed.

Enemy air activity was much reduced, still more victories arrived, on 25 July when *ten.* Fucini with the help of *cpr.* Venier shot down a Brandenburg near Cornuda, on 27 July when Mecozzi claimed a large two-seater near Sernaglia, on 12 August, as *cap.* Riva with Costantini of the 91ª Squadriglia shot down an enemy airplane at S, Lucia di Piave, on 31 August Chiri, Fucini and Rennella shot down a small two-seater at Mandrie. The tempest that ravaged airfields of both sides on 9 September destroyed Hanriots 607 and 7577 at San Luca.

More duels took place in October 1918, on the 6ᵗʰ Mecozzi shot down a two-seater at Susegana, in the same day Riva, Mecozzi and *serg.* Gardini fought agains a formation of "*one DFW and seven D.5*" and shot down two of them, *serg.* Morfino attacked two enemies but his engine failed and he crash landed returning to base.

During the final offensive, starting on 24 October the 78ª Squadriglia flew 142 sorties, shooting down some enemies (from four to nine, according to different reports, in those hectic days claims overlapped again) firing 10,000 rounds and dropping 140 light bombs on the retreating enemies. *Ten.* Fucini, *cpr.* Morfino and *sergenti* Chiri and Codeghini returned with badly damaged airplanes. On 28 October eight fighters bounced *ten.* Carlo Pasquinelli and badly wounded him. He managed to return to base, but died of his wounds on 9 November. On 30 October Capparucci was hit and had to force land at San Fior di Sopra, an enemy airfield. Codeghini landed next to him, picked him up and flew him to safety straddled behind him.

On Victory Day, 4 November, the 78ª Squadriglia was at San Luca, part of the XXIII Gruppo, with the same pilots

Above: Antonio Riva, here with cpr. Morfino in his Hanriot, showing a red pennant. Riva was born in Shanghai, his Chinese name was 李安東. After the war he returned to China where he married an American girl and instructed Chinese pupils to fly. Falsely accused of being a spy, he was shot in Beijing in 1951.

plus *ten.* Natale Sgarlata and *serg.* Alfredo Tagliapietra, with available Hanriots 11409, 13229, 13280, 19200, 19214, 19229, 19276, 19295, 19299. 606, 614 773, 812, 6092, 19385, 19322, 19330,19331 19359, 19376, 20949, 13351, and a single Nieuport 27, 19770.

In the period from November 1917 to the armistice, the 78ª Squadriglia flew 784 offensive patrol sorties, 1,964 cruise and 839 escort flights, 217 strafing, 31 bomb dropping and 273 leaflet dropping sorties, had 337 air combats with 70 victories. Overall during the war, it flew a total of 1,296, fighter, 2,420 cruise, 1,054 escort sorties, having 442 air combats and 88 recognized victories.

Cap. Riva, had the Cross of the *Ordine Militare di Savoia*, the Silver Medal went to *cap.* Riva, *tenenti* Fucini, Masiero (two), Mecozzi, Pasquinelli *serg.m.* Schiona (two) *sergenti* Bocca, Capparucci, Chiri, Codeghini (two), Gandini, Germino, Gritti, Rennela (two) and *cpr.* Morfino and Venieri, the Bronze Medal to *cpr.* Bulgheroni and *serg.m.* Fornagiari.

A new tragedy happened on 21 December: *serg.* Antonio Chiri, despite the warnings of his commander, was flying low level aerobatics over the airfield at S. Giacomo di Veglia, but in a pass too low he killed two children and a soldier, and wounded three other people.

In 1919 *cap.* Vincenzo Velardi became the commander; this unit was not disbanded, but survived, equipped with Hanriots, until the creation of the Regia Aeronautica in 1923.

Identified Victory Claims of the 78ª Squadriglia

Date	Place	Pilots	Victim	Unit
12.11.1916	Asiago	*S.ten.* Di Rudinì	Enemy aircraft FTL	
29.11.1916	Val Sugana	*S.ten.* Di Rudinì	Enemy aircraft FTL	
30.11.1916	Valdagno	*Serg.* Vola	Enemy aircraft FTL	
19.3.1917	Gallio	*Serg.* Chiri	Hansa Br. C.I 27.55	Flik 21
3.5.1917	Isonzo	*Serg.* Chiri	Hansa Br. C.I 129.40?	Flik 34?
19.5.1917	Lential	*Cap.* Bolognesi	Hansa Br. C.I 29.70	Flik 24
3.6.1917	M. Zebio	*Cap.* Bolognesi (& Weiller, Olphe Gaillard, EE)	Hansa Br. C.I 26.47?	Flik 14?
14.6.1917	M. Armentera	*Serg.* Nardini	KD.1 28.35?	Flik 21?

Above: The right side of a Hanriot showing the Italian, Belgian, and American flags. Presumably on the left side there were the French, British, and maybe Japanese flags.

Date	Place	Pilot	Victory	Unit
14.6.1917	M. Armentera	*Serg.* Nardini	Hansa Br. C.I 26.29?	Flik 24?
17.6.1917	Val d'Assa	*Serg.* Magistrini	Enemy aircraft FTL	
19.6.1917	Val d'Astico	*Serg.* Fornagiari	Hansa Br. C.I 29.73	Flik 17
18.7.1917	Asiago	*Serg.* Nardini, *serg.* Magistrini	Hansa Br. C.I 229.11	Flik 24
18.7.1917	Asiago	*Serg.* Nardini, *serg.* Magistrini	Albatros D.III 53.33 FTL	Flik 24
18.7.1917	Asiago	*Serg.* Nardini, *serg.* Magistrini	Albatros D.III 53.38 FTL	Flik 24
22.8.1917	Ternova	*Serg.* Fornagiari	Two-seater	
26.8.1917	Loque	*Serg.* Chiri	Fighter	
31.8.1917	Loque	*Serg.m.* Fornagiari	Enemy aircraft	
6.9.1917	Gorizia	*Serg.* Nardini	Enemy aircraft	
24.9.1917	Zagorje	*Serg.* Rennella	Aviatik Berg C.I 38.17	Flik 32
26.9.1917	Grahovo	*Serg.* Rennella (& gunners of 10ª Sq. Caproni)	Fighter?	
2.10.1917	Podmelec	*Serg.* Fornagiari	DFW?	FA(A) 219?
3.10.1917	Mesnjak-Auzza	*Serg.* Fornagiari (& Piccio, 91ª)	Hansa Br. C.I 329.20	Flik 53
16.10.1917	Mount Nero	*Serg.* Magistrini	DFW	FA(A) 232
7.11.1917	Cividale	*S.ten.* Masiero	Alb. D.V	Jasta 31
13.11.1917	Arcade	*S.ten.* Masiero, *serg.* Chiri (& Fucini, 76ª)	DFW	FA(A) 232
19.11.1917	Arcade	*S.ten.* Masiero	Alb.?	
20.11.1917	Moriago	*S.ten.* Masiero, *serg.* Chiri	DFW	FA(A) 219
21.11.1917	Vidor	*Serg.* Rennella	Enemy aircraft	
10.12.1917	Noventa di P.	*S.ten.* Masiero, *serg.* Chiri (& Scaroni, 76ª)	Aviatik C.I 37.24	Flik 58?
14.12.1917	Val Seren	*S.ten.* Masiero	Two-seater	
26.12.1917	Camalò	*Cap.* Riva (& Scaroni, Michetti, 76ª)	DFW C.V	FA(A) 219
26.12.1917	Biadene	*Ten.* Brenta (& Scaroni, 76ª)	AEG BG 4/19	
26.12.1917	Falzè	*Ten.* Masiero, *serg.* Fornagiari	DFW C.V	
26.12.1917	Signoressa	*Cap.* Riva	DFW C.V	

Above: Ermenegildo Bocca, another gallant pilot, came from Argentina.
Below: In the final months of the war, the 78ª Squadriglia introduced gaudy personal markings. This is the airplane of *cpr.* Severino Venier.

Above: American visitors admiring the Hanriot of Mario Fucini, with black skulls for each of his victory claims.

26.12.1917	Musano	*Serg.* Fornagiari (& Comandone, 82ª)	DFW C.V	
14.1.1918	Val di Pez	*Serg.* Rennella	Two-seater?	
15.1.1918	Arsiè	*Serg.* Rennella, *cap.* Riva, *serg.* Brenta	Fighter	
24.1.1918		*Serg.* Rennella		Flik 60/J?
27.1.1918	Asiago	*Cap.* Riva	Alb. D.III	Flik 55/J?
27.1.1918	San Gaetano	*Serg.m.* Fornagiari		FA 17?
3.2.1918	Val Brenta	*Serg.* Codeghini	Fighter?	
18.2.1918	M. Lisser	*Serg.m.* Fornagiari, *serg.m.* Schiona	Phönix D.I 128.08	Flik 39/D?
21.2.1918	Gallio	*Serg.m.* Fornagiari, *serg.* Chiri	Albatros D.III 153.158	Flik 55/J
21.2.1918	Ghirano	*Cap.* Riva	Hansa Br. C.I 369.40	Flik 45/D FTL
17.3.1918	Val Seren	*Serg.* Rennella	Enemy aircraft	
18.3.1918	Conegliano	*Ten.* Masiero	Kite Balloon	
19.3.1918	Colmirano	*Serg.* Codeghini	Kite Balloon	
4.4.1918	Montello	*Serg.* Chiri	Enemy aircraft	
1.5.1918	Fontanelle	*Serg.* Rennella	Enemy aircraft	
1.5.1918	Cimadolmo	*Cap.* Riva, *serg.* Rennella	Phönix C.I 121.08	Flik 52/D?
17.5.1918	Breda di Piave	*Ten.* Fucini, *serg.* Rennella (& Avet, 70ª)	Hansa Br. C.I 229.30	Flik 12/Rb?
17.5.1918	San Biagio	*Serg.* Chiri (& Nardini, 91ª, Reali, 79ª)	Albatros D.III 153.221	Flik 61/J?
24.5.1918	Pederobba	*Ten.* Mecozzi	Enemy aircraft	
26.5.1918	Virago	*Ten.* Mecozzi, *serg.* Capparucci	Two-seater	
26.5.1918	Ormelle	*Ten.* Mecozzi, *serg.* Capparucci	Fighter	
30.5.1918	Lovadina	*Serg.* Rennella	Albatros D.III 153.219	Flik 41/J?
13.6.1918	Col di Guardia	*Serg.* Capparucci, *serg.* Codeghini	Fighter	
15.6.1918	S. Giovanni	*Serg.m.* Fornagiari	Hansa Br. C.I 329.48	Flik 26/D?
15.6.1918	Maserada	*Cap.* Riva, *ten.* Mecozzi	Hansa Br. C.I 69.61 369.69?	
16.6.1918	Pilonetto	*Cap.* Riva, *ten.* Fucini, *sold.* Venier	Hansa Br. C.I 369.61	Flik 38/D
16.6.1918	Nervesa	*Ten.* Fucini	Albatros D.III 153.222	Flik 41/J?
16.6.1918	Nervesa	*Ten.* Fucini, *serg.* Bocca	Hansa Be. C.I 29.32	Flik 41/J?
16.6.1918	Barco	*Serg.* Codeghini	Aviatik D.I 138.115	Flik 56/J
18.6.1918	S. Salvatore	*Serg.m.* Fornagiari	Hansa Br. C.I 369.42	Flik 44/D?

Above: The Hanriot of *serg*. Oreste Codeghini, marked with two crossed swords, in flight.

Above: The Hanriot of *serg.m*. Antonio Chiri had a black tail.

Above: Hanriot Hd.1 14935 of *serg.m.* Mario Mey, from Florence, carried the red flower of that city.

19.6.1918	Nervesa	*Serg.* Codeghini	Fighter	
19.6.1918	Villa Jacur	*Ten.* Mecozzi, *ten.* Moresco	Two-seater	
19.6.1918	Villa Jacur	*Ten.* Mecozzi	Fighter	
19.6.1918	Barco	*Ten.* Mecozzi, *ten.* Moresco	Kite balloon BK20?	
20.6.1918	Nervesa	*Serg.* Codeghini, *ten.* Brenta	Fighter	
20.6.1918	Nervesa	*Ten.* Brenta	Fighter?	
20.6.1918	Nervesa	*Serg.* Codeghini, *ten.* Brenta	Albatros D.III 153.169?	
20.6.1918	Montello	*Serg.* Rennella, *serg.m.* Gandini	Fighter	
22.6.1918	Colle Capitello	*Serg.* Codeghini	Hansa Br. C.III 369.120	Flik 38/D?
23.6.1918	Barbisano	*Serg.* Rennella	Fighter	
23.6.1918	Nervesa	*Ten.* Fucini, Chiri, *cpr.* Venier	Enemy aircraft	
(16.7.1918	Monastir	*Ten.* Moresco	Camel D8102	45 Squadron
25.7.1918	Sernaglia	*Ten.* Fucini, *cpr.* Venier	Brandenburg	
27.7.1918	Sernaglia	*Ten.* Mecozzi	Hansa Br. C.I 169.141	Flik 52/D
12.8.1918	Susegana	*Cap.* Riva (& Costantini, 91ª)	Phönix 128.11	Flik 40/P?
20.8.1918	Moriago	*Serg.* Chiri	Two-seater	
23.8.1918	Falzè	*Serg.m.* Fornagiari	Hansa Br. C.I 429.27	Flik 67/DS
31.8.1918	Mandre	*Serg.* Chiri, *ten.* Fucini, *serg.* Rennella	Enemy aircraft	
6.10.1918	Susegana	*Ten.* Mecozzoi	Phönix C.I 121.61	Flik 57Rrb?
6.10.1918	M. Saver	*Ten.* Mecozzi, *cap.* Riva, *serg.m.* Gandini	Albatros D "K"	
6.10.1918	Isola Cremona	*Cpr.* Morfino	Two-seater	
27.10.1918	San Polo	*Serg.* Codeghini	Bomber	
27.10.1918	Mandre	*Serg.* Chiri (& Cerutti, 79ª)	Fighter	Flik 74/J?
27.10.1918	San Polo	*Serg.* Chiri, Rennella, Mey	Two-seater	
27.10.1918	Vazzola	*Ten.* Fucini, *serg.* Capparucci	Fighter	Flik 56/J?
27.10.1918	Pieve di Soligo	*Cap.* Riva, *cpr.* Morfino	Two-seater	
27.10.1918	Fontanelle	*Serg.* Chiri	Bomber	
28.10.1918		*Ten.* Fucini	Fighter	
28.10.1918	Vazzola	*Cap.* Riva (& White, McEwan, 28 Sqn. RAF)	Hansa Br. C.I 369.70	Flik 35/D?
29.10.1918	Oderzo	*Cap.* Riva, *cpr.* Morfino	Hansa Br. C.I 369.175	

Above: A simple diamond was the insignia of *serg.m.* Luigi Capparucci on Hanriot 7479.

Above: Flying a different, later production Hanriot, Capparucci retained his diamond insignia.

Above: Another version of the red flower of Florence on the Hanriot of *serg.m.* Mario Mey.

Casualties and Combat Losses of the 78ª Squadriglia

Date	Place	A/c	Pilot	Cause
14.11.1916	Nove	Ni.11	*Serg.* Chiri UNH	Ground fire
22.1.1917	Istrana	Ni.11 2158	*Serg.* Vola KIC	Accident
26.6.1917	Fossalunga	Ni.11 1664	*Serg.* Fornagiari UNH	Accident
1.8.1917	Istrana	Ni.17 2303	*S.ten.* Buffa KIC	Accident
14.11.1917	Maser	Hd.1 6120	*Asp.* Aquilino KIA	Enemy aircraft
27.1.1918	Val Brenta	Hanriot	*Serg.m.* Germino WIA	Fighters
11.6.1918	San Luca	Hd.1 7555	*Serg.* Morfino WIC	Accident
15.6.1918	Cusignana	Hanriot	*Cpr.* Bulgheroni WIA	Ground fire
16.6.1918	Nervesa	Hanriot	*Serg.* Bocca WIA	Fighters
28.10.1918	Papadopoll	Hanriot	*Ten.* Pasquinelli DOW	Fighters
30.10.1918	San Fior	Hd.1 11335	*Serg.* Capparucci UNH	Ground fire

Above: Capparucci and Codeghini re-enacting their dramatic escape.

Above: French-built Hanriot 606 of *cap*. Riva.

79ª Squadriglia

Above: A Nieuport 11 of the flight of the 79ª Squadriglia at Padua, with three white bands as unit marking.

Formation of the 79ª Squadriglia began in November 1916 at the Centro Formazione Squadriglie of Arcade and this unit was declared ready for operations on 12 January 1917. The next day it flew to its assigned base, Istrana airfield, for missions of standing patrols, escort and offensive patrols over the Asiago Plateau. This unit was equipped with 80 hp Nieuport 11s, its commander was *cap.* Francesco Chimirri with the pilots *tenenti* Cesare Bertoletti and Umberto Mazzini, *s.ten.* Alberto Moresco, *maresciallo* Giovanni Attili, *caporali* Marziale Cerutti, Attilio Imolesi, Giovanni Nicelli, Antonio Reali and *soldato* Vittorio Melloni.

Weather conditions precluded flights before 16 January and only on 20 January there were the first combat sorties, standing patrols over the plateau. The unit then flew patrol and alarm flights above Asiago and Val Sugana, without meeting the enemy. At the end of February *ten.* Bertoletti was reassigned to the 70ª Squadriglia. On 4 March three fighters flew over Treviso dropping leaflets for the National Loan.

On 28 March 1917 the 79ª Squadriglia detached its 3ª Sezione, including Moresco, Attili and Cerutti, to Padua, for the defence of that city. On 4 April finally there was the first sighting of the enemy, *cpr.* Nicelli over Primolano and *cpr.* Reali over Grigno both spotted enemy aircraft which got away. Escort missions for Caproni bombers became frequent.

On 10 April the squadron passed under the control of the newly formed X Gruppo, but it remained in that organization only one month, as on 10 May, when the Comando d'Aeronautica of the 4ª and 6ª Armata was formed, it passed to VII Gruppo, made available to the newly formed 4ª Armata, formerly Comando Truppe Altipiani, but still maintaining its detached flight at Padua, which flew also missions over Venice.

In late April another flight was deployed at Bolzano Bellunese, to participare in the 10th Offensive of the Isonzo. On 26 April *serg.* Imolesi, flying a Nieuport marked with a horse shoe, contributed to the eighth victory of *cap.* Baracca who shot down Brandenburg C.1 129.17.

The 79ª Squadriglia got two new pilots, *sergenti* Andrea Teobaldi and Paolo Benvenuti.

In the first half of June 1917 this unit supported the Italian offensive known as the Battle of the Ortigara. On 2 June there was the first air combat, *serg.* Reali freed two Caudrons from the threat of an enemy fighter and then had an inconclusive duel with a faster two-seater in the Asiago area. The next day Reali, flying Nieuport 11 2110, attacked in the morning an enemy two-seater near Borgo Roncegno and saw its observer, probably wounded, slumping in his cockpit. Reali was confident of having hit the engine too, and he claimed a victory, the enemy falling near Borgo, which for lack of confirmations was not credited to him. In the following days encounters with enemy aircraft became more frequent. On 6 June *ten.* Moresco flew a patrol mission over Treviso at night. On June 10 seven fighters flew together to escort a raid of Capronis. On 14 June Cerutti scored his, and his unit's, first confirmed victory. Flying Ni.11 2269 for

Above: A Nieuport 11 of the 79ª Squadriglia at Nove di Bassano; the steeples of the churches are useful to identify the different towns in Veneto.

a standing patrol over the plateaus with *ten*. Moresco, he spotted an Austrian airplane near Mount Verena, attacking it together with his companion. After a few rounds the gun of Moresco jammed, Cerutti shot it down. Ground observers confirmed the result of this air combat, the victim was Brandenburg C.I 28.35. On 15 June *cap*. Chimirri landed at Nove di Bassano with engine problems, when he took off again to return to Istrana he stalled and was badly wounded. Command of 79ª Squadriglia passed to *ten*. Bertoletti, first temporarily then on 10 September, when he was promoted to captain, definitively.

On June 22, Cerutti fought against an enemy airplane and saw it going down out of control with its propeller stopped. Several Austrian aircraft were spotted that always escaped thanks to their higher speed. At the end of June Nicelli and Imolesi were assigned to the flight detached at Padua. On July 12 *ten*. Mazzini had a long duel with two fighters, his gun jammed but he managed to get away: an Austrian pilot, *Zgsf*. Telessy of Flik 21 flying Albatros 53.39 claimed a victory.

On 5 August *m.llo* Attili, on Ni.17 3132 in flight over the Plateau, crashed and was badly wounded. A new pilot replaced him, *ten*. Federico Comirato. On August 18 Mazzini had a duel with an enemy fighter, with a heated exchange of fire which proved inconclusive. This dogfight may correspond with a Nieuport forced down claimed by Johann von Morpurgo of Flik 21 flying 53.29. That same day *serg*. Reali met two enemy aircraft, he forced a two-seater to go down out of control and a fighter to retreat with damages. Reali's

Ni.17 also was hit. The next *ten*. Bertoletti had a similar encounter with a two-seater and a very determined fighter, which was inconclusive.

All through the summer the 79ª Squadriglia, effectively barring the sky over Asiago, flew many offensive patrol and escort missions and had many combats, all of them inconclusive, often on account of jammed guns.

On 26 September 1917 *ten*. Mazzini and *serg*. Imolesi faced a two-seater with a fighter escorting it, Imolesi shot down Br. C1 129.29 of Flik 21, the fighter was driven off, it was Albatros D.3 53.29, its pilot, Telessy again, claimed an enemy "Spad" shot down, but both Italian pilots safely returned to base. On 30 September and 1 October *serg*. Nicelli had inconclusive duels with Austrian fighters.

In the period of Caporetto the 79ª Squadriglia has heavily committed. On 25 October Imolesi had a long duel with an enemy, but his gun jammed three times; Comirato survived the attack of a fighter and Nicelli attacked a two-seater, fired 270 rounds and forced it to land in its territory.

On 26 October Cerutti, during a Caproni escort mission went to the rescue of a Nieuport under attack (Poli, of 70ª Squadriglia) and shot down a fighter that crashed at Valzano.

On October 30 Cerutti was in action escorting SPs on the opposite side of the front, over Monfalcone where he attacked a seaplane which was seen alighting on the Isonzo River.

In early November the 79ª Squadriglia began receiving new equipment, Nieuport 27 fighters with 120 hp engines directly supplied by France. On 2 November 1917 the unit

Above: Nieuport 11s of the flight of the 79ª Squadriglia at Padua.

moved from Istrana to Nove di Bassano. Its defense flight at Padua remained, as the Supreme Command had now moved there, after leaving Udine.

On 7 November Nicelli forced down Brandenburg 29.71 of Flik 24/F, that turned over near Fonzaso, its crew was captured, Nicelli also had to land with a failing engine, but he did so safely.

On 17 November Imolesi had a tough dogfight with Austrian fighters, his gun jammed but he managed to escape, *Zgsf.* Alexander Kasza of Flik 55/J on Albatros 153.19 claimed a Nieuport. The next day Cerutti drew away four enemies that were trying to attack a Farman. The names of these gallant sergeants come up frequently, but all pilots of the 79ª Squadriglia, including *cap.* Bertoletti were flying a high number of missions. On 23 November Cerutti spotted some unknown airplanes, he noticed that they carried French roundels and waved but didn't trust them, so he maneuvered around them firing warning shots to make them land, which they did, at the airfield of their liking, Castelgomberto. They were Dorand AR of Escadrille AR 14 and the French command strongly recommended to the Italians a course on aircraft recognition. On 24 November Cerutti attacked two enemy two-seaters with a fighter as escort and shot both of them down north of Mount Grappa. On the 27th an enemy two-seater attacked Cerutti, the Italian pilot fought back, firing 400 rounds and saw his enemy with leaking tanks make an emergency landing at Alano di Piave.

The 79ª Squadriglia, still based at Nove, was assigned to the XV Gruppo, made available to the Comando Truppe degli Altipiani. The flight at Padua in November returned to join the rest of the unit. Actions during this period were intense, mostly escorts to bombers and two-seaters as the final actions of the enemy offensive took place on the northern front. A new pilot arrived, *sold.* Remo Bozzetti, who immediately took up the pace of the squadron, flying one or

two missions each day. On 7 December 1917, *serg.* Nicelli shot down an enemy airplane over Mount Verena, a victory that was confirmed. On 13 December, in a series of combats, the 79ª Squadriglia claimed two victories, one by Imolesi with Ciotti, and one by Nicelli, but it may be a duplication of the same victory over Brandenburg 229.09 of FlG.1.

On 16 December the pilots of this unit could not protect a SAML of 115ª Squadriglia shot down by the fighters of Flik 55/J, which Nicelli, with a jammed gun, tried to deter just manoeuvring. On 20 December *serg.* Reali, who the day before had crash landed, scored his first confirmed victory, a two-seater that was dropping leaflets, ineffectively protected by a fighter, which he watched crashing in Val d'Assa.

On 28 December *cap.* Bertoletti who was in Padua was wounded during an enemy air raid over the airport, while his driver Guido Balma was killed.

During 1917 the 79ª Squadriglia flew about 1,500 combat flights and had 69 combats. On 1 January 1918 *ten.* Mazzini was interim commander, with pilots *ten.* Federico Comirato, *s.ten.* Melloni, *sergenti* Cerutti, Giuseppe Ciotti, Imolesi, Nicelli, Reali, *caporalmaggiore* Edmondo Lucentini, *soldati* Remo Bozzetti and Riccardo Ferrero.

Some Hanriots arrived, joining the Ni.27s. On 5 January 1918, Cerutti claimed a fighter shot down on Mount Corno. On the 10th Cerutti and Reali, escorting a SAML, engaged five fighters, Reali shot down one, getting his Nieuport badly shot up, Cerutti with a jammed gun could not help him. On January 11 there was a big air battle, with *cpr.m.* Lucentini, Imolesi ad Ciotti facing five fighters and then attacking three two-seaters one of which was shot down. Lucentini had to drop out of the fight with a jammed gun, this was possibly the Nieuport claimed by *StFw.* Richard Mueller, of Flik 15 on Berg 138.07. On 14 January Ciotti and Reali claimed a two-seater, which a fighter failed to protect, shot down in Valstagna, this claim was confirmed.

Above: Personnel of the flight of the 79ᵃ Squadriglia at Padua, only the front part of the cowling is painted in green, white, and red, the rest in a light color.

From 28 to 31 January 1918 the 79ᵃ Squadriglia was engaged during the reconquest of the "three mountains" (Col del Ross, Valbella and Col d'Echele) that the Austrians had taken in December, the first successful Italian counter-offensive. On January 28, during the battle, Cerutti shot down two enemies, his 7ᵗʰ and 8ᵗʰ victories, and Reali claimed two more in the early afternoon while Nicelli attacked five enemies and saw one go down out of control. The unit got a new pilot, *asp.* Salvadore Occhipinti, who at his first mission crashed on landing wrecking his fighter.

On 30 January, Nicelli and Reali shot down two enemies, respectively their 7ᵗʰ and 11ᵗʰ victories. That day Italian fighters claimed ten victories. Two days later, Reali, while escorting a SP., attacked a formation of five enemies claiming one shot down. On 4 February five pilots, Nicelli, Reali, *serg.* Fortunato Sicco, Ciotti and Lucentini escorting S.P.3s of 33ᵃ Squadriglia had a combat with six enemy aircraft, claiming three shot down over Valstagna. An observer of the 26ᵃ Squadriglia said that he saw two going down, one painted all black. In the afternoon Reali had another combat over Valstagna, claiming a victory that didn't have confirmation. No doubt on 5 February for the victory of Nicelli and Cerutti, their 11ᵗʰ and 9ᵗʰ, against a two-seater, as the airplane came down in Italian territory and its two airmen were captured.

On 24 February, the 79ᵃ Squadriglia had five combats,

Cerutti shot down an airplane on the south slope of Mount Grappa, and Nicelli also claimed a victory. In the afternoon, however, five pilots could not protect an SP.3 of the 26ᵃ Squadriglia from a Austrian fighters of Flik 60/J which shot it down.

On 10 March *serg.* Imolesi had an accident, crashing on Nove airfield with his Ni.27 and dying of wounds three days later. He was credited with six victories.

On 11 March Reali claimed a victory against a fighter crashing in a wood near Mount Erio. On 15 March 1918 the 79ᵃ Squadriglia moved from Nove to San Luca di Treviso, together with the 78ᵃ Squadriglia of the same XV Gruppo. On 25 March three victories were claimed, at Cornuda, Valdobbiadene and San Pietro di Feletto.

On 4 May *serg.* Nicelli engaged in an engine test flight saw a group of Austrian fighters over the lines and atttacked them together with Sopwith Camels of RAF No. 66 Squadron, two Albatros were shot down with the death of Oblt. Patzelt and Korp. Fritsch of Flik 68/J. The next days, flying aerobatics for visiting Allied officers, Nicelli crashed, when a wing of his Nieuport folded.

Nicelli was not forgotten, the airport of Venezia Lido is still named after him.

On 17 May Reali and Lucentini took part with other pilots in the combat in which *serg.* Nardini of 91ᵃ Squadriglia shot down the Austrian ace Frank Gräser.

Above: *Sergente* Imolesi in a Nieuport 17 adorned with a horse shoe. This fighter is fitted with a Vickers and a Lewis gun.

Above: *Serg.* Cerutti, wearing a woman's stocking as a hat, and *serg.* Imolesi in front of a Nieuport 17, that is armed with just a Lewis; the Vickers gun is missing.

In mid-June 1918 the 79ᵃ Squadriglia was assigned to the *Massa da Caccia*, the fighter force assembled to face the coming Austrian offensive. The pilots flew without rest, four sorties a day was the norm, they claimed several victories and strafed and bombed the enemy troops; on 17 June ground fire wounded *ten.* Mario Olivieri who made an emergencly landing with Ni.27 11363 just across the lines. There were many claims, *ten.* Giovambattista Toffoletti claimed three fighters in a single combat on 20 June, three more on 21 June, Reali claimed a dozen, some of these claims were accepted. The *Massa da Caccia* was disbanded on 29 June and the squadron reported again to the XV Gruppo.

On 30 June with interim commander *cap.* Mazzini were the pilots *ten.* Comirato, Toffoletti, *s.ten.* Angelo Federici, *s.ten.* Francesco Fusconi Pagnani, *sergenti* Cerutti, Ciotti, Carlo Gaffuri, Lucentini, Reali, Fortunato Sicco, Umberto Soliani, *caporali* Attilio Aime and Augusto Rustici, *soldati* Bozzetti, Riccardo Ferrero and Carlo Rossi. The unit now had 12 Ni.27s and five Hanriots.

On 7 July it was assigned, together with the 78ᵃ Squadriglia, to the new XXIII Gruppo, an all-fighters command based at San Luca. *Ten.* Toffoletti died on 21 July: coming back from leave, he stopped at Poggio Renatico offering to ferry a new fighter to San Luca for 78ᵃ Squadriglia, and he crashed on take-off on Hanriot 19240.

On 3 September *cap.* Mazzini was transferred, *ten.* Eugenio Mossi was interim commander until 8 September, then *cap.* Mario Omizzolo became the commander. The 79ᵃ

Squadriglia was very active in the weeks before the final offensive. On 4 October *serg.* Reali scored his 11ᵗʰ and final confirmed victory, shooting down Albatros D.III 253.51 of Flik 56/J in cooperation with *serg.* Lucentini. Pilot *Korporal* Fritz Berggold jumped with a parachute but lost his life. On 8 October an anti-aircraft shell killed *cap.* Omizzolo flying Ni.27 19775 near S. Stefano di Valdobbiadene. Ten. Mossi became interim commander again until the 17ᵗʰ, as *cap.* Arturo Freddi Cavalletti assumed command. Two final victories were claimed in the final days of the war, on 26 October while escorting Caproni triplanes Cerutti shot down a fighter, on 27 October, Cerutti with *serg.* Chiri of 78ᵃ Squadriglia claimed another fighter near Cittadella di Piave.

On the day of cessation of hostilities, the 79ᵃ Squadriglia at San Luca with commander *cap.* Freddi Cavalletti had pilots *tenenti* Comirato, Vittorio Melloni, Mossi, Carlo Ravedati, *s.ten.* Arnaldo Brandolini, Federici and Fusconi Pagnani, *sergenti* Gino Andreutti, Cerutti, Ciotti, Gaffuri, Lucentini, Soliani, *caporali* Dino Pini, Rossi and Rustici, *carabiniere* Franco Bianchi, *soldati* Domenico Bertone, Ferrero and Giacomo Savioli. It was equipped with 18 Nieuport 27s and three Hanriots.

The 79ᵃ Squadriglia late in the war had as its emblem a black she-wolf. During 1918 this unit flew 2,910 combat missions and sustained 158 air combats. Its total for the war was 4,830 combat sorties, 178 combats, 63 claims (88 acccording to other sources). The Air Force Command officially credited this unit with 47 victories.

Above: The pilots of of the flight of the 79ᵃ Squadriglia around December 1917, from the left *serg.* Imolesi, *serg.* Reali, *ten.* Comirato, *ten.* Mazzini, the commander *cap.* Bertoletti, *s.ten.* Melloni, *serg.* Cerutti, *cpr.* Lucentini (probably) and *serg.* Ciotti.

Two of its pilots received two *Medaglie d'Argento*: Cerutti and Nicelli; one Silver Medal was assigned to Ciotti, Lucentini, Olivieri, Reali, Rossi, Rustici and Toffoletti. Freddi Cavalletti, Lucentini, Mossi and Soliani received the *Medaglia di Bronzo*. The 79ᵃ Squadriglia was not disbanded after the war, and remained in service when the Regia Aeronautica was formed, in 1923.

Identified Victory Claims of the 79ᵃ Squadriglia

Date	Place	Pilots	Victim
26.4.1917	Gradisca	*Serg.* Imolesi (& Baracca, Gorini 70ᵃ)	Hansa Br. C.I 129.17, Flik 35
3.6.1917	Borgo Cima 12	*Serg.* Reali	Two-seater
14.6.1917	Mount Verena	*Serg.* Cerutti, *ten.* Moresco	Hansa Br. C.I 28.35, Flik 21
22.6.1917	Val d'Assa	*Serg.* Cerutti	Enemy aircraft OOC
18.8.1917	Asiago	*Serg.* Reali	Two-seater NC
26.9.1917	Asiago	*Serg.* Imolesi	Hansa Br. C.I 129.29, Flik 21/D
26.9.1917	Cima 12	*Serg.* Imolesi, *ten.* Mazzini	Albatros D.III 53.29, Flik 21/D
25.10.1917	Mount Lisser	*Serg.* Nicelli	Hansa Br. C.I 129.22, Flik 21/D
26.10.1917	Valzano	*Serg.* Cerutti (& Poli, 70ᵃ)	Fighter Jasta 31?
30.10.1917	Isonzo	*Serg.* Cerutti	K225?
7.11.1917	Arsiero	*Serg.* Nicelli	Hansa Br. C.I 29.71, Flik 24/F
24.11.1917	Fonzaso	*Serg.* Cerutti	Hansa Br. C.I 29.05, Flik 24/F
24.11.1917	M. Grappa	*Serg.* Cerutti	Hansa Br. C.I 229.16, Flik 17/D
27.11.1917	Alano di Piave	*Serg.* Cerutti	Two-seater
7.12.1917	Col d'Echele	*Serg.* Nicelli	Enemy aircraft
13.12.1917	Asiago	*Serg.* Nicelli	Hansa Br. C.I 229.09, FlG 1?

Above: The ace *serg.* Giovanni Nicelli.

13.12.1917	Ghertele	*Serg.* Imolesi, *serg.* Ciotti	Hansa Br. C.I 229.09, FlG 1?
20.12.1917	Val d'Assa	*Serg.* Reali	Two-seater, Flik 24/F?
5.1.1918	Mount Corno	*Serg.* Cerutti	Fighter
10.1.1918	Mount Lisser	*Serg.* Reali	Fighter
11.1.1918	Lusiana	*Serg.* Ciotti, *serg.* Imolesi,	Hansa Br. C.I 129.25, Flik 15/F?
14.1.1918	Valstagna	*Serg.* Reali, *serg.* Imolesi	Enemy aircraft
25.1.1918	Mount Zebio	*Serg.* Reali	Two-seater
28.1.1918	Val Ronchi	*Serg.* Cerutti	Fighter
28.1.1918	Melette	*Serg.* Cerutti, *serg.* Reali	Fighter
28.1.1918	Cima Echele	*Serg.* Reali	Hansa Br. C.I 129.31? Flik 21/D?
30.1.1918	Casara Melegon	*Serg.* Reali	Enemy aircraft
30.1.1918	Cima Echele	*Serg.* Nicelli, *serg.* Reali	Hansa Br. C.I 29.07? Flik 45/D?
1.2.1918	Asiago	*Serg.* Reali	Two-seater
4.2.1918	Valstagna	*Serg.* Reali, Ciotti, Nicelli, Lucentini	Fighter
4.2.1918	Valstagna	*Serg.* Nicelli	Fighter
5.2.1918	Sassorosso	*Serg.* Cerutti, *serg.* Nicelli	Hansa Br. C.I 29.16, Flik 45/D
11.2.1918	Asiago	*Serg.* Cerutti	Phönix D.I 328.06, Flik 24/F
13.2.1918	Marcesina	*Serg.* Nicelli	Enemy aircraft
24.2.1918	Crespano V.	*Serg.* Cerutti	Phönix D.I 128.09, Flik 39/D
24.2.1918	Cismon	*Serg.* Nicelli, *ten.* Comirato	Phönix D.I 328.12, Flik 60/J
11.3.1918	Monte Erio	*Serg.* Reali	Phönix D.I 228.06?, Flik 60/J?
25.3.1918	Cornuda	*Serg.* Ciotti	Aviatik C.I 137.14, Flik 45/D
25.3.1918	Valdobbiadene	*Serg.* Ciotti, *serg.* Cerutti	Enemy aircraft
25.3.1918	S. Pietro di Fel.	*Serg.*Cerutti	Enemy aircraft
8.4.1918	Lovadina	*Serg.* Reali (& artillery?)	Two-seater
12.4.1918	Collalto	*Serg.* Reali	Kite balloon
1.5.1918	Pieve di Soligo	*Serg.* Reali	Enemy aircraft
4.5.1918	Vidor	*Serg.* Nicelli (& Birks, Apps, 66 Sqn. RAF)	Albatros D.III 153.182, Flik 68/J
4.5.1918	Ciano	*Serg.* Nicelli (& Birks, Apps, 66 Sqn. RAF)	Albatros D.III 153.210, Flik 68/J
31.5.1918	S. Salvatore	*Serg.* Reali	Not confirmed
10.6.1918	Falzè di Piave	*Serg.* Reali, *sold.* Rustici	Not confirmed
15.6.1918	Falzè di Piave	*Serg.* Reali, *ten.* Olivieri	Enemy aircraft
15.6.1918	Farra di Soligo	*Serg.* Reali, *ten.* Toffoletti, *serg.* Ciotti	Hansa Br. C.I 329.48, Flik 26/D?

Above: Fighters of the of the flight of the 79ª Squadriglia at Nove di Bassano in early 1918, with a Ni.27 with unusual supports for a gun over the top wing, two Ni.17 and a Hanriot, in the background a SVA of the 2ª Sezione.

16.6.1918	Mandre	*Ten.* Olivieri	Two-seater
17.6.1918	Farra di Soligo	*Ten.* Toffoletti	Two-seater
18.6.1918	Ponte alla Priula	*Serg.* Reali	Enemy aircraft
20.6.1918	Canareggio	*Serg.* Reali	Fighter
20.6.1918	Susegana	*Serg.* Reali, *ten.* Toffoletti	Fighter
20.6.1918	Susegana	*Ten.* Toffoletti	Fighter
21.6.1918	Susegana	*Serg.* Cerutti, *serg.* Reali, *ten.* Toffoletti	Hansa Br. C.I 269.22, Flik 65/DS
21.6.1918	Susegana	*Serg.* Cerutti, *serg.* Reali, *ten.* Toffoletti	Two-seater
21.6.1918	Susegana	*Serg.* Cerutti, *serg.* Reali, *ten.* Toffoletti	Two-seater
22.6.1918	Montello	*Serg.* Reali (& Baracchini, 81ª)	Albatros D.III, Flik 42/J?
22.6.1918	Montello	*Serg.* Reali (& Baracchini, 81ª)	Fighter
22.6.1918	Montello	*Serg.* Reali (& Baracchini, 81ª)	Fighter
24.6.1918	Ponte a. Priula	*Serg.* Cerutti, *serg.* Lucentini, *cpr.m.* Rossi	Hansa Br. C.I 369.67, Flik 4/D?
1.7.1918	Collabrigo	*Serg.* Reali	Enemy aircraft
4.7.1918	Susegana	*Sold.* Rossi	Enemy aircraft
4.7.1918	Oderzo	*Serg.* Cerutti, *serg.* Soliani	Kite balloon
4.7.1918	S.Maria Feletto	*Ten.* Toffoletti	Kite balloon
5.7.1918	Mandre	*Serg.* Soliani, *sold.* Rustici	Two-seater
19.7.1918	Falzè	*Serg.* Lucentini (& Eleuteri, 70ª)	Hansa Br. C.I 169.138 Flik 67/S?
30.7.1918	Conegliano	*Serg.* Reali	Two-seater OOC
9.8.1918	Lower Piave	*Serg.* Ciotti, *cpr.* Rossi	Two-seater
11.9.1918	Ponte alla Priula	*Serg.* Cerutti	Two-seater
11.9.1918	Susegana	*Cap.* Omixzzolo, *serg.* Reali	Enemy aircraft
3.10.1918	Ponte alla Priula	*Serg.* Lucentini, *cpr.* Rustici	Enemy aircraft
4.10.1918	Ormelle	*Cpr.* Rustici (& Keller, 91ª)	Kite balloon
4.10.1918	Fontigo	*Serg.* Reali, *serg.* Lucentini (& pilots70ª)	Albatros D.III 253.51, Flik 56/J
26.10.1918	Mandre	*Serg.* Cerutti	Aviatik D.I 338.26, Flik 74/J
27.10.1918	Cittadella	*Serg.* Cerutti (& Chiri, 78ª)	Fighter Flik 74/J?

Above: Nieuport 27 with a personal insignia. This picture was identified as the airplane of *serg.* Cerutti, but it is not necessarily so.

Casualties and Combat Losses of the 79ª Squadriglia

Date	Place	Aircraft	Pilot	Cause
15.6.1917	Nove di Bassano	Nieuport	*Cap.* Chimirri WIC	Accident
5.8.1917	Conso	Ni.17 3132	*M.llo* Attili WIC	Accident
10.3.1918	San Luca	Ni.27	*Serg.* Imolesi KIC	Accident
5.5.1918	Porcellengo	Ni.27 11353	*Serg.* Nicelli KIC	Accident
5.5.1918	?	Ni.27	*S.ten.* Occhipinti WIA	?
17.6.1918	Piave	Ni.27 11363	*Ten.* Olivieri WIA	Ground fire
21.7.1918	Poggio Renatico	Hd.1 19240	*Ten.* Toffoletti KIC	Accident
8.10.1918	S. Stefano di V.	Ni.27 19775	*Cap.* Omizzolo KIA	Ground fire

Right: The 79ª Squadriglia was flying the Hanriot as late as 1926. The serial is 21032

Above: The sergeants of the XXIII Gruppo showing their medals: sitting, form the left, Fornagiari, Reali, Cerutti, Rennella, and Aime, standing, Chiri. (Archives Franz Selinger)

Above: *Serg*. Cerutti with his Nieuport 27 19750 with the monogram MIR and the ace of clubs.

Above: A line-up of Nieuport 27 fighters of the 79ª Squadriglia with the insignia of the she-wolf. The fourth one carries the monogram VM, for pilot Vittorio Melloni, the seventh one FPF for Francesco Pagnani Fusconi.

Above: Nieuport 27 serial 19768 of the 79ª Squadriglia. (Archive Pierluigi Moncalvo)

80ª Squadriglia

Above: Variations of the Happy Hooligan cartoon adorned the Nieuports of the 80ª Squadriglia until the Command forbade them. (Archive Angelo Emiliani)

The 80ª Squadriglia was formed at the Centro Formazione Squadriglie at Arcade and was mobilized on 28 February 1917, flying to Santa Maria la Longa, becoming combat ready on 12 March 1917. It belonged to the I Gruppo, made available to the 3ª Armata, on the southern part of the front. Its commander was *cap.* Mario Gordesco, coming from 75ª Squadriglia, and its pilots were *tenenti* Raoul Da Barberino and Guido Keller, *s.ten.* Guido Sambonet, *serg.m.* Amleto Degli Esposti, *sergenti* Michele Allasia, Felice Avon, Alvaro Leonardi and Abbondio Viganò.

It was equipped with Nieuport 80 hp serials 2139, 2140, 2142, 2147, 2152, 2157, 2172 and 2174.

On 15 March Leonardi and Viganò were deployed at Cascina Farello, near Aquileia, to provide local air defense together with a flight on detachment from 77ª Squadriglia; from there, or from nearby Aiello airfield, they flew until 30 May. The 80ª Squadriglia was engaged in cruise, escort and patrol flights over the Carso front. On 17 March *ten.* Keller protected a Caudron from the attack of two enemies, while *serg.* Allasia escorting a Voisin fought with an enemy plane, but his gun jammed. On that day, Italian anti-aircraft fire hit the Nieuport 2193 of *ten.* Da Barberino, that was struck off charge. On 18 March both *serg.m.* Degli Esposti and *serg.* Allasia had inconclusive duels with enemy fighters. The squadron was very active, all pilots flying escort and patrol missions shuttling among S. Maria la Longa, Aiello and Cascina Farello. They shared the last field with the French pilots of Escadrille N 382 and they occasionally escorted

seaplanes of the Navy. On 10 April Allasia fought two Brandenburgs and a fighter, but his gun jammed. Two days later, he met another enemy and drove it off.

The first victory arrived on 24 April 1917: *ten.* Keller shot down Br. C1 129.04 that fell in the Vippacco River with the death of its pilot, *Korp.* Rudolf Kousal, while the observer Julius Gyorffy was captured. On 25 April 25, among the many war missions, with escorts to Voisins of the 25ª Squadriglia, Allasia had duels with two enemies and drove them away, his Nieuport was hit many times. This could correspond to a claim by *OfStV.* Julius Arigi of FlG 1 who flying 28.06 claimed a Nieuport forced down near Monfalcone.

On 30 April 1917 the 80ª Squadriglia moved from S. Maria la Longa to Aiello. In May there were constant flights on the frontline and many inconclusive encounters with enemy airplanes. On 17 May Allasia was wounded by anti-aircraft fire, he force-landed at Doberdò and was hospitalized. After many inconclusive encounters, on 24 May *serg.* Leonardi together with Olivari of the 70ª Squadriglia forced down the Austrian seaplane L136 from a group that were attacking monitors of the Royal Navy, the Austrian naval airmen were captured.

In the morning of 26 May *ten.* Keller fought with an enemy airplane, then attacked another over Oppachiasella and noticed the observer desisting from fighting, after having put some bullets in his Nieuport, and the airplane going down trailing smoke.

Above: The "Fortunello" (Happy Hooligan) on Nieuport 2140 was rather gruesome.

The 80ª Squadriglia had gaudy personal insignia, with Fortunello (the American Happy Hooligan cartoon character) in many variations, but in May the Aviation Command complained: "*It is absolutely not tolerable, for obvious and many reasons, that puppets, caricatures or any other grotesque figure be applied to the airplanes, which are in evident contrast with the grave and serious purposes for which the airplanes are intended.*" So Happy Hooligan had to go, and a big star replaced him.

On 30 May 1917, the flight detached at Cascina Farello was called back and the squadron reunited at Aiello. In the first half of June 1917 new pilots arrived, *ten.* Carlo Molinari and *asp.* Giovanni Ancillotto. On 13 June there was one more skirmish over Merna, and Sambonet returned with his fighter hit. On 21 June Ancillotto had his first duel, an enemy plane escaped. On 25 June Keller and Leonardi drew away two fighters trying to attack a Voisin they were escorting, getting the praise of the command of the I Gruppo. On 29 June seven pilots of the 80ª escorted Capronis bombing the enemy lines beyond Hermada. In June this unit flew 162 war missions and had nine combats. On 7 July *ten.* Sambonet escorting a Caudron attacked a two-seater and shot it down over Mount Stol, soldiers recovered parts of the burned wreck, showing serial 112.2, but Austrian sources provide no identification for this event. On 13 July *serg.* Allasia fought against a seaplane that he saw going down in a spin and alighting off Prosecco, *serg.* Leonardi in the same area had another duel with an Austrian airplane.

On 16 July the unit delivered its Nieuport 11s to La Comina and re-equipped with the Nieuport 17 with 110 hp engines, getting twelve of them. *Ten.* Keller and *serg.* Viganò were transferred to the 77ª Squadriglia. On 28 July Leonardi met a fighter and a two-seater, the fighter ran away, but the other plane daringly attacked the Ni.17. Leonardi fired back and watched it spinning down, but it was a ruse, and close to the ground his gallant opponent straightened its flight and returned to Prosecco.

At the end of July 1917, the 80ª Squadriglia with commander Gordesco had the pilots *tenenti* Da Barberino, Sambonet, Carlo Molinari, *s.ten.* Ancillotto, *sergenti* Allasia, Avon, Degli Esposti, Leonardi. In July 1917 it flew 205 war missions, had 14 combats and claimed two victories. They flew dropping leaflets, like the ones with photos showing the good treatment of Austrian prisoners.

On 10 August two victories were claimed, together with pilots of the 91ª Squadriglia: *serg.m.* Degli Esposti near Jamiano and *serg.* Allasia over Dosso Faiti. As the 11th Batlle of the Isonzo was raging, the unit resumed its detachment of a flight at Cascina Farello. The 80ª Squadriglia flew 21 combat missions on 18 August, with two combats, 23 on the 19th with one combat, and so on the following days. On 20 August commander Gordesco, who flew as frequently as his pilots, finally had a combat, over Voiscizza, his opponent went down in a steep dive but was not claimed as shot down. In the evening he led a big formation on an escort to Capronis, and then he strafed enemy trenches with *ten.* Da Barberino repeating this feat the following days when up to eight fighters flew escorts and then strafed. After days

Above: Nieuport 2174 of the 80ᵃ Squadriglia. The man in its cockpit is *serg.m.* Camillo Sirigatti, a reconnaissance pilot.

of intense action, the number of sorties hardly decreased in September. There were two duels on 9 September, and *serg.* Avon came back with his fighter hit after a duel. The pilots began flying one daily weather reconnaissance flight.

On 1 October *s.ten.* Ancillotto and *serg.* Allasia went to Pordenone to train in night combat missions and in the night of 4 October Ancillotto flew for 75 minutes over Monfalcone looking for raiders. On 22 October the commander of the 3ᵃ Armata, the Duke of Aosta, came to Aiello for a ceremony assigning the Silver Medal to *cap.* Gordesco and *serg.* Allasia. A new pilot, *serg.* Nello Parlanti, arrived.

The 80ᵃ Squadriglia was heavily engaged during the retreat of Caporetto. On 26 October there were 24 combat flights, Ancillotto and Leonardi shot down at Doberdò Lake the seaplane K212, Ancillotto the seaplane K367, and the next day also K366. On 27 October the order to retreat arrived, nine fighters took off for La Comina, five were burned. The 80ᵃ Squadriglia flew some missions from La Comina, then on 1 November it moved to Arcade. On 2 November *serg.* Allasia shot down an enemy near Codroipo. The next day Ancillotto also claimed a victory, identified as a DFW C.5 of Fl. Abt. 14. On 6 November Leonardi, together with Rizzotto of the 77ᵃ Squadriglia, shot down Brandenburg C.1 229.24 of Flik 12, its pilot was taken, the observer died. On 7 November Allasia and *serg.* Avon (77ᵃ Squadriglia) claimed another victory while escorting a

SAML near Conegliano.

On 8 November, the 80ᵃ Squadriglia became part of the new XIII Gruppo and moved with its ten Nieuport 17s to Marcon airfield, together with the 77ᵃ Squadriglia. On 10 November *cap.* Gordesco took command of XIII Gruppo and *cap.* Da Barberino became the commander of the squadron. The 80ᵃ received a large number of pilots, some of them from the disbanded 84ᵃ Squadriglia, who were immediately sent into battle, as air activity was very intense, with up to 12 escort missions in a day. On 16 November *cap.* Da Barberino was wounded in a flight accident, and *ten.* Sambonet became the interim commander. At the end of November the pilots were *tenenti* Sambonet, Giovanni Mazzia, (in hospital), Renato Mazzucchelli, *s.tenenti* Francesco Carabelli, Eolo Restelli, *brigadiere* Ernesto Cabruna, *serg.m.* Degli Esposti, *sergenti* Mario Banino, Leonardi, Elia Liut, Nello Parlanti, Rodolfo Piermattei, Cesare Rapalli, Giovanni Riva and Francesco Rossi.

At the end of November 1917, the first Hanriot Hd.1 arrived in flight from Padua, serials 6138 and 6162. In November 1917 the 80ᵃ Squadriglia flew 242 combat sorties, had nine combats and claimed 5 victories. In this period there was some confusion between the units based at Marcon, and pilots such as Ancillotto and Cabruna (now *maresciallo*) were quoted in the documents of both 77ᵃ and 80ᵃ.

Above: A smiling Fortunello on Nieuport 2157. (Archive Massimiliano De Antoni)

The activity of the 80ᵃ in December 1917 was very intense. Its equipment was now mainly Hanriots, with fewer Nieuport 17. On 8 December *Ten* Restelli shot down an enemy plane near Susegana. The historical journal of the squadron reports another victory by Restelli and Piermattei on the 16ᵗʰ while escorting a Savoia Pomilio over the Piave. The fighters also strafed the enemy positions and they were often deployed to Padua to fly Caproni escort missions from there. On 30 December *serg.* Banino had a combat over Susegana and returned with his plane shot up (this may correspond to a claim for a Camel by *Leut.* Von Stenglin of Jasta 1 over Conegliano).

In December 1917 the 80ᵃ Squadriglia flew 163 war sorties, had 7 combats with three victory claims. Since its formation to the end of the year its total amounted to 2,409 combat sorties with 128 air combats.

In January 1918 new pilots arrived: *s.ten.* Giorgio Romano and *tenenti* Carlo Alberto Conelli de Prosperi and Giorgio Zoli. In January activities were reduced, also on account of the weather and there were some accidents, like on 15 January, when Cabruna smashed Hanriot 507, but the arrival of new Hd.1s was constant.

In the night of 26/27 January isolated airplanes bombed Marcon, little damage was produced but two men were killed and more wounded of the personnel of the other squadrons

on that field, 77ᵃ, 83ᵃ e 118ᵃ. New pilot arrived, *cpr.* Giuseppe Caldarelli, *s.tenenti* Giuseppe Pascoli and Serafino Ravetta.

On 5 February *sergenti* Leonardi and Piermattei had a combat with an enemy aircraft that was seen going down steeply. On 1 March command passed from *ten.* Sambonet to *ten.* Giorgio Zoli, until 30 April, when *cap.* Umberto Gelmetti arrived as effective commander. More new pilots arrived in March: *s.tenenti* Pietro Molino and Giorgio Romano, *sold.* Luigi Corti. The hard-working *serg.* Leonardi, a veteran of this unit, was promoted to *aspirante*. In March activity was constant with formation patrol flights over the Piave, with frequent ground strafing. On 24 March there was a combat, *ten.* Molino met two enemy fighters, *asp.* Leonardi shot down one of them, *sold.* Corti was hit and force landed near Roncade.

In the spring of 1918, the 80ᵃ Squadriglia was very active, patrolling all along the Piave River, from Ponte della Priula to the coast, daily engaged against enemy kite balloons, and *cap.* Gelmetti always concluded his sorties with ground strafing. On 3 April he attacked a Drachen, he fired 250 rounds until his gun jammed, but ground fire repeatedly hit his fighter, that returned safely but was disabled.

On 3 May *cap.* Gelmetti went to Florence and picked up Voisin 1317 of the local 105ᵃ Squadriglia, to be used for

Above: The left side of Nieuport 2157 showing a roundel with the inscription *"Asso?.. Macchè!! Due di coppe"* (An ace? Not at all! Two of clubs, that is, the lowest card.) This was possibly the airplane of commander Gordesco.

spy missions beyond enemy lines. On 8 May new pilots arrived, *cap*. Filippo Serafini, *ten*. Guido Baricalla, *serg*. Giuseppe Cao and *sold*. Ottavio Sottani. On 13 May *s.ten*. Leonardi and *ten*. Sambonet were detached for a week to Padua for the air defence of that city. Since mid-May *cap*. Raul Silvagni and Attilio Pierro flew with this unit.

On 17 May *cap*. Gelmetti flew a long offensive patrol on a Spad loaned from 77ª Squadriglia, but an engine failure forced him down near Arcade. On 23 May *ten*. Conelli, *s.ten*. Pascoli and *s.ten* Leonardi shot down an Aviatik C.1 at Noventa. On 25 May *cap*. Silvagni crashed Hanriot 6266 as he was taking off for another voluntary sortie and was badly wounded.

On 31 May *cap*. Gelmetti flew the first secret mission with the Voisin for the so-called "Giovane Italia" network of agents, taking off at 1 a.m. and safely returning 2 hours later after landing in enemy-held territory. *Serg*. Giuseppe Cao was wounded in an accident at take-off.

On 7 June *cap*. Achille Pierro was appointed as new commander of the 80ª Squadriglia, while Gelmetti took command of the 5ª Sezione SVA. The squadron was assigned to the *Massa di Manovra*, to contrast the coming Austrian offensive, and they participated with air superiority and ground strafing missions. *Ten*. Guido Baricalla did not return from one such mission on 15 June, he landed his intact Hanriot 6273 beyond the enemy lines and was captured, the Hanriot later got Austrian registration 00.72. On 17 June *cap*. Gelmetti shot down Phönix C.1 121.22, which was later recovered as the front advanced.

On 1 July 1918, the force of the 80ª Squadriglia with *cap*. Pierro included *tenenti* Carlo De Rossi, Giorgio Romano, Zoli, *s.tenenti* Ettore Dario, Leonardi, Giuseppe Pascoli, Serafino Ravetta, *sergenti* Avon. Piermattei, Giuseppe Pizzoccheri, *caporali* Luigi Corti, Telemaco Pillotti, Ottavio Sottani, Giovenale Testa, *soldati* Vincenzo Bonanni, Giovanbattista Gaiaudo, and Silvio Grassi.

In the night of 23 July Austrian airplanes bombed Marcon, but causing no damage. In the summer the new mission of dropping leaflets was added. On 8 September a huge storm hit the war zone, wrecking many aircraft on both sides, three Hanriots on the 80ª in flight made an emergency landing at Musette and were wrecked, but the pilots were unhurt.

During the final offensive of late October 1918, the 80ª Squadriglia flew 227 sorties and *cpr*. Ernesto Beretta claimed one final victory. Its performance during the war had

Above & Below: Alvaro Leonardi on Nieuport 2123. A perfect replica of this fighter, belonging to the Vintage Aviator Collection, is now flying at Hood Aerodrome, New Zealand. (James Fahey)

been impressive: 4,637 war flights, 177 air combats, and 30 confirmed air victories plus several Drachens driven down and one flamed, for the loss of one pilot in captivity but not a single pilot or airplane due to enemy action. Leonardi was awarded two *Medaglie d'Argento*, Degli Esposti and Piermattei one each, while Conelli de Prosperi, Serafini and Grassi received one *Medaglia di Bronzo*.

The 80ᵃ Squadriglia was disbanded at the end of January 1919.

Above: From the left, Sambonet, Keller, unknown, and Gordesco in Nieuport 11 2157.

Identified Victory Claims of the 80ª Squadriglia

Date	Place	Pilots	Victim
24.4.1917	Rubbia	*Ten.* Keller (& Appiani, Arrigoni, 76a)	Hansa Br. C.I 129.04, Flik 12
24.5.1917	Grado	*Serg.* Leonardi (& Olivari, 70ª)	Lohner L136, SFS Trieste
26.5.1917	Oppachiasella	*Ten.* Keller	Hansa Br. C.I 129.18, Flik 23?
7.7.1917	Mt. Stol	*Ten.* Sambonet (& Rizzotto, 77ª)	112.2 ??
13.7.1917	Trieste	*Serg.* Allasia	Seaplane ftl
10.8.1917	Jamiano	*Serg.* Degli Esposti (& Ranza, 91ª)	Hansa BR. C.I 69.92, FlG 1
10.8.1917	Mt. Stol	*Serg.* Allasia (& Sabelli, 91ª)	Hansa BR. C.I 229.25, FlG 1
20.8.1917	Comen	*Cap.* Gordesco	Enemy a/c OOC
26.10.1917	Brestovica	*Ten.* Ancillotto	SFS Trieste K367
26.10.1917	Lake Doberdò	*Serg.* Leonardi, *ten.* Ancillotto (& Lombardi, 77ª)	SFS Trieste K212
27.10.1917	Lake Doberdò	*Serg.* Leonardi, *ten.* Ancillotto (& Lombardi, 77ª)	SFS Trieste K366
2.11.1917	Codroipo	*Serg.* Allasia	Enemy aircraft
3.11.1917	Oderzo	*Ten.* Ancillotto (& Lombardi, 77ª)	DFW C.V, FA 14
6.11.1917	Conegliano	*Serg.* Leonardi (& Rizzotto, 77ª)	Hansa Br. C.I 229.24, Flik 12
7.11.1917	Livenza	*Serg.* Allasia (& Avon, 77ª)	FA 204 (A)?
27.11.1917	Zenson	*Serg.* Leonardi	Alb. D Jasta 1?
5.12.1917	Salgareda	*Serg.m.* Degli Esposti (& Cabruna 77ª, Carabelli 83ª)	Hansa Br. C.I 69.17, Flik 32?
8.12.1917	Susegana	*Ten.* Restelli	Enemy aircraft
16.12.1917	Piave	*S.ten.* Restelli, *serg.* Piermattei	Enemy aircraft
5.2.1918	Piave	*Serg.* Leonardi, *serg.* Piermattei	Enemy aircraft n.c.

Above: Nieuport 11 2225; the Lewis gun has a 97-round magazine. (Collection Carmelo Biz)

Above: The 80ᵃ Squadriglia turned to a more serious insignia, a simple star. This Ni.11, 2225, actually shows two stars. (Collection Carmelo Biz)

Above: Nieuport 17 3592 with an elaborate version of the star, insignia of the 80ª Squadriglia. (Archive Luigino Caliaro)

24.3.1918	Vendrome	*Asp*. Leonardi	Alb. D.III 153.138, Flik 42/J?
23.5.1918	Noventa	*Asp*. Leonardi, *ten*. Conelli de Prosperi, *s.ten*. Pascoli	Aviatik C.I 37.56, Flik 22/D
17.6.1918	Fossalta di Piave	*Serg*. Sottani	? Flik 34/D
17.6.1918	Meolo	*Cap*. Gelmetti	Phönix C.I 121.22?
18.6.1918	Monastir	*Asp*. Leonardi, *s.ten*. Pascoli, *cpr*. Corti	Hansa Br. C.I 369.41, Flik 19/D
19.6.1918	Monastir	*Cap*. Gelmetti (& Serafini, Sambonet 77ª)	Aviatik C.I 137.40, Flik 5/F
20.6.1918	S.Donà di Piave	*Serg*. Piermattei, *cpr*. Sottani (& Cabruna, 77ª)	Hansa Br. C.I 329.39, Flik 22/D
21.6.1918	Ceggia	*Serg*. Piermattei (& Cabruna, 77ª)	Kite Balloon
23.6.1918	Ceggia	*Cpr*. Corti?	Enemy aircraft?
15.7.1918	S.Donà di Piave	*S.ten*. Leonardi, *cpr*. Testa	HansaBr.C.I 429.01, Flik 49/D?
20.8.1918	Campo Bernardo	*S.ten*. Leonardi, *cpr*. Sottani	Ufag C.I 161.05, Flik 5/F?
31.8.1918	Grassaga	*Serg*. Sottani, *cpr*. Gaiaudo	Enemy aircraft?
14.9.1918	Roncade	*Serg*. Corti (& Lamperti, Albertazzi, 77ª)	Phönix D.I 228.08, Flik 46?
29.10.1918	Conegliano	*Cpr*. Beretta	Fighter?

Casualties and Combat Losses of the 80ª Squadriglia

Date	Place	Aircraft	Crew	Cause
17.5.1917	Doberdò	Ni.11	*Serg*. Allasia WIA	Ground fire
24.3.1918	Roncade	Hanriot	*Sold*. Corsi UNH	Fighters
25.5.1918	Marcon	Hd.1 6266	*Cap*. Silvagni WIC	Accident
15.6.1918	?	Hd.1 6273	*Ten*. Baricalla POW	?

Above: A ceremony for the award of medals at Aiello airfield, probably on 2 October 1917, with an apparently new Nieuport 17 of 80ª Squadriglia. The Duke of Aosta, commander of the 3ª Armata, is in the center, with crossed arms, to his right *Gen*. Maggiorotti and to his left *Col*. Moizo, of the air force command. It is remarkable that after two and a half years of war so few medal ribbons are to be seen.

Above: Hanriots of the 80ª Squadriglia at Marcon.

Above: The Hanriot of *ten*. Guido Baricalla captured on 15 June 1918. On the white background of the star there is the Latin motto *"Alere flammam"*, keep high the flame. (Archives Zoltàn Ciròk)

Above: Seventeen Hanriots, both Italian and French-built, can be seen, equipping the 80ª Squadriglia in late 1918. (Collection Fabio Bianchi)

Above: The pilots of 80ª Squadriglia with *cap*. Pierro in the center, near the end of the war. Italian fighter squadrons at this time had 18 pilots, and were scheduled to have 36 in 1919.

Below: *Cap*. Gelmetti getting out of a Hanriot with a variation of the burning star insignia, standing is *ten*. Ancillotto. (Archive Franz Selinger)

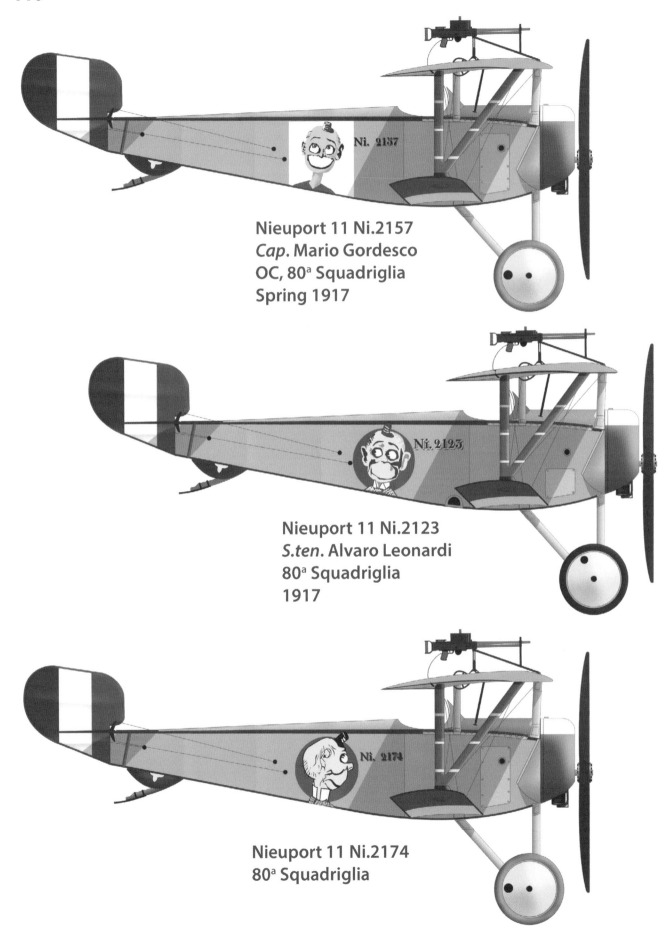

Nieuport 11 Ni.2157
Cap. Mario Gordesco
OC, 80ª Squadriglia
Spring 1917

Nieuport 11 Ni.2123
S.ten. Alvaro Leonardi
80ª Squadriglia
1917

Nieuport 11 Ni.2174
80ª Squadriglia

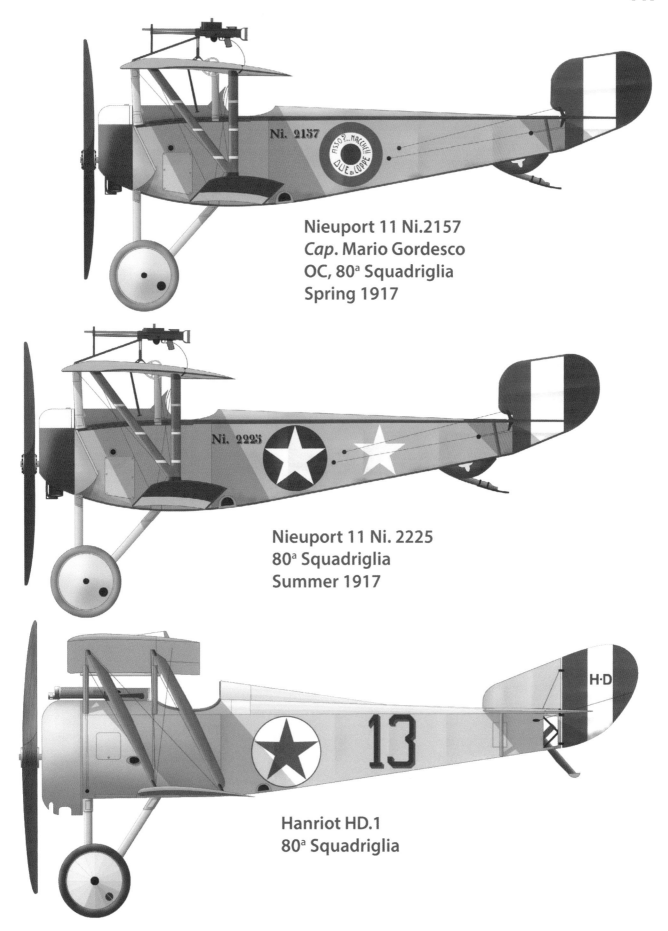

Nieuport 11 Ni.2157
Cap. Mario Gordesco
OC, 80ª Squadriglia
Spring 1917

Nieuport 11 Ni. 2225
80ª Squadriglia
Summer 1917

Hanriot HD.1
80ª Squadriglia

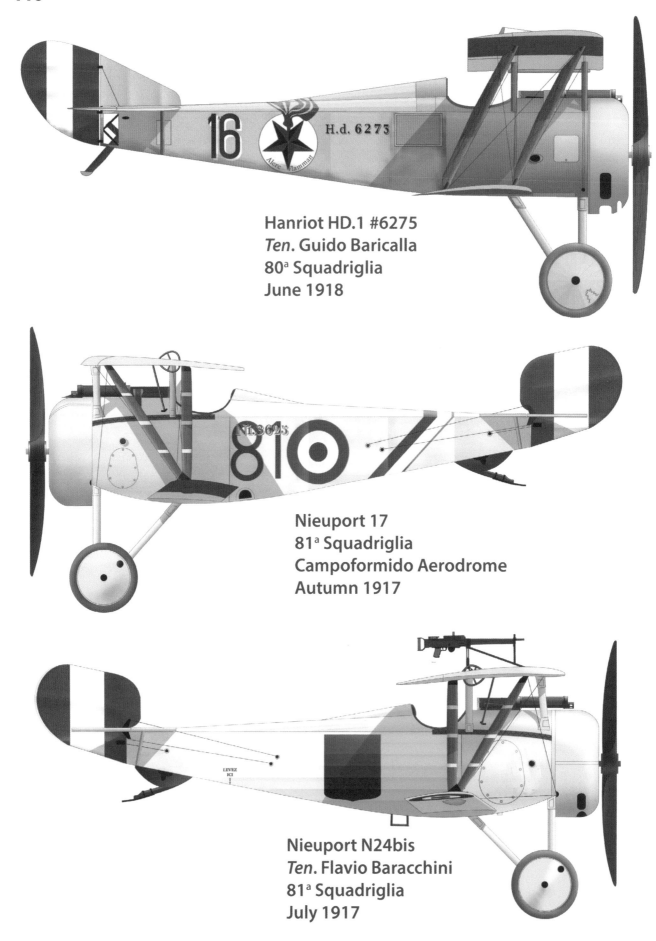

Hanriot HD.1 #6275
Ten. Guido Baricalla
80ᵃ Squadriglia
June 1918

Nieuport 17
81ᵃ Squadriglia
Campoformido Aerodrome
Autumn 1917

Nieuport N24bis
Ten. Flavio Baracchini
81ᵃ Squadriglia
July 1917

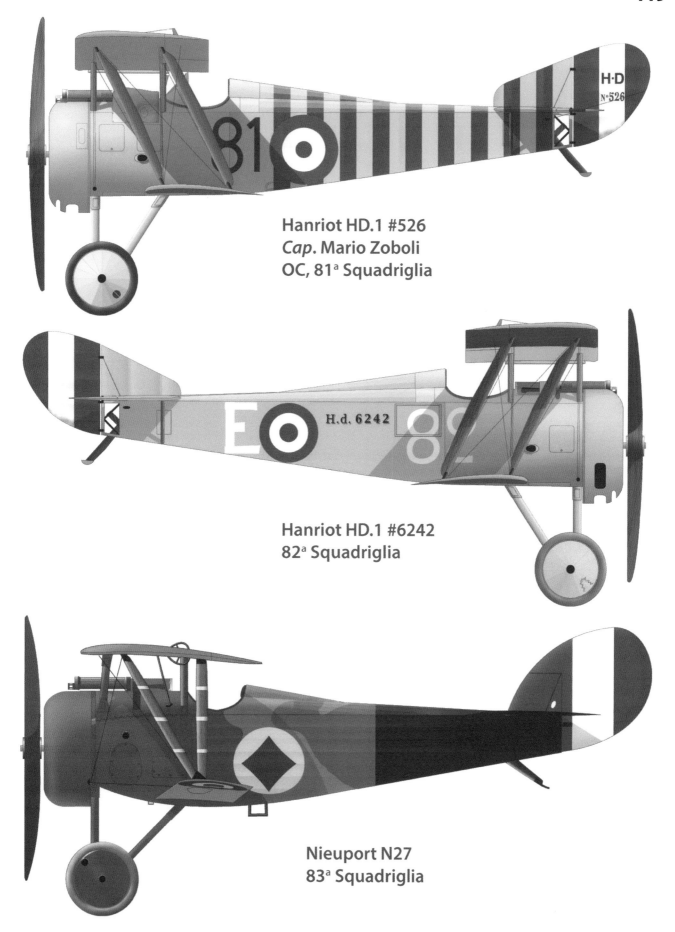

Hanriot HD.1 #526
Cap. Mario Zoboli
OC, 81ª Squadriglia

Hanriot HD.1 #6242
82ª Squadriglia

Nieuport N27
83ª Squadriglia

81ª Squadriglia

Above: A line-up of Nieuport 11s, possibly of the 81ª Squadriglia.

The 81ª Squadriglia was established at the Centro Formazione Squadriglia of Arcade on 20 March 1917 and it deployed at Langoris airfield, also called Borgnano, 3 miles west of Gorizia, on 20 April. It was assigned to the II Gruppo, made available to the 2ª Armata, its commander was *cap.* Antonio Bosio, with pilots *ten.* Gastone Novelli, *s.tenenti* Vincenzo Arone, and Flavio Torello Baracchini, *sergenti* Riccardo Ciotti, Paolo Nicosia, Ennio Sorrentino, *cpr.* Paolo Avenati, and *sold.* Paolo Simoncini, flying Nieuport 11s with serials 2143, 2179, 2180, 2186, 2191, 2192, 2194, 2195, 2201, 2215, 2220. During the ferry flight *serg.* Ciotti crashed on Ni.11 2194 and died of his wounds three days later. *Cap.* Bosio was soon shifted to the 75ᵃ, and *cap.* Salvatore Calori replaced him.

On 23 April the new squadron flew its first combat mission and the next day *serg.* Sorrentino and *cpr.* Avenati had the first air combat. On 27 April *ten.* Alessandro Buzio arrived as a replacement for *serg.* Ciotti.

On 1 May there was the first victory, as *serg.* Sorrentino claimed an enemy over Vippacco, who had himself claimed a Nieuport shot down. One pilot stood out, the bold *s.ten.* Baracchini, his first claim, on 15 May, was not confirmed, and in fact his adversary managed to return, but series of victories followed in May and June, while the 10ᵗʰ Battle of the Isonzo was raging. On 23 May, in a big battle in which the Austrians shot down a Caproni, he forced down a Brandenburg of FlG 1, and another one two days later, in just over a month he scored nine air victories. On 14 June the old (32 years) *maresciallo* Arturo Guglielmi, a veteran of Nieuport monoplanes, was killed in a take-off accident.

On 24 June *cap.* Calori went to the 76ᵃ Squadriglia and on

4 July *cap.* Mario Zoboli replaced him as commander. On 14 July Baracchini also went to the 76ᵃ Squadriglia.

On 9 July the 81ᵃ Squadriglia, together with the 76ᵃ, became part of the VI Gruppo, reporting to the 4ᵃ Armata operating north of the 2ᵃ Armata and on 10 August it formed, with the 78ᵃ, the Sottogruppo Aeroplani (airplanes sub-group) of Borgnano.

In July the first Nieuport 17 were received, and by mid-August the unit had a dozen of them. A new pilot, *carabiniere* Lino Montello Chiaventone arrived from the 36ᵃ Squadriglia, but he was wounded in a crash and, when recovered, he was posted as instructor at the seaplane school at Sesto Calende.

When the enemy smashed the Italian lines at Caporetto, Borgnano was abandoned, with some complete fighters falling in enemy hands, like Ni.17 3625, that got the Austrian serial 00.59. The 81ᵃ Squadriglia moved to Arcade on 31 October and to Istrana on 9 November, now equipped with Nieuport 27s. On 3 November *serg.* Sorrentino claimed two seaplanes shot down at Grado, Austrian data don't confirm these claims, but the Command admitted both of them and the War Bulletin reported them. On 17 November *serg.m.* Ettore Bontempi was wounded in a crash landing at Camalò after an air combat with the Austrian pilot Sandor Kasza of Flik 55/J.

On 26 December the 81ᵃ Squadriglia took part in the succesful Battle of Istrana, but details of its participation are not available, at least one victory was credited to *ten.* Sorrentino, possibly over an Austrian fighter in another part of the front. During 1917 the 81ᵃ Squadriglia had flown 1,650 sorties, sustained 150 air combats and had 15 confirmed victories.

On 1 January 1918 the unit with commander *cap.* Zoboli had pilots *tenenti* Giuseppe Lucci, Sorrentino, Lamberto Toncher, *s.ten.* Antonio Bogliolo, *serg.m.* Mario Baldaccini and Alfredo Sozzini, *sergenti* Gino Allegri, Alessandro Borgato, Alberto Rettori, *caporali* Raffaele Tarducci, Attilio Venuti, *carab.* Montello Chiaventone, and *sold.* Giovanbattista Gays.

On 15 January *serg.* Rettori, flying Nieuport Ni.27 5800 in a cruise patrol, failed to return to Istrana. He had landed by mistake at San Fior di Sopra, then a base of German fighters, and was captured. The Germans chivalrously dropped a note reporting what had happened.

On 2 February 1918 the 81ᵃ Squadriglia moved to Isola di Carturo, and on the 17ᵗʰ to Casoni, where it started to re-equip on the Hanriot Hd.1. A new pilot, *serg.* Alfonso Giacomelli smashed three Nieuport in less than a month, and was removed from flying service. On 25 March *cap.* Zoboli was transferred to the Comando Aviatori in Turin, and *cap.* Renato Mazzucco became the new commander. New pilots came in April, *sergenti* Carlo Corti and Silvio Mellone.

On 22 April *serg.* Sorrentino, in an escort mission, attacked some fighters, claiming one shot down in flames over Asolone, but was himself wounded and force landed with his airplane shot up. 50 years later, describing this combat in a magazine, he said his opponents were the von Richthofen squadron. For this feat, the King of Italy awarded him his third Silver Medal "on the field", and yet the squadron diary does not report anything.

On 1 May another pilot was lost, *serg.* Silvio Mellone who got lost and ran out of fuel on Nieuport 27 5836, landing at San Pietro in Campo, then base of Flik 53/D. On the 14ᵗʰ *cpr.* Bruno Angeli was wounded in a landing accident. On 31 May *ten.* Baracchini, now holder of Italy's highest decoration, the *Medaglia d'Oro al Valor Militare*, returned, and just 2 days later, on 2 June, he claimed an enemy reconnaissance airplane at Susegana.

In June 1918 the 81ᵃ Squadriglia contributed to the air offensive that was instrumental in stopping the Austrian offensive. On 15 June 15 combat missions were flown, and three victories were claimed, two by Baracchini. On June 18 thirteen fighters escorted Capronis bombing Nervesa, then they went down to strafe, ground fire hit Hanriot 7589 of *ten.* Lucci who crash landed and suffered a broken clavicle, also the Hanriot of *magg.* Lombard, commander of VI Gruppo, was hit. On 19 June there were 16 offensive and 21 escort flights, *serg.* Corti flamed a Drachen. On June 20 there were six free hunting sorties, ten strafing and no less than 31 escort sorties, Austrian fighters attacked and shot down in flames Hanriot 605 of *serg.* Nava, despite the intervention of *serg.* Corti who claimed an enemy fighter shot down. Again, there were 30 combat sorties on 21 June, and Baracchini flamed a Drachen with a Le Prieur rocket. On the 22ⁿᵈ Baracchini, flying Nieuport 27 11383 of the 79ᵃ Squadriglia, together with *serg.* Reali of 79ᵃ Squadriglia, claimed one enemy in flames and two out of control on the left bank of

Above: The crash of Nieuport 2194 in which *serg.* Riccardo Ciotti lost his life on 20 April 1918.

Piave River. On 25 June Baracchini with *serg.* Corti attacked six fighters over Oderzo, and the ace shot down one of them, but on the way back a bullet from the ground hit him in the belly, putting him out of the war. The official final list in 1919 assigned him 21 confirmed victories. Baracchini died in 1928 in an accident in his laboratory preparing signal flares for aviation use.

The score for the 81ᵃ Squadriglia in June was 385 combat flights, 34 combats and 14 planes or kite balloons destroyed. According to the Comando Superiore di Aeronautica, in June 1918 the Italian airmen shot down 86 airplanes and five balloons, the British 61 airplanes and two balloons, plus anti-aircraft artillery brought down three more planes; overblown figures, surely, but the defeat of the K.u.k. Luftfahrtruppen was total.

On 30 June 1918 the 81ᵃ Squadriglia had *capitani* Mario Ponis and Arturo Freddi Cavalletti, *ten.* Manillo Zerbinati, *s.tenenti* Michele Borea d'Olmo and Antonio Bogliolo, *serg.m.* Alfredo Sozzini and Mario Baldaccini, *sergenti* Ciampitti, Corti, Genta, Oliveti, Ungaro, *cpr.* Astolfi, and a strength of 14 Hanriots, 562, 6128, 6272, 6283, 6287, 7451,7483, 7514, 7522, 7526, 7557, 7591, 13221, 13259, and five Nieuport 27s, 5801, 5834, 5835, 5852, 5858. On 17 July *cap.* Ponis left, and became commander of the 85ᵃ Squadriglia in Albania. On 14 July *ten.* Bogliolo, *serg.m.* Sozzini and *serg.*

Above: Baracchini, standing behind the rudder of his Nieuport 11 2179, being congratulated after scoring a victory.

Oliveti shot down an Austrian fighter together with Camels of RAF No. 28 Squadron and claimed one out of control. On 14 July an enemy fighter was shot down together with British pilots of No. 45 Sqn., and a Drachen was shot at, but not flamed.

On 31 July an Austrian fighter attacked Ciampitti and Astolfi over Valdobbiadene, but the two Italian pilots shot it down in flames; it is believed that their victim was the 27 victories ace Oblt. Frank Linke-Crawford on Aviatik Berg D.1 115.32.

On 30 August *serg.* Ciampitti flying on Hd.1 13272 attacked a Drachen, but ground fire stopped his engine and he smashed his plane landing just across the river. Activity was always intense, with many missions dropping leaflets and special newspapers for the civilians in the enemy-occupied territory. Enemy activity was reduced, however, and only on 22 October could three rookie pilots claim a victory,

a bomber out of a formation of five over Val Seren. Il 26 October the 81ª Squadriglia was assigned to the *Massa da Caccia*, taking part in the final battle and scoring on that day its final victory, by *serg.* Corti over Col dell'Orso.

When the war ended, it was still at Casoni, with commander *cap.* Mazzucco and the pilots *cap.* Renato Formilli, *tenenti* Bogliolo, Carlo De Angeli, Borea d'Olmo, Zerbinati, *sergenti maggiori* Baldaccini, Bontempi, Sozzini, *sergenti* Astolfi, Corti, Genta, *caporali* Pietro Bertini, Paolo Compagnoni, Carlo Madassani, Riccardo Mella, Angelo Menconi, Umberto Olendini, Glicerio Reviati, and *sold.* Giuseppe Biagetti. During 1918 it had flown 2,468 war sorties, sustained 80 air combats and had 19 confirmed victories. For the whole war, its contribution was 4,118 combat sorties, 230 air combats and 34 victories. It was disbanded in the spring of 1919.

Above: Another view of Baracchini with Nieuport 2179 that shows a cartoon character painted on the deck of the fuselage.

Identified Victory Claims of the 81ª Squadriglia

Date	Place	Pilots	Victim	Unit
1.5.1917	Vippacco	*Serg.* Sorrentino	Hansa Br. C.I 27.64	Flik 2?
15.5.1917	Aisovizza	*S.ten.* Baracchini	Hansa Br. C.I 129.46	Flik 23
20.5.1917	Vodice	*S.ten.* Baracchini (& Piccio, 91ª)	Hansa Br. C.I 229.10	Flik 12
23.5.1917	San Marco	*S.ten.* Baracchini	Hansa Br. C.I 69.09	FlG 1 FTL
25.5.1917	Aisovizza	*S.ten.* Baracchini	Hansa Br. C.I129.38	FlG 1
3.6.1917	Sober	*S.ten.* Baracchini	Hansa Br. C.I 129.02	Flik 4?
3.6.1917	Aisovizza	*Ten.* Novelli (& Olivari, Poli, 91ª)	Hansa Br. C.I 129.02	Flik 4?
6.6.1917	Gargano	*S.ten.* Baracchini (& Olivari, 91ª)	Hansa Br. C.I 229.19	FlG 1
18.6 1971	Aisovizza	*S.ten.* Baracchini	Hansa Br. C.I 129.14	Flik 32
19.6.1917	Schoenpass	*S.ten.* Baracchini, *ten.* Novelli	Hansa Br. C.I 29.63	Flik 19
22.6.1917	San Marco	*S.ten.* Baracchini, *ten.* Novelli (& Piaggio, 77ª)	Hansa Br. C.I 229.05	Flik 35
31.7.1917	Plava	*Ten.* Buzio	Hansa Br. C.I 229.03	Flik 32?
3.11.1917	Grado	*Serg.* Sorrentino	Seaplane	
3.11.1917	Grado	*Serg.* Sorrentino	Seaplane	
27.11.1917	Val di Marie	*Serg.* Allegri	Fighter OOC	
26.12.1917	Finer	*Serg.* Sorrentino	Albatros D.III 153.111	Flik 41/J?
14.1.1918	Foza	*Cap.* Zoboli	Two-seater	

Nieuport 17 3587 of the 81ª Squadriglia. (Archive Luigino Caliaro)

The Nieuport 17 of ace Baracchini showing his insignia, a black shield. (Archive Luigino Caliaro)

Above: The black shield of Baracchini now appearing on a rare Nieuport 24 bis.

25.1.1918	Godellana	*Ten.* Lucci, *serg.* Sorrentino, *serg.* Borgato	Albatros D.III 153.70	Flik 55/J?
31.1.1918	Sassorosso	*Ten.* Lucci, *serg.* Sorrentino, *serg.* Borgato	Possible	
18.2.1918	Asolone	*Cap.* Zoboli (& *serg.* Contardini, 82ª)	Phönix D.I 128.08	Flik 39/D?
17.3.1918	Val Seren	*Serg.* Sorrentino	Enemy a/c	
3.4.1918	Premador	*Ten.* Baracchini (& Scaroni, Nannini 76ª)	Kite balloon	BK 20
22.4.1918	Asolone	*Serg.* Sorrentino	Fighter?	
9.5.1918	Val Calcina	*Serg.* Sorrentino	Two-seater OOC	
2.6.1918	Susegana	*Ten.* Baracchini	Two-seater	
15.6.1918	Conca di Alano	*Cap.* Mazzucco, *serg.* Oliveti, *cpr.* Astolfi	Two-seater	
15.6.1918	Moriago	*Ten.* Baracchini, *cap.* Mazzucco	Hansa Br. C.I 369.113	Flik 38/D?
15.6.1918	Susegana	*Ten.* Baracchini	Fighter	
19.6.1918	S. Salvatore	*Serg.* Corti	Kite balloon	
20.6.1918	Piave	*Serg.* Corti	Fighter	
21.6.1918	San Pietro	*Ten.* Baracchini	Kite balloon	BK 4?
22.6.1918	Piave	*Ten.* Baracchini (& Reali, 79ª)	Hansa Br. C.I 269.02	Flik 65?
22.6.1918	Piave	*Ten.* Baracchini (& Reali, 79ª)	Enemy aircraft OOC	
22.6.1918	Piave	*Ten.* Baracchini (& Reali, 79ª)	Enemy aircraft OOC	
25.6.1918	Fontanelle	*Serg.* Genta	Fighter OOC	
25.6.1918	Colfosco	*Ten.* Baracchini, *serg.* Corti	Phönix D.IIa 222.02	Flik 43/J?
7.7.1918	Montebelluna	*Ten.* Bogliolo, *serg.m.* Sozzini (& RAF pilots)	Albatros D.III 153.257	Flik 30/J
7.7.1918	Moriago	*Ten.* Bogliolo, *serg.m.* Sozzini (& RAF pilots)	Fighter OOC	
14.7.1918	Conegliano	*Serg.* Corti, *ten.* Zerbinati	Kite balloon	BK20
14.7.1918	Arsiero	*Serg.* Corti (& Howell, 45 Sqn. RAF)	Albatros D.III 153.249	Flik 3/J
31.7.1918	Conca di Alano	*Cpr.* Astolfi, *serg.* Ciampitti	Aviatik D.I 115.32	Flik 60/J
22.10.1918	Val Seren	*Cpr.* Compagnoni, *sold.* Beviati, *sold.* Pianciola	Bomber	
26.10.1918	Mount Solarolo	*Serg.* Corti	Two-seater	

Above: Nieuport 17 3625 fell in Austrian hands, together with Pomilio PD 3818. (Archive Jiry Cejka)

Above: Captured Nieuport 17 3606, that got the Austrian serial 00.60. (Archive Zoltàn Cziròk)

Above: Nieuport 27 11339 of *serg.m.* Mario Baldaccini, with the insignia of the "2 of spades".

Casualties and Combat Losses of the 81ª Squadriglia

Date	Place	Aircraft	Crew	Cause
20.4.1917	Borgnano	Ni.11 2194	*Serg.* Ciotti KIC	Accident
14.6.1917	Borgnano	Ni.11	*M.llo* Guglielmi KIC	Accident
28.8.1917	Blanchis	Ni.17	*Serg.* Pellanda KIC	Accident
17.11.1917	Camalò	Ni.27	*Serg.m.* Bontempi WIA	Fighters
15.01.1918	San Fior	Ni.27 5800	*Serg.* Rettori POW	Fighters
22.4.1918	Asolone	Hd.1	*Serg.* Sorrentino WIA	Fighters
1.5.1918	San Pietro	Ni.27 5836	*Serg.* Mellone POW	Lack of fuel
20.6.1918	Montello	Hd.1 605	*Serg.* Nava KIA	Fighters
25.6.1918	Piave	Hd.1	*Ten.* Baracchini WIA	Ground fire
30.8.1918	Cornada	Hd.1 13272	*Serg.* Ciampitti UNH	Ground fire

Above: The Nieuport 27 5800 of *serg.* Rettori that fell in German hands on 15 January 1918. (Archive Jan Zahalka)

Above: Nieuport 27 5836 that fell in Austrian hands on 1 May 1918 had a beautiful insignia with a horseshoe and a horse's head on its left side.

Above: The same airplane on its right side showed a horseshoe, but the horse's head had not been painted yet. (Archive Jan Zahalka)

Above: Hanriots and a Ni.27 of the 81ᵃ Squadriglia at Casoni. The first Hd.1 seems to have a black shield insignia.

Above: Four Hanriots and, in the middle, a Ni.27 armed with four Le Prieur rockets.

Above: Fighters of the 81ª Squadriglia at Casoni: the first one is Hanriot 6287 of *cpr*. Astolfi, the second one Hd.1 of *serg*. Genta, the third one is Ni.27 5836 of *serg*. Melloni, that fell in enemy hands on 1 May 1918.

Left: An unidentified Hanriot of the 81ª Squadriglia in flight.

Above: Hanriots and Nieuports of the 81ª Squadriglia at Casoni.

Above: As the fortunes of war turned for the better, the Hanriots of the 81ª Squadriglia, like the ones of the sister unit 76ª Squadriglia at Casoni, received ever more gaudy personal markings.

Above: *Cap*. Mazzucco, commander of the 81ª Squadriglia, with his striped Hanriot Hd.1.

Above: The well-known star-studded Hanriot of *ten*. Bogliolo.

Above: A piglet and a child are painted on the Hanriot of *s.ten*. Michele Borea d'Olmo, unfortunately hiding the serial number.

82ª Squadriglia

Above: Andrea Teobaldi with Nieuport 2297. This gallant pilot was an instructor at the Gabardini flying school after the war. In World War 2 he piloted transport airplanes on the dangerous route from Sicily to North Africa.

The 82ª Squadriglia was established at the Centro Formazione Squadriglie of Arcade in March 1917 and on 11 April it was assigned to the new X Gruppo, together with 70ª and 91ª Squadriglia. Its first commander was *ten.* Giuliano Parvis, an "*irredento*", that is, an Italian of Austrian citizenship, his real name being Giorgio Pessi. In August 1918 he went to the United States as part of the Italian aeronautical mission, flying Capronis, and died in 1933 at the controls of an airliner. The unit moved to Santa Caterina on 25 May with Nieuport 11 serials 1704, 2189, 2198, 2208, 2211, 2219, 2221, 2235 and 2236.

On 26 May *serg.* Gaetano Aliperta had the first inconclusive combat with an enemy aircraft. On 9 June, as Parvis went to the 78ª Squadriglia, *ten.* Antonio Fochessati became the new commander. Its pilots included *s.ten.* Aldo Anesini, *sergenti* Montalto Ercoli, Giampiero Vecco, Pietro Zanatta, in June *serg.* Andrea Teobaldi arrived.

In June 1917 the 82ª Squadriglia, the rookie unit in the Group, exercised in patrol flights. In one such flight, *serg.* Zanatta made a forced landing for engine failure, but struck a soldier who was killed. 96 combat flights were flown, with four combats.

On 2 July 1917 *cap.* Pietro Cavadini became the commander. On 7 July five of its Nieuports escorted the Capronis bombing the mercury plant at Idria, and this mission was repeated on 28 July. *Serg.* Giulio Poli, formerly of the 70ª Squadriglia, claimed a victory on 16 July. Another escort mission to bombers attacking Assling took place on 14 August. *Ten.* Renato Rossetti, *sergenti* Teobaldi and Zanatta had combats, *serg.* Aliperta in his post-war memories described a successful duel with a fighter, which was not reported in contemporary records, nor in the motivation of his Silver Medal, which credits him with a victory on 28 July. On 14 August, during an escort mission he fought against an enemy fighter that was hit in the radiator and landed at Aidussina (Heidensschaft) being destroyed, likely it was KD 28.66 of Flik 12 with pilot Oblt. Benno Fiala Ritter von Fernbrugg.

On 17 August a flight of 82ª Squadriglia was detached at Borgnano for the large offensive against the Bainsizza. The fighters escorted formations of Capronis attacking Grahovo on successive missions on 23, 29 and 31 August.

Above: A Nieuport 11, an Hanriot, and a Nieuport 17 of the 82ª Squadriglia at Padua. In the background there are three Capronis and two SVAs of the 87ª Squadriglia.

On 7 September *ten.* Fochessati was again interim commander of the 82ª Squadriglia. On 28 September *serg.* Aliperta forced down a fighter at S. Lucia di Tolmino, a German Albatros D.5 that Italian artillery destroyed on the ground. On 1 October while trying to intercept an enemy raid, with *s.ten.* Michele Riello and *serg.* Teobaldi, *serg.* Aliperta was bounced, with two bullets in his body he made an emergency landing at Oleis.

On 25 October *ten.* Fochessati fought alongside *magg.* Piccio, the Group commander, shooting down in flames a German two-seater over Castelmonte. On 26 October *serg.* Zanatta was wounded in an accident; he was in hospital when the enemy arrived and he became a prisoner of war.

The 82ª Squadriglia retreated to Padua, then on 5 November to Arcade, meanwhile re-equipping with Hanriots.

On 6 November *serg.* Alessandro Contardini while escorting a SAML claimed an enemy shot down near Mortegliano. On that same day *serg.* Agostino Buttazzoni during a Caproni escort mission force-landed for engine failure between the lines, torched his airplane and returned. The next day, 7 November, the same Buttazzoni went missing, after a duel with German fighters, and crash landed near Portobuffolè, but in the following days he managed to rejoin his unit.

On 10 November the 82ª Squadriglia moved to Istrana, with a few Hanriots. At that date, under *ten.* Fochessati there were the pilots *tenenti* Flaminio Avet, Alberto Camandone, Giovanni Pirelli, Alessandro Resch, Renato Rossetti, *s.ten.* Michele Riello, *sergenti* Paolo Benvenuti, Mario D'Urso,

Poli, Teobaldi and *sold.* Clemente Panero. On 20 November *serg.* Poli claimed a victory, and on the 27th *ten.* Camandone claimed an enemy out of control over Asiago. On 29 November *sold.* Panero shot down an Albatros Austrian fighter, that fell in Italian territory, confirming the claim.

On 8 December a British pilot doing some stunt flying too low with a Sopwith Camel hit *ten.* Rossetti, who suffered bruises and a broken finger.

During the air battle of Istrana, 26 December, seven pilots of the 82ª Squadriglia took off, and *ten.* Camandone, *sergenti* Benvenuti, D'Urso, Teobaldi, and *sold.* Panero shared many claims of that confused engagement with their comrades of 76ª and 78ª Squadriglia and of No. 28 Squadron, RFC. Four Hanriots of the squadron, 6094, 6100, 6136, 6177 were destroyed on the ground. During 1917 the 82ª Squadriglia flew 889 combat sorties and had 47 air combats.

On 1 January 1918 *sold.* Panero flying Hanriot 6127 drew away, and possibly hit, a fighter that was threatening the SAML under his escort over Asiago. On 3 January *ten.* Avet became interim commander for two weeks, then he was assigned to the 70ª Squadriglia. On 9 January the squadron moved from overcrowded Istrana to San Pietro in Gu, with its Hanriots 6095, 6108, 6127, 6137, 6167, 6649, 6151 and 7214.

On 12 January *serg.* Teobaldi fought against five enemy fighters during a Caproni escort mission, and watched the forced landing of Ca 4226 of the 2ª Squadriglia that he had freed from the pursuing enemies. On 28 January a new pilot, destined to fame, *s.ten.* Arturo Ferrarin with serg. Croci of 70ª Squadriglia shot down an enemy on the Melette

Right: Giorgio Pessi, a.k.a. Giuliano Parvis, in the United States, in front of a Standard-built Caproni 600 hp at Hazelhurst Field.

mountains, where a big battle was going on, *sold*. Panero attacked a fighter and a two-seater, and believed to have shot down both of them. On 29 January *magg*. Ferruccio Coppini became commander of the 82ª Squadriglia.

On 22 February *sold*. Panero crashed on take-off with Hanriot 6137 and died of his wounds on 19 March. The international Riviera Airport at Villanova d'Albenga is named after him.

On 14 March 1918 the 82ª Squadriglia returned to its former base at Istrana. On 4 April Teobaldi, Benvenuti, Ferrarin, Camandone and Contardini had a large combat against a patrol of seven Austrian fighters in the area of Ponte della Priula, and chased them off.

In May *serg*. Poli went away, becoming a test pilot at Macchi. On 2 May Ferrarin claimed a victory, that was not confirmed, actually he was not credited with any victory during the war; the next day Teobaldi shot down an airplane near Grave di Papadopoli, and this claim was validated.

On 21 May the 82ª Squadriglia moved from Istrana to Gazzo, west of the Brenta River, not too close to the front.

At the beginning of summer 1918 with commander *magg*. Coppini were the pilots *capitani* Luigi Aglietti, Salvatore Breglia, Francesco Fassi, Giulio Cesare Paldaoff, Pompeo Vaccarossi, *tenenti* Camandone, Umberto Garelli, Pirelli, Rossetti, *s.ten*. Ferrarin, *sergenti* Benvenuti, Mario Jacazio, Gaspare Monetti, Agostino Roggeri, Eugenio Spano,

Above: Hanriot Hd.1 "M" at Istrana in the days of the air battle of 26 December 1917.

Teobaldi and *soldati* Guido Colombatto and Chiaffredo Monetti. The number of pilots of a fighter squadron had doubled since the year before. Being part of X Gruppo, which reported directly to the Supreme Command, the 82ª Squadriglia was specifically tasked with the escort of Caproni bombers. On 7 June twelve Hanriots were deployed to Ganfardine airfield for an escort mission to a bombing of Pergine airfield on 8 June, while a raid to Gardolo airfield on the 10th was cancelled for bad weather, which precluded all flights until the 15th, when the Austrian offensive began. The 82ª Squadriglia was very active, on 17 June *cap.* Vaccarossi was wounded and he force landed with a rifle bullet in his arm. On 18 June Austrian fighters attacked Fassi, Breglia, Paldaoff, Camandone and Benvenuti as they were strafing the gangways across the Piave River between Zenson and Salgareda. Hanriot 7452 of *cap.* Fassi was shot down in flames, all the other ones were damaged, Camandone and Breglia reported possible victories. During the battle, the 82ª Squadriglia was assigned to the *Massa da Caccia,* then it returned to the X Gruppo.

In the last summer of the war the fighters of the 82ª Squadriglia flew to escort Caproni bombers attacking the enemy airfields. On 29 July *ten.* Rossetti drew away two Albatros D.3 attacking a Caproni over Mansuè, Camandone also reported a fighter shot down near Lake Santa Croce, and also *cap.* Tosi and *ten.* Rossetti again, claimed one each, over Comina and Pasiano. In August two Ansaldo Balilla arrived, 16497 and 16554, for operative evaluation, and in late September the unit received also Spad 1154, 1257, 1295

and 3049.

On 23 October the *Massa da Caccia* was reformed, and the 82ª Squadriglia became part of it. On 29 October *ten.* Camandone shot down a fighter near Vittorio Veneto, while *serg.* Spano was wounded in an accident. On the 30th *cpr.* Brignoli attacked and maybe shot down a fighter that was threatening British reconnaissance airplanes near Fontanafredda.

On 4 November at Gazzo airfield with commander *magg.* Coppini were the pilots *capitani* Luigi Bellei, Tosi and Vaccarossi, *tenenti* Camandone, Ferrarin, Riccardo Gatti, Francesco Pietrosemolo *s.tenenti* Guido Gobbi, Giuseppe Martini, *m.llo* Gaspare Monetti, *serg.m.* Romeo Sartori (another future test pilot at Macchi) and Eugenio Spano, *serg.* Agostino Roggeri, *caporali* Annibale Annibali, Uberto Bianchini, Bignoli, Santo Conte, Antonio Gerazzio, *soldati* Michele Lucciola, and Guido Colombatto.

Its airplanes were 15 Hanriots (known serials 609, 621, 774, 794, 7475, 11418, 11425, 11428, 13335, 14918, 19287, 19391, 20962) five Spads, 1265, 1257, 1527, 1660 and 3049, and one Balilla, 16514.

The scoreboard of the 82ª Squadriglia for the conflict reported 664 escort sorties, 2,086 standing patrols, 317 flights on alarm, 14 reconnaissance flights, 160 strafing and leaflet dropping sorties, and 115 air combats, with 27 claimed victories.

In December interim commander was *cap.* Ermanno Bartolini and in that same month the 82ª Squadriglia was disbanded.

Above: A line-up of Hanriots: the first one, serial 6649, is French-built and was the usual mount of *serg.* Teobaldi; next it Macchi-built 13311, marked with a small "R".

Identified Victory Claims of the 82ª Squadriglia

Date	Place	Pilots	Victim
16.7.1917	Brestovica	*Serg.* Poli	Enemy aircraft
28.7.1917	Aidussina	*Serg.* Aliperta	Fighter
14.8.1917	Idria	*Serg.* Aliperta	KD 28.66, Flik 12
28.9.1917	S. Lucia di T.	*Serg.* Aliperta	Albatros D.V, Jasta 31
25.10.1917	Castelmonte	*Ten.* Fochessati (& Piccio, 91ª)	DFW, FA 39?
26.10.1917	S. Lorenzo di M.	*Serg.* Teobaldi (& Costantini 91ª, Fanti 76ª)	DFW C.V, FA 39
6.11.1917	Mortegliano	*Serg.* Contardini	Hansa Br. C.I 69.30, Flik 34/D?
20.11.1917	Cima Verzena	*Serg.* Poli	Enemy aircraft
27.11.1917	Asiago	*Ten.* Camandone	Enemy aircraft OOC
29.11.1917	Molca	*Sold.* Panero	Albatros D.III 53.33, Flik 24
26.12.1917	Volpago	*Serg.* Benvenuti	Enemy aircraft
26.12.1917	Musano	*Ten.* Camandone (& Fornagiari, 78ª)	Enemy aircraft
26.12.1917	Camalò	*Serg.* Teobaldi	DFW, FA 2
26.12.1917	Camalò	*Serg.* Benvenuti, *serg.* D'Urso	Enemy aircraft
26.12.1917	Montello	*Sold.* Panero	Enemy aircraft
1.1.1918	Valstagna	*Sold.* Panero	Fighter
28.1.1918	Melette	*S.ten.* Ferrarin (& Croci, 70ª)	German aircraft?
28.1.1918	Val Brenta	*Sold.* Panero	Two-seater
28.1.1918	Val Brenta	*Sold.* Panero	Fighter
18.2.1918	Asiago	*Asp.* Contardini (& Zoboli 81ª)	Phönix D.I 128.08, Flik 39/D?
3.5.1918	Grave di P.	*Serg.* Teobaldi (& No.66 Sqn. RAF)	Phönix D.I 228.38, Flik 63/J?
18.6.1918	Zenson	*Ten.* Camandone	Enemy aircraft
18.6.1918	Noventa	*Cap.* Breglia	Enemy aircraft
29.7.1918	Pordenone	*Cap.* Tosi (& Haines, 45 Sqn. RAF)\	Aviatik D.I 138.62, Flik 72/J
29.7.1918	Lago S. Croce	*Ten.* Camandone (& Jones, 45 Sqn. RAF)	Aviatik D.I 138.98, Flik 72/J
29.7.1918	Pasiano	*Ten.* Rossetti	Fighter OOC
30.10.1918	Fontanafredda	*Cpr.* Bignoli	Fighter OOC

Above: *S.ten.* Arturo Ferrarin; no confirmed victory was credited to him, but he became one of the great pilots in the history of aviation. (Archive Tebaldi)

Casualties and Combat Losses of the 82ª Squadriglia

Date	Place	Aircraft	Crew	Cause
1.10.1917	Tolmino	Nieuport	*Serg.* Aliperta WIA	Fighters
26.10.1917	S. Caterina	?	*Serg.* Zanatta WIC, POW	Accident
6.11.1917	?	Hd.1	*Serg.* Buttazzoni UNH	Accident
7.11.1917	Portobuffolè	Hd.1 7211	*Serg.* Buttazzoni UNH	Fighters
22.2.1918	S. Pietro in Gu	Hd.1 6137	*Sold.* Panero KIC	Accident
17.6.1918	Piave	Hd.1	*Cap.* Vaccarossi WIA	Ground fire
18.6.1918	S. Andrea	Hd.1 7452	*Cap.* Fassi KIA	Fighters
29.10.1918	?	Hanriot	*Serg.m.* Spano WIC	Accident?

Above: An immaculate Hanriot, the *sottotenente* pilota in front is not known. (Archives Giulio Cristiani)

The fatal accident of Hanriot Hd.1 6137 of
soldato Clemente Panero at San Pietro in Gu.

Above: Pilots of the 82ª Squadriglia, the first from the left is s.ten. Ferrarin. (Archive Caliaro)

Below: An Hanriot Hd.1 "P" of 82ª Squadriglia, it is a French machine, construction number 506, its Italian military serial was 11392.

83ª Squadriglia

Above: *Ten.* Bonomi, commander of the 2ª Sezione, 83ª Squadriglia, after his harmless crash on 27 May 1917.

The 83ª Squadriglia Nieuport was a peculiar unit, because it was created at the Centro Formazione Squadriglie of Arcade on 5 May 1917, with different *sezioni* (flights) which operated separately. The 1ª Sezione was formed to operate on the front of Macedonia, and it sailed on 16 May 1917 from Taranto. On 1 June its first airplane, Nieuport 2273, was assembled at Dudular. The personnel of this flight included the commander *s.ten.* Giovanni Righi, and *sergenti* Giovanni Contò and Giovanni Miracca. On 8 June it moved to Kremsan (near the current border between Greece and Northern Macedonia) where the 47ª Squadriglia Farman was based, equipped with Nieuport 11 and 17 and one Spad. On 22 June the first fighter mission was flown, and *s.ten.* Righi

and *serg.* Miracca had a combat. On 1 August 1917 *ten.* Ernesto Bonavoglia became the commander.

In September *serg.* Miracca claimed a German Albatros, then on 5 October, *ten.* Bonavoglia, flying a Spad, hit a German plane and forced it to a crash landing in the plain of Resia, Macedonia. On 10 December 1917 the Sezione was upgraded to Squadriglia, taking the designation 73ª, that was available after the former unit with that number became 121ª Squadriglia. In its brief existance, the 1ª Sezione of 83ª flew 189 combat flights, had 15 combats and claimed two victories. A *Medaglia d'Argento* was awarded to *ten.* Bonavoglia.

Identified Victory Claims of the 1ª Sezione – 83ª Squadriglia

Date	Place	Pilots	Victim
9.1917	Macedonia	*Serg.* Miracca	German aircraft
5.10.1917	Prestq Lake	*Ten.* Bonavoglia	German aircraft

The 2ª and 3ª Sezione of the 83ª Squadriglia were formed at the Centro Formazione Squadriglie at Arcade and in May 1917 they were sent respectively to S. Pietro in Campo,

Belluno, and Cavazzo Carnico, in the North.

The 2ª Sezione at S. Pietro in Campo, Belluno, had as commander *ten.* Vittorio Bonomi, later a constructor of

Above: *Ten.* Ernesto Bonavoglia had a long career, first with the 76ª Squadriglia, culminating in the command of the 73ª Squadriglia in Macedonia.

sailplanes, with *sergenti* Arturo Dell'Oro (a volunteer from Chile) and Mario Pereno with Nieuport 11s 2209, 2233, 2245 and 2262 and belonged to the newly formed XII Gruppo together with the 48ª Squadriglia Caudron and the 3ª Sezione of 113ª. It flew its first war sortie on 10 May 1917, its task being to escort the Caudron G.4s of the 48ª Squadriglia. On 13 May the unit had its first contact with the enemy, when *serg.* Dell'Oro shot at an enemy aircraft over Belluno. On 19 May *serg.* Pereno fired at close range at an enemy airplane and drove it off. On 27 May *ten.* Bonomi flying a standing patrol had an engine failure and crashed his fighter, with no harm to himself. On 4 June 1917 Bonomi had a combat over Cortina d'Ampezzo, but his gun jammed, on 8 June Pereno had a combat over Alleghe. On 14 June Bonomi had a duel between Borgo and Strigno, close to where the Ortigara battle was raging, the Italian's fighter was hit, and almost crashed on landing, the crew of a

Brandenburg of Flik 24 claimed a victory.

On 13 July again *serg.* Pereno had a combat and was forced to retreat on account of a jammed gun. On 18 July Pereno made a forced landing with a failed engine, was wounded and hospitalized, returning to the unit one month later. Once again on 6 August commander Bonomi had an engine failure and crashed his Nieuport near Nebbiù. On 11 August the Sezione received three new Nieuport 17s, 3618, 3626, 3632, which were tested and then replaced the Ni.11s. On 20 August *serg.* Pereno left, being reassigned to the 84ª Squadriglia, *serg.* Albino Giannotti, coming from that same unit, replaced him. On 1 September 1917 Arturo Dall'Oro with Nieuport 17 3626 voluntarily rammed an enemy airplane. The *Medaglia d'Oro* was the reward for his sacrifice. His victims were Müller and Cerny of Flik 45. The three airmen were solemnly buried together, and then an Italian airplane dropped photos of the funeral at the Austrian airfield of Brixen. On 10 September a new pilot arrived, *serg.* Michele Signorini. All through September 1917 this small unit flew many standing patrol and escort missions for the 48ª Squadriglia.

The 3ª Sezione arrived at Cavazzo Carnico on 16 May, being formed by *ten.* Pietro Danieli and *serg.* Antonio Pellanda, and flew its first war mission on 19 May, when serg. Pellanda had a duel. Passing under the command of *ten.* Vincenzo Arone, the 3ª Sezione was assigned to the VI Gruppo, of which it was the only fighter compoment until the arrival of 76ª and 81ª Squadriglia in July. In June it had pilots *sergenti* Tommaso Masala and Giuseppe Magnetti.

After Caporetto, the 83ª Squadriglia moved three airplanes to Feltre. On 26 October *serg.* Signorini had a combat with an enemy airplane, with no results. *Ten.* Bonomi took command of the squadron. The two fighters still at S. Pietro in Campo, Belluno, went to Casoni on 2 November. On 6 November 1917 *serg.* Giannotti had a combat and claimed a victory, for which no confirmation was found. On 11 November 1917 both the 2ª Sezione and the 3ª from Cavazzo Carnico moved to Marcon, that is, from the extreme North to the extreme South of the front. The two joined flights became part of the XIII Gruppo, with commander *ten.* Bonomi and pilots *ten.* Arone, *sergenti* Signorini, Giannotti, Magnetti and Masala. In November, when weather allowed it, these pilots flew escort missions for SAML and SP two-seaters. On 24 November the unit had a combat, three pilots, Giannotti, Magnetti and Masala made forced landings without damaging their fighters, which were all recovered. On 27 November Bonomi had a duel with an enemy fighter. On 30 November the unit received a Nieuport 11 equipped with Le Prieur rockets.

On 5 December *s.ten.* Francesco Carabelli attacked a Drachen and then took part in the destruction of an enemy airplane, possibly Brandenburg 69.17 of Flik 32/B together with Cabruna and Degli Esposti, of 77ª and 80ª Squadriglia. *Serg.* Albino Giannotti on 8 December shot down a Drachen at Grisolera using the Ni.11 with Le Prieur rockets. Observation balloons were not important when the front was

Above: Arturo Dell'Oro rammed an enemy airplane, losing his life. The Gold Medal, Italy's highest decoration, was assigned for his heroic feat.

along the Isonzo River and observation posts could be placed on the mountains, but they became essential spotting for the artillery when the frontline moved to the flat terrain along the Piave River.

On 15 December 1917 *ten.* Vittorio Bonomi was the interim commander, with pilots *ten.* Arone, *s.ten.* Carabelli, *sergenti* Buri, Magnetti, Masala, Giovanni Riva, Francesco Rossi. In late December the unit received Ni.27s, usually called Super Nieuport. The 3ª Sezione was re-named 1ª, as the unit with that name in Macedonia had now become 73ª Squadriglia.

In January 1918 new pilots arrived, *ten.* Marinello Nelli, *sold.* Eugenio Caminada, *serg.* Raffaele Capo (from Argentina) and *cap.* Giulio Moroni who became the new

Above: Nieuport 11s of the 3ᵃ Sezione, 83ᵃ Squadriglia, at Cavazzo Carnico.

commander. On 12 March *sergenti* Rossi and Riva took part in a combat in which *brig.* Cabruna scored a victory.

In March 1918 the 83ᵃ Squadriglia had pilots *tenenti* Rino Corso Fougier and Enrico Gadda, *sergenti* Masala and Magnetti, *cpr.* Donadio, *sold.* Caminada, with Nieuport 27s 5826, 5900, 5851, 5913, 5906, 5889, 5917, 5854 and Nieuport 17 3707.

On 18 March the unit moved from Marcon, leaving the XIII Gruppo, and went back to the North, once again divided in two Sezioni, with the 1ᵃ Sezione at San Pietro in Gu, assigned to the VII Gruppo, reporting to the Comando di Aeronautica della 6ᵃ Armata, which had moved there leaving Nove to the French squadrons. The 1ᵃ Sezione had pilots *tenenti* Fougier, who became the commander on 22 March, Gadda, *sergenti* Caminada, Masala and Magnetti, *cpr.* Donadio.

The 2ᵃ Sezione was sent to Castenedolo, assigned to the IX Gruppo, in the sector of the 1ᵃ Armata. Its commander was *ten.* Nelli, then *cap.* Serafino Battaini, with pilots *cap.* Bruno Lodolo, *ten.* Pierfausto Barelli, *serg.m.* Eligio Cruciani, *sergenti* Raffele Capo, Angelo Comolli, Giovanni Riva, Francesco Sodani, and in April it received *sergenti* Cesare Giordano, Guido Branca, Carlo Campana, *caporali* Guido Roncuzzi and Raffaele Tarducci and *soldati* Stefano Borla and Giosuè Lombardi, flying Nieuport Ni.27 5820, 5685, 5842, 5894, 5892, 5814, 5893, 5883 and 5821

On 23 April 1918 *ten.* Enrico Gadda, of the 1ᵃ Sezione returning from a mission on Ni.27 5889 was killed in an accident. The 83ᵃ Squadriglia flew many escort missions and

cruises, and had a few inconclusive combats.

In May the 1ᵃ Sezione consisted of *cap.* Fougier, *ten.* Enrico Rizzi, *s.ten.* Giovanni Menegoni, *m.llo* Giulio Martinotti, *sergenti* Alessandro Aprà, Adamo Bortolini, Magnetti, Masala, Rossi, *cpr. maggiori* Donadio and Lemmi, *cpr.* Silvio Vischioni, *soldati* Caminada, Luigi Bello and Rodolfo Maggia. On 23 May *s.ten.* Menegoni, *serg.* Bortolini and *cpr.m.* Donadio attacked an enemy formation over Val Seren, and a two-seater went down out of control, most likely Phönix C.1 121.82 of Flik 11/F, its crew unhurt.

The 2ᵃ Sezione in May had *capitani* Lodolo, Nelli, Battaini and Nilo Tibaldi, *serg. maggiori* Eligio Cruciani and Amedeo Poggiali, *sergenti* Guido Branca, Carlo Campana, Capo, Angelo Comolli, Cesare Giordano, Francesco Sodani, Riva, *cpr.m.* Roncuzzi, *cpr.* Raffaele Tarducci and *soldati* Borla and Lombardi, a weird combination of four captains and eleven troopers. On 20 May 1918 the 2ᵃ Sezione became the 74ᵃ Squadriglia at Castenedolo, while the 1ᵃ Sezione was upgraded to Squadriglia and moved to Poianella, one mile away from San Piero in Gu.

On 16 June 1918 during the battle of the Piave *m.llo* Martinotti and *serg.* Aprà had a combat with a fighter that was hit but managed to return to its field. On the 18ᵗʰ *cpr.* Lemmi was hit and badly wounded while strafing and force landed his Hanriot 6529. On 22 June *serg.* Magnetti, with the support of *sergenti* Rossi and Donadio, had a confirmed victory at Villa Premuda. In total during the Battle of the Piave the 83ᵃ Squadriglia flew 262 offensive patrol sorties and 122 escort flights, shot 63,800 rounds and dropped 42

S.E. il Gen: di Robilant osserva un Neuport da caccia

Above: General Di Robilant, commander of the 4ª Armata, visiting the 2ª Sezione, 83ª Squadriglia, at San Pietro in Campo.

bombs.

The squadron during the summer had a mixed complement of Nieuport 27s and Hanriots. It received new pilots *cpr.m.* Camillo Trabucco and *soldati* Umberto Galassi, and Romeo Sartori who on 13 August suffered the attack of a trigger-happy British Sopwith Camel pilot.

In the late summer of 1918, there were more victories: on 11 August *serg.* Rossi and *sold.* Galassi claimed a victory over Val d'Assa, on 21 August, *ten.* Menegoni, *serg.* Aprà and Galassi claimed a two-seater, on 14 September *cap.* Fougier, *ten.* Bortolini and Sartori claimed a fighter over Arsiè, and on 16 September Fougier claimed a "small two-seater" over Val di Nos. On 18 September the same commander Fougier fought against seven enemies over Feltre, with one possibly disabled.

On 4 October the 83ª Squadriglia became part of the new XXIV Gruppo, together with the 2ª Sezione SVA, based at Poianella. It flew reconnaissance flights over enemy airfields, and more victories were claimed: on 22 October Masala and Donadio shot down an enemy at Bocchetta di Po, and on the 28th Masala, Bortolini and Sartori claimed another victory over Mount Verena.

On 4 November 1918 seven fighters together with four SVAs of the 2ª Sezione flew over Trento over the Italian troops entering the city and dropped flowers. On that date the 83ª Squadriglia was at Poianella, reporting to the Comando d'Aeronautica of the 6ª Armata. During 1918 it had flown over 2,500 combat sorties. The *Medaglia d'Argento* was assigned to *cap.* Fougier, *ten.* Gadda, *s.ten.* Menegoni, *sergenti* Donadio, Magnetti, Martinotti, Francesco Rossi, *cpr.m.* Lemmi, the *Medaglia di Bronzo* to *ten.* Rizzi, *sergenti* Aprà, Bortolini, Capo, *soldati* Galassi and Sartori.

In February 1919 the 83ª Squadriglia was in the VII Gruppo at Poianella, having three Nieuports and 14 Hanriots. On 26 February *cpr.m.* Sabatino Lemmi was killed in a flying accident. The 83ª Squadriglia was disbanded on 25 March 1919.

Above, Below, & Facing Page: The brand-new Nieuport 17s of the 2ª Sezione, 83ª Squadriglia.

Identified Victory Claims of the 83ª Squadriglia

Date	Place	Pilots	Victim
1.9.1917	Belluno	*Serg*. Dall'Oro	Hansa Br. CI. 69.29, Flik 45
6.11.1917	Front of 18° CA	*Serg*. Giannotti	Enemy aircraft
5.12.1917	Salgareda	*S.ten*. Carabelli (& Cabruna, Degli Esposti, 80ª)	Hansa Br. C.I 69.17, Flik 32/B
8.12.1917	Grisolera	*Serg*. Giannotti	Kite Balloon, BK 8
12.3.1918	San Donà	*Serg*. Rossi, *serg*. Riva (& Cabruna, 77ª)	Aviatik C.I 214.04, Flik 49/D?
23.5.1918	Val Seren	*Cpr.m*. Donadio, *s.ten*. Menegoni, *serg*. Bortolini	Phönix C.I 121.82, Flik 11/F
16.6.1918	Riva Grassa	*Serg*. Aprà, *m.llo* Martinotti	Fighter
22.6.1918	Villa Premuda	*Serg*. Magnetti, *serg*. Rossi, *serg*. Donadio	Enemy aircraft
11.8.1918	Val d'Assa	*Serg*. Rossi, *sold*. Galassi	Enemy aircraft
21.8.1918	Val d'Assa	*Ten*. Menegoni, *serg*. Aprà, *sold*. Galassi	Two-seater
14.9.1918	Arsiè	*Cap*. Fougier, *ten*. Bortolini, *sold*. Sartori	Fighter
16.9.1918	Val di Nos	*Cap*. Fougier	Two-seater
22.10.1918	Bocchetta di Po	*Serg*. Masala, *serg*. Donadio	Enemy aircraft
28.10.1918	Monte Verena	*Serg*. Masala, *serg*. Bortolini, *sold*. Sartori	Enemy aircraft

Casualties and Combat Losses of the 83ª Squadriglia

Date	Place	Aircraft	Crew	Cause
1.9.1917	Belluno	Ni.17 3626	*Serg*. Dell'Oro KIA	Ramming
23.4.1918	S. Pietro in Gu	Ni.27 5889	*Ten*. Gadda KIC	Accident
18.6.1918	Piave	Hd.1 6259	*Cpr*. Lemmi WIA	Ground fire

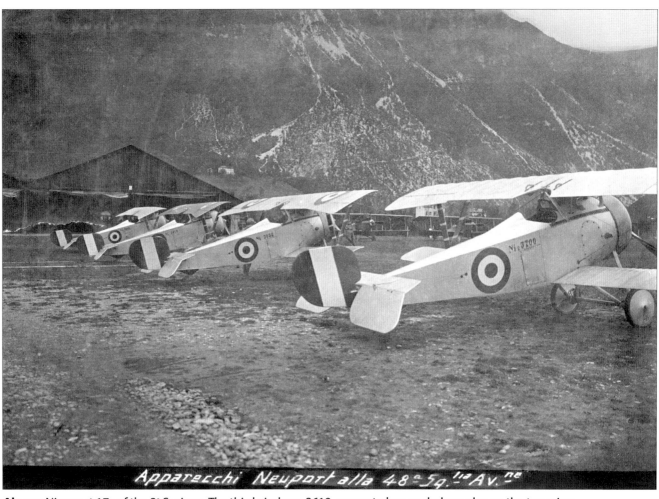

Apparecchi Neuport alla 48ª Sq.ᵈ ᴵᵃAvⁿᵉ

Above: Nieuport 17s of the 3ª Sezione. The third airplane, 3619, seems to have a darker color on the top wing.

Below: *Ten*. Rino Corso Fougier, who became commander of the Italian Air Force in 1941, with Nieuport 27 19779.

Above: Nieuport 27s of the 83ª Squadriglia, showing the unit's insignia, a red diamond, and white paint on the rear fuselage. (Archive Luigino Caliaro)

Above: Behind these Ni.27s of the 83ª Squadriglia at Poianella two Hanriots can be seen.

Above: A Nieuport 27 of the 83ª Squadriglia, called *"Baby"*. (Collection Mario Bobbio)

Above: Another striped Ni.27 of the 83ª Squadriglia. The red diamond remained as unit insignia until 1927. (Collection Mario Bobbio)

Above: A line-up of the fighters of the 83ª Squadriglia. Also one Hanriot has it back fuselage painted white.

Above: Hanriot Hd.1 6259 with the diamond insignia of the 83ª Squadriglia. (Archive Mario Federighi)

84ª Squadriglia

Above: Nieuport 11s of the 84ª Squadriglia.

The 84ª Squadriglia Nieuport was formed in June 1917, at Arcade and on 2 July it deployed at Santa Maria La Longa, where it mobilized, that is, was declared combat ready, with commander *cap.* Giovanni Fancello, and assigned to the I Gruppo. Its pilots were *tenenti* Giovanni Mazzia and Renato Mazzucchelli, *serg.m.* Leonida Schiona, *sergenti* Albino Giannotti and Francesco Rossi, using Nieuport 11s with serials 3209, 2294, 2296, 2129, 2191, 2308 and 3244. Its main war mission was to provide escorts for the Voisins of 25ª Squadriglia and the Caudrons of V Gruppo. Schiona had a long career, as a flying instructor in Yemen and then as airline commander.

The 84ª Squadriglia flew many escort flights, *sergenti* Giannotti and Rossi had a combat on 13 July, and *serg.m.* Schiona on the 14th, over Duino. In the night of 16 July, the unit removed the machine guns from the airplanes and prepared for defense, as the two Regiments of the Brigata Catanzaro, resting at Santa Maria la Longa, mutinied after receiving the order to go back to the first line. This revolt was terminated and decimation of the soldiers was ordered, the worst such event in the Italian war. Gabriele d'Annunzio was a witness, and he cried. "*You are innocent, condemned only*

by fate!" and he dropped flowers on the mass grave of those soldiers (current research indicates that 16 were shot).

The 84ª Squadriglia received *ten. pil.* Felice Martinengo and *brig.* Ernesto Cabruna. The commander *cap.* Fancello crashed to his death on 22 July 1917 during a test flight. On 6 August also Cabruna crashed, his plane was wrecked but he was unhurt. Likely, *ten.* Martinengo was then the interim commander. The unit received *serg.* Mario Pereno in late August, while *serg.* Giannotti went to the 83ª. On 26 September 1917 the 84ª Squadriglia was sent to Aiello, remaining part of the I Gruppo. On 26 October it was temporarily assigned to the X Gruppo and retreated to La Comina. It was still equipped with Nieuport 11s, but his pilots were tasked with flying to safety the better fighters of 77ª and 80ª Squadriglia, and nine Ni.11s were abandoned, together with three new Ni.17s and one Spad that had just arrived and were still crated. With a few pilots and no airplanes, the short-lived 84ª Squadriglia was disbanded on 11 Novembre 1917.

A new 84ª Squadriglia Hanriot was being formed at Ponte San Pietro on 15 October 1918 but this order was cancelled on the 30th.

Above: The fatal crash of the 84ª Squadriglia's commander, *cap*. Fancello, on 22 July 1917.

Above: Gabriele d'Annunzio at Santa Maria La longa visiting the aviators of the 84ª Squadriglia.

85ª Squadriglia

Above: A minor accident for a Nieuport 11 of the Sezione Nieuport in Albania; the pilot is *cpr.* Guido Gerard.

A Sezione Nieuport for the XVI Corpo d'Armata deployed in Albania was established on 23 September 1916 at Durazzo (Durres). Its commander was *ten.* Giovanni Sabelli, with pilots *sergenti* Antonio Lovadina (a test pilot for Fiat after the war) and Antonio Palpacelli. It was based at Tahiraqua field and was assigned to the VIII Gruppo when it was formed, 9 December 1916. Initially it flew very little, on account of bad weather and the bad conditions of the airfield, and it began sorties in February 1917.

In May 1917 the Sezione Nieuport in Albania had pilot *ten.* Sabelli, *ten.* Adriano Bacula (chief test pilot of SIAI Marchetti in later years), *serg.* Lovadina, *serg.m.* Palpacelli, *serg.* Lorenzo Cortesi and *cpr.* Guido Gerard. Later it also had *sergenti* Mario Banino and Luigi Sauda, with Nieuports 2121, 2252, 2257, 3218, 3225, 3290.

The flight became 85ª Squadriglia on 25 September 1917 at Piskupi, with *cap.* Ernesto Pellegrino as commander and was now equipped with Nieuport 17s, having received Ni.17s 3176, 3568, 3627, 3671, 3676, 3677, 3678, 3680, 3681, 3682.

At the end of the year, it had commander *cap.* Pellegrino, pilots *ten.* Bacula, *s.tenenti* Vinicio Muraro and Prospero Freri, *aspiranti* Nicola Cena and Natale Ravasso, *serg.* Cortesi and *cpr.* Gerard. During 1917 it flew 97 combat sorties, during which it had some combats, all in October (on the 13th *ten.* Bacula and *asp.* Gerard, 15th and 18*th ten.* Bacula,

26th *asp.* Cena, whose Ni 3680 was hit, 28th *serg.* Cortesi) which were all inconclusive due to gun jamming or other reasons. On 19 December six Nieuports flew together with five SAMLs of the 116ª Squadriglia escorting two Capronis of the 11ª Squadriglia that bombed enemy emplacements at the Bridge of Kupi.

On 1 January 1918 the 85ª Squadriglia had on strength *cap.* Pellegrino, *tenenti* Muraro and Freri, *s.tenenti* Albrigo Balbi, Cena, Raffele Castellano, Silvio Ciappi, Mario Ghislanzoni and Natale Ravasso, and *serg.* Lorenzo Cortesi. On 16 January *cap.* Mario Sarrocchi became interim commander. In February this unit moved from Tahiraqua to Piskupi (Peshkepi).

On 17 April two enemy airplanes shot down and killed *serg.* Cortesi. In May Hanriots arrived, to replace the Nieuports, serials 6276, 6281, 6286, 7453, 7464 and 7468. At the end of May, no less than two dozen more Hanriots arrived from Italy, serials 7501, 7476, 7546, 7492, 7497, 7511, 7494, 7513, 7493, 7491, 7543, 7540, 7576, 7521, 7568, 7519, 7469, 7490, 7505, 7528, 7508, 7525, 13238 and 13244.

On 15 June *cap.* Pellegrini returned to Italy, the new commander, *cap.* Mario Ponis, arrived on 17 July. Also, more pilots came, *cpr.* Camillo Trabucco, *ten.* Mario Nascimbene and *ten.* Giuseppe Cartoni. On 6 July the 85ª Squadriglia sent its fighters to escort the Capronis of 11ª Squadriglia

Above: Nieuport 17 3568 in Albania; in the center of the roundel there is a personal insignia, too small to be deciphered. This fighter returned to Italy and was assigned to the flying school at Busto Arsizio.

bombing the areas of Parajbor and Fjeri, the next day the Caproni escort was repeated, and in the afternoon the fighters escorted the bomber seaplanes of the 257ª Squadriglia.

In September the 85ª Squadriglia moved a flight, under the command of *ten.* Arrigo Tessari (chief of the Aeronautica Nazionale Repubblicana in 1944) to Durazzo, just reconquered, having also two Pomilio PE, that effectively supported the advance of Italian troops in a badly charted and harsh terrain.

During the war, the 85ª Squadriglia flew 925 combat sorties, had one loss but no victory. The *Medaglia d'Argento* was assigned to *ten.* Nicola Cena, *serg.* Lorenzo Cortesi, *cap.* Alberto Livi (aggregated as commander of the VIII Gruppo), and *asp.* Castellano, the Bronze Medal was given to *serg.* Cortesi, twice, *ten.* Cartoni, also twice, *ten.* Cena, *serg.* Gerard, *ten.* Ravasso and *cap.* Sarrocchi.

In December 1918 the 85ª Squadriglia was still at Piskupi under the command of *ten.* Cartoni. It flew mail flights among the towns of Albania, its force now consisting of *ten.* Cartoni, commander, with *capitani* Alberto De Angelis, Galliena and Milanesi, *ten.* Proia, *sergenti* Giulio Farlini, Luigi Giannini, Francesco Gritti and Migliarina. It was disbanded on 10 October 1919, but a Sezione remained, that was assigned to the Squadriglia Mista di Valona, that was in action during the Albanian insurrection in June-July 1920. For these final operations *ten.* Cartoni received the *Medaglia d'Argento*.

Above & Below: The long line-up of the Nieuport 17s of the 85ᵃ Squadriglia at Tahiraqua, Albania.

Above: The Hanriots of the 85ª Squadriglia received a variety of not particularly beautiful personal markings. This is Hd.1 19304.
Below: A detail of the emblem of 19304.

Above: Another version of the cartoon from the book by Oronzo Marginati. The words mean "Bring my regards to him".

Below: Another personal insignia, probably referring to a famous vaudeville artist, Ettore Petrolini.

Above: A *sottotenente* of the 85ᵃ Squadriglia with his Hanriot marked with the four aces.

Above: A red dragon on the sides of Hanriot 7501, while three stars, green, red, and white, are painted on the top fuselage.

Above: Happy Hooligan was as popular on Italian airplanes in World War 1 as Donald Duck was in World War 2.

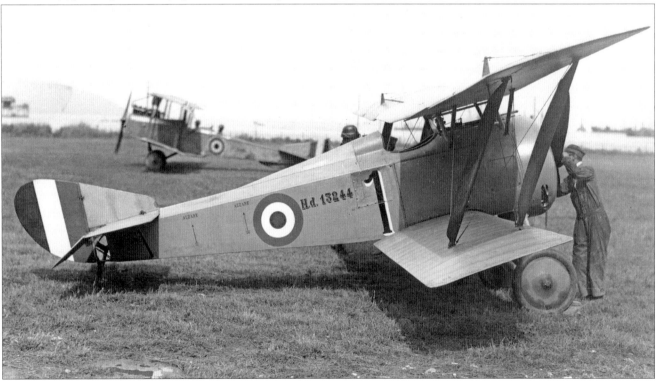

Above: Hanriot Hd.1 #13244 at Valona; a Pomilio PD is in the background.

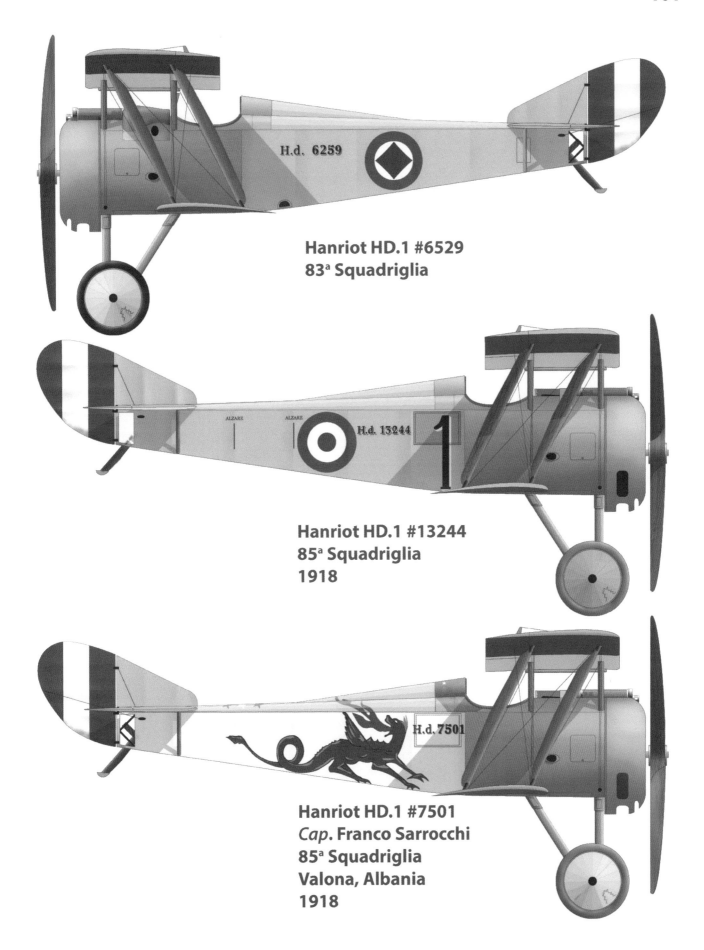

Hanriot HD.1 #6529
83ª Squadriglia

Hanriot HD.1 #13244
85ª Squadriglia
1918

Hanriot HD.1 #7501
Cap. **Franco Sarrocchi**
85ª Squadriglia
Valona, Albania
1918

86ª Squadriglia

Formation of this unit, to be equipped with the Ansaldo SVA, began in August 1917 as 181ª Squadriglia, but when this number was assigned to the Caproni triplane squadron, it became 86ª Squadriglia SVA, at the Centro Formazione Squadriglie of Ponte S. Pietro at the command of *cap.* Alberto De Bernardi, being established in December 1917. In January 1918 it was officially formed, with *cap.* Palma di Cesnola as commander, but it always flew with independent *sezioni,* assigned to different Armies. Therefore the 86ª existed as a paper unit until June 1918, but it was never activated. Its 1ª Sezione initially was based at Nove di Bassano, with pilots *ten.* Andrea Costantini, *ten.* Ferruccio Marzari, *s.ten.* Emilio Benini and *s.ten.* Giovanni Ranucci, assigned to the XV Gruppo, with SVA 6809, 6810, 6811

and 6812, its 2ª and la 3ª Sezione were at San Pelagio with *s.tenenti* Giorgio Orsini and Carlo Magno Grandinetti, *sergenti* Gino Allegri and Giuseppe Caiero, SVA 6797, 6816, 6814, 6818 and 6821. On 2 February 1918 an official formation order was issued, for a squadron with 18 "narrow chord wing" SVAs and con 18 pilots but, as said, the unit never formed, and therefore its events are reported referring to its individual *sezioni SVA.*

On 15 October 1918 a new 86ª Squadriglia was reported in formation with 24 Ansaldo A.1Balilla, ten of them already available, at Ponte San Pietro. It received men and airplanes from the 88ª and 92ª when formation of these two units was cancelled, but on 31 January 1919 also formation of the 86ª was cancelled.

Above: Plenty of SVAs were available at Campo San Pietro for the training of SVA pilots. A civilian flying school or military pilots operated there in the Twenties.

87ª Squadriglia

Above: Japanese officers examine the SVA of the 87ª Squadriglia at Ghedi.

Formation of a new squadron with Ansaldo SVA began in August 1917, to be named 182ª, but as this number was assigned to a Caproni Triplane unit, it became 87ª Squadriglia, Meanwhile, pilots of the 91ª Squadriglia had tested the SVA, and described it as not adequate as a fighter. In December 1917 the formation of the 87ª Squadriglia as a long-range reconnaissance unit was approved.

The 87ª Squadriglia was activated on 2 February 1918 at Ponte San Pietro it was planned as a unit with 18 pilots and 18 "narrow wings" SVAs, its commander was *cap.* Piero Masprone (for whom no previous assignment is known), with pilots *tenenti* Giordano Bruno Granzarolo, Aldo Finzi and Antonio Locatelli, *s.tenenti* Francesco Ferrarin, Carlo Fornasari, Alberto Grazzini, Lionello Marani and Guglielmo Vianini. Most of its pilots were from the Veneto region, partly occupied by the enemy, and therefore highly motivated, the Supreme Command gave it the name "Serenissima", like the Republic of Venice, and its red flag with the winged Lion of St. Mark was painted on the fuselages. Its pilots were all officers, and had fully trained on the SVA.

The 87ª Squadriglia was initially based at San Pelagio, part of X Gruppo, on 21 February it was moved to Ghedi, reporting to the Comando Raggruppamento Squadriglie da Bombardamento, that is, as a unit with strategic missions, administratively reporting to the XI Gruppo. Locatelli flew

the first mission on 30 March, a photo reconnaissance flight over Val Lagarina. On 5 May there was a formation flight over Trento and the power plant at Stenico was bombed, as the SVAs were fitted to carry three 162-mm bombs.

Meanwhile, in the night of 10 March 1918, Zeppelin LZ 104 bombed Naples. The Commissariato d'Aeronautica asked for the cooperation of the Navy to check if an airship hangar was in construction at Sebenico, and Palli with his SVA 11720 was sent to Brindisi. The Regia Marina much appreciated his excellent photographs, and in May and June Palli flew several missions taking pictures of the Austrian warships in harbor and at sea.

On 9 May *ten.* Michelangelo Riccardini was wounded in a forced landing of SVA 11806, that turned over, *s.ten.* Vincenzo Contratti also wrecked SVA 11723 in a forced landing, but was unhurt. On 21 May Ferrarin and Locatelli flew to Friedrichshafen, 470 miles in 4 hours 14 minutes, and took pictures of the Zeppelin works. In those days the 87ª Squadriglia returned to San Pelagio and received new pilots, *tenenti* Ludovico Censi, Piero Massoni, Domenico Pastorello, *s.tenenti* Umberto Garelli, Giuseppe Sarti and Gioacchino Sartor, *serg.* Gino Allegri. A complete photo survey of the front was completed. On 24 June leaflets were dropped over Zagreb. The 87ª Squadriglia took part in the mass interforce bombardment of Pola, 17 July, sending 9 SVAs, three of which had to turn back for engine troubles. The motivation

Above: Natale Palli in his SVA 11720 at San Nicolò, Venice, during his series of missions for the Navy. Behind is a Hanriot Hd.1 of the local 241ᵃ Squadriglia. Palli died in this SVA on 20 March 1919, crashing in the Alps while trying to reach Paris.

of a Silver Medal to *ten*. Finzi reports an air victory over a two-seater near Mori on 30 June, but no documents are available.

The 87ᵃ Squadriglia as an élite unit was an asset, but with limitations. The commander of CSA, *gen.* Bongiovanni, writing on 25 May to all aviation commands praising the deeds of the 87ᵃ Squadriglia, added: "*However, I must warn the gallant SVA pilots of the danger of excessive individual initiatives and remind them that in war all actions must be coordinated and with specific purposes, according to instructions that only superior authorities can determine, while isolated feats turn into a sterile waste of energies. Finally, I remind that no individual daring could justify the violation of an order.*"

A very special operation had been considered for a long time, a flight over Vienna. D'Annunzio had been agitating for it since 1915, and a Caproni was prepared and tested for a long-range flight, before the commands discovered it and forbid the initiative of the poet. Now with the SVA the feat was possible, and *cap.* Masprone began the preparation. A special SVA with two seats was to be prepared to take along d'Annunzio, with his seat directly over the fuel tank. The first one crashed at Marcon on 7 July, killing pilot *cap.* Luigi Bourlot and *cap.* Leonardo Rizzani. Another one was prepared, 12736, assigned to *cap.* Natale Palli. The flight was carefully prepared, under control of the over-excited poet. Two first attempts, on 2 and 8 August, had to turn back because of bad weather, then d'Annunzio made the pilots swear that they would complete the feat or die, and eleven SVAs took off on 9 August, with Palli and d'Annunzio in the lead, followed by Allegri, Censi, Contratti, Granzarolo, Ferrarin, Finzi, Locatelli, Masprone, Massoni and Sarti.

Contratti and Ferrarin had to turn back with failing engines, and also *cap.* Masprone had to give up, smashing his SVA in a forced landing, and being wounded, the other eight reached Vienna. Sarti had problems also, and force landed near Wiener Neustadt, burning his SVA 11801 before being taken prisoner. Over Vienna, leaflets were dropped with a message from d'Annunzio, rather stilted and convoluted, and a much simpler message written by Ugo Ojetti, a journalist who ran the office of psychological warfare, then the Italian planes turned back, vainly followed by Austrian fighters, and safely returned to San Pelagio. This feat was amply reported in Italy and abroad, and is still remembered today.

The resources of the 87ᵃ Squadriglia had been strained, however, a mission on 16 August could not be flown because only two airplanes were efficient, out of a total of 24 (6840, 6846, 6775, 6778, 11713, 11714, 11722, 11721, 11726, 11736, 11737, 11777, 11779, 11780, 11800, 11805, 11806, 11853, 11895, 11911 11912, 11916, and 12736). A latent contrast between the commander and Finzi and Locatelli surfaced. Masprone, a good organizer but a weak commander, who flew very little, with only one combat mission, was removed on 23 August, and on 7 September *cap.* Palli became the new commander. Finzi was sent to the 1ᵃ Sezione SVA and Locatelli to the Stormo SVA of the Squadriglia Siluranti Aeree of d'Annunzio in Venice.

Cap. Palli brought the squadron back to shape, and on 24 and 31 August airplanes from the 87ᵃ Squadriglia bombed Franzenfeste. Another excellent pilot arrived, *ten.* Ferruccio Marzari. On 14 September seven SVAs bombed depots at Osoppo, and on the 17ᵗʰ the railroad yards at Casarsa. The 87ᵃ Squadriglia was now assigned to the IV Gruppo.

Above: The Zeppelin works at Friedrichshafen in a photograph taken on 21 May 1918.

From 26 September to 2 October Palli and d'Annunzio went with SVA 12736 to the French front, where the poet talked about his next dream: a flight to Berlin. After the war, documents report of SVA Type Vienna and SVA Type Berlin, most likely versions with larger fuel tanks.

On 5 October, returning from a mission to Aviano, the SVAs of *ten*. Vianini and *s.ten*. Allegri collided, the former managed to land, but Allegri was killed, he was awarded the *Medaglia d'Oro*.

On 22 October *ten*. Francesco Pierattini on SVA 11726 failed to return from a bombing mission over Casarala, wounded by ground fire and a prisoner.

The squadron was intensively employed in the final offensive, with many missions every day; on 27 October long-serving *ten*. Vincenzo Contratti, at his second sortie in the day, was shot down and killed, victim of Oblt. Hautzmayer of Flik 61/J, *ten*. Domenico Pastorello was the victim of ground fire, wounded and taken prisoner.

At the end of the conflict the 87ᵃ Squadriglia with commander *cap*. Palli had the pilots *tenenti* Gioacchino Criscuoli, Granzarolo, Massoni, Vianini, *s.tenenti* Francesco Costa San Severino and Alberto Grazzini, with 14 SVAs. Its war activites amounted to about 200 combat sorties. Two of its pilots had the *Medaglia d'Oro*, Allegri and Locatelli, two Silver Medals were awarded to Allegri, Contratti, Granzarolo, Finzi and Marzari, one to Censi, Palli, Sarti and Vianini. Costa S. Severino, Ferrarin, Marani, Pastorello and Sartor received the Bronze Medal.

It was not disbanded, and remained active up to World War II, always carrying the flag with the Lion of St. Mark.

Casualties and combat losses of the 87ᵃ Squadriglia

Date	Place	Aircraft	Pilot	Cause
9.8.1918	Wiener N.	SVA 11801	*Ten*. Sarti POW	Accident
5.10.1918	San Pelagio	SVA 11805	*S.ten*. Allegri KIC	Collision
22.10.1918	Casarsa	SVA11726	*Ten*. Pierattini WIA, POW	Ground fire
27.10.1918	Portobuffolè	SVA	*Ten*. Contratti KIA	Fighters
27.10.1918	Meduna	SVA	*Ten*. Pastorello WIA, POW	Ground fire

Above: Antonio Locatelli in a SVA equipped with bomb racks at Padua, in September 1918. The pilot standing is Gino Allegri. (Archive Roberto Mantiero)

Above & Below: Antonio SVAs of the 87ª Squadriglia at San Pelagio. The fourth one is a shorter span SVA 3.

Above: The pilots who flew over Vienna. From the left, Granzarolo, Allegri, Locatelli, Palli, d'Annunzio, Massoni, Finzi, Censi.

Above: SVA 12736 with d'Annunzio and Palli; during the flight to Vienna it did not yet carry the insignia of the Lion of St. Mark.

Above: The pilots of the 87ª Squadriglia just after landing. From the left, Granzarolo lighting a cigarette, Censi, Finzi, d'Annunzio, Palli, Locatelli.

Above: D'Annunzio posing with SVA 12736. His personal insignia showed the war flag of the Republic of Venice, the Lion has closed the book and is holding a sword. The tail was blue with the seven golden stars of Ursa Minor.

Above: Leaflets dropping over Vienna; the Cathedral of St. Stephen is on the upper right.

Above: The SVA 12736 of d'Annunzio. The Latin motto below the Lion reads: "*Iterum rudit leo*", the lion roars again.

Above: SVA 12736 in France, during d'Annunzio and Palli's visit to the front. Behind is a Spad 13 of French Escadrille SPA 154.

Facing Page, Below: The leaflets of Vienna were in Italian and German, this is the "short" message of Ugo Ojetti.

Above: Long serving pilot Gino Allegri, whom d'Annunzio called Fra' Ginepro, earned a Gold Medal, three Silver, and one Bronze medal.

Below: SVA 6841 of the 87ª Squadriglia equipped with racks for two bombs on the side of the fuselage.

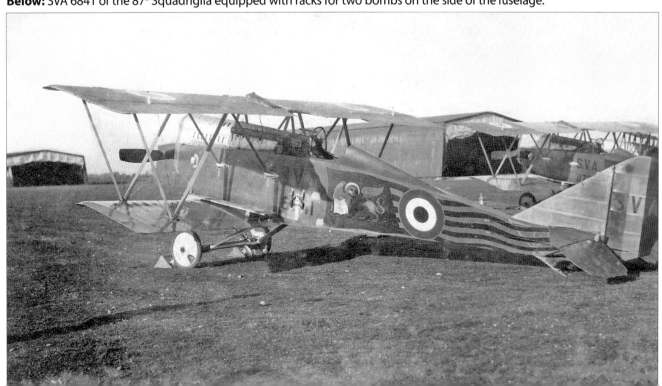

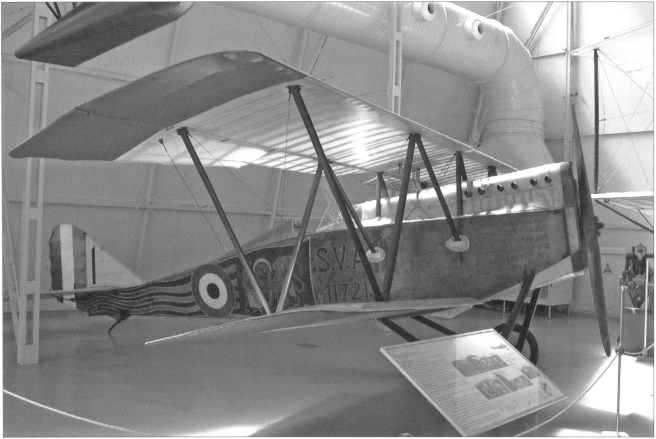

Above: A third original SVA of the 87ᵃ Squadriglia, 11777, is preserved in the Museo Aeronautico "Gianni Caproni" in Trento. Both 11721 and 11777 were modified after the war with an enlarged radiator.

Facing Page, Above: The SVA was donated to d'Annunzio and is preserved at Vittoriale, his villa on the Garda Lake, now a national museum. The volunteers of GAVS, Group of Friends of Historical Aircraft, are here seen planning its careful restoration.

Facing Page, Below: A second original SVA of the 87ᵃ Squadriglia, 11721, is preserved at the Historical Museum of the Italian Air Force at Vigna di Valle, near Rome.

Above: Two Ansaldo Balilla, 16552 and 16553, decorated with St. George slaying a dragon, were donated to Locatelli and Palli; both of them survive in museums. This is Palli's 16553 at San Pelagio airfield. The castle in the background is now home to an aviation museum. (Courtesy Melley)

Born in 1863 in Pescara, Gabriele d'Annunzio was an Italian poet, novelist, and playwright who occupied a prominent place in Italian literature, and dominated the Italian cultural and political life. Gaining success very young, he influenced society with his decadent and symbolistic works, with his production as journalist and also with his scandalous lifestyle.

In 1897 he was elected to the Chamber of Deputies, joining the ranks of the left. His excessive lifestyle forced him to move to France in 1910 to escape his creditors. He returned to Italy in 1915, giving speeches demanding his country's entry in the war on the side of the Allies.

During the war, donning his old uniform of a cavalry officer, using his friendship with politicians and high-ranking officers, he managed to take part in dangerous actions on land, at sea, and particularly in the air. While his enemies, and they were many, still criticized his lifestyle, he gave proof of boundless courage. At the beginning of the war, he was flown over Trento and Trieste, where he dropped messages. An accident on a seaplane in 1916 forced him to live in darkness for six months and caused him the loss of one eye.

He returned to flying, taking part in bombing missions in 1917, in daring naval actions, and in countless ceremonies, where he mesmerized the audiences with his speeches, while his behavior with the other aviators was the one of a witty comrade.

In the fall of 1917, he was the leader of a dangerous night mission of Caproni bombers across the Adriatic Sea. In 1918 he forced the commands to set up a squadron of torpedo bombers, based in Venice, with which to attack the Austrian fleet in its bases, and at the same time he realized his wartime dream, a raid against Vienna, in which only leaflets were dropped. He was the constant creator of new words, mottoes, and insignias.

When peace arrived, and his popularity was immense, he was disappointed that the Versailles peace conference assigned to Italy less territory than the British and French

Above: D'Annunzio flying with Glenn Curtiss in Rome, September 1909, the beginning of the poet's passion for aviation.

Above: D'Annunzio with his beloved daughter Renata.

had promised in 1915. The city of Fiume, now Rijeka, Croatia, with an Italian ethnic majority, was occupied by Allied troops.

In September 1919 d'Annunzio rebelled, and marched into the city followed by thousands of soldiers, occupied it, and turned it into a small independent state, with him

D'Annunzio giving a speech to aviators at Aviano, July 1917. Everybody was spellbound by his oratory art, except Francesco Baracca.

Above: The cover of *Notturno*, a book that the poet wrote in 1916, dictating to his daughter Renata, that deals with the naval aviators of Venice.

Above: The "Casetta rossa", the little red house where d'Annunzio lived in Venice during the war.

Above: D'Annunzio with a group of pilots who had rebelled and joined him in Fiume.

as ruler. More and more soldiers defected and joined him, forcing the government to forbid all flights and to order the removal of magnetos from airplanes to preclude further desertions. As ruler of Fiume, while his enthusiastic followers experimented with drugs and homosexuality, he issued an idealistic and modern Constitution, and Fiume was the first country to recognize the Soviet regime in Russia.

In December 1920 the weak democratic government of Italy finally put an end to this carnival, and warships and the regular army restored order. Fiume became an independent state, and in 1924 the city became part of Italy.

Fearing that d'Annunzio could march on Rome, the government gave him a villa on Lake Garda, called Vittoriale, where d'Annunzio lived his final years in luxury.

Meanwhile, the Fascist leader Benito Mussolini had taken power, his nationalistic policies had been inspired by d'Annunzio, the poet was able to go along with the dictatorship, but he never liked the Duce.

In 1937 he tried to approach Mussolini to warn him against an alliance with Hitler, whom d'Annunzio called "the house painter corporal" but Mussolini refused to even talk with him. D'Annunzio died in 1938; his villa is now a museum and a center of historical research.

Left: The room where d'Annunzio wrote in the Vittoriale villa.

Above: D'Annunzio with the Caproni "Ace of spades" and his crew, Pratesi, Pagliano, and Gori.

Above: All the objects that d'Annunzio collected have been preserved; this the "room of the Leda".

Above: In the Twenties the Italian government provided a Macchi M.18 for the amusement of d'Annunzio, who called it "*Tarabuso*", bittern.

Above: D'Annunzio's bedroom at the Vittoriale.

Above: The Vittoriale at Gardone, on a hill overlooking the Lake of Garda.

Left: D'Annunzio on Caproni Ca. 2378 after bombing Pola, August 1917.

Above: Contemporary painting of a SVA of the 87ª Squadriglia as indicated by the Lion of St. Mark.

Left: The lion of Venice at war, holding a sword while the Gospel is closed.

SVA 10 #12736
Cap. Natale Palli / Gabriele D'Annunzio
87ª Squadriglia *La Serenissima*
August 1918

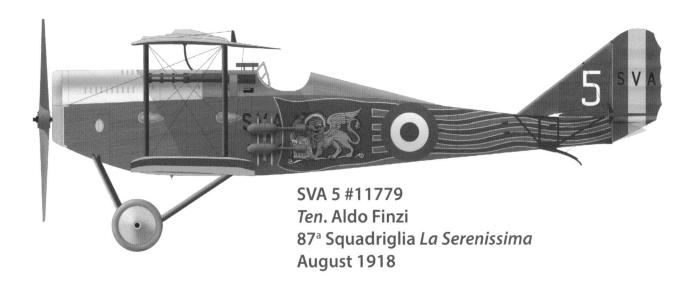

SVA 5 #11779
Ten. Aldo Finzi
87ª Squadriglia *La Serenissima*
August 1918

SVA 3 #12181
89ª Squadrilgia
Homs, Libya
1919

88ª Squadriglia

The 88ª Squadriglia was formed as a paper unit at Ponte San Pietro on 31 March 1918, consisting of the Sezioni SVA autonome 4ª, 5ª and 6ª. Later on, these flights were activated individually, as had already happened with the 86ª Squadriglia, and thus the 88ª as such did not really exist.

Another 88ª Squadriglia was again in formation at Riva di Chieri on 15 October 1918, now to be equipped with Ansaldo A.1 Balilla. On 7 December 1918 its formation was cancelled.

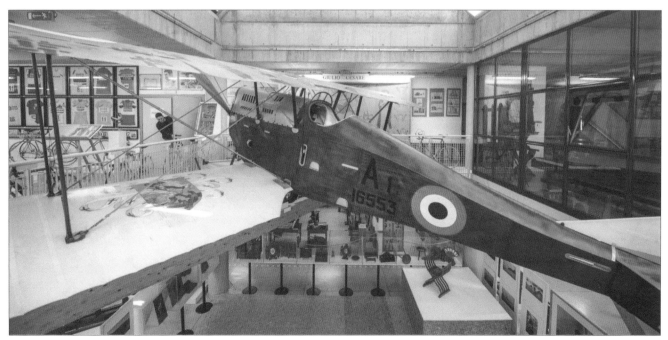

Above: The Ansaldo Balilla 16553 gifted to Antonio Locatelli is now exhibited in the Museum Tino Sana in Almenno San Bartolomeo. (Courtesy Visit Bergamo)

89ª Squadriglia

Above: An Ansaldo SVA and men of the 89ª Squadriglia at Busiago. (Courtesy Associazione Caputmundi)

The 89ª Squadriglia was established on 6 July 1918 with 18 SVA 6 "wide chord wings" and a gun over the top wing, as an experimental unit. On 16 August at Ponte San Pietro, it received the pilots *cap.* Francesco Forquet, *tenenti* Carlo Roccari and Roberto Lordi, *s.ten.* Emilio Bocciarelli, *sergenti* Stefano Bassini, Mario Calzolari, Arturo Rabbia, Giacomo Sasso, Vincenzo Stanganini, *caporali* Francesco Catania, Ezio Manfredi, Ferruccio Saita, Pietro Santin. Its first two *Sezioni* were assigned to the Supreme Command, but the squadron, now equipped with SVA 5s produced by Savoia, was mobilized only on 14 October 1918, based at Busiago in the reborn XX Gruppo SVA of which *cap.* Fourquet became the commander. Commander of the 89ª Squadriglia then was *ten.* Roccari with pilots *tenenti* Luigi Diaz, Fernando Lombardi, Lordi, *s.ten.* Bocciarelli, *sergenti* Bassini, Angelo Borroni, Stanganini, *caporali* Catania, Manfredi, Aristide Piselli, and Santin. The XXII Gruppo reported directly to the Supreme Command.

During the Battle of Vittorio Veneto, the 89ª Squadriglia flew many missions dropping bombs on airfields, railroads and troops, flying two missions each day with all its pilots, together with its twin unit, the 90ª Squadriglia. Its airplanes were often damaged and made emergency landings on other airfields. On 1 November *ten.* Lombardi was missing, but he returned the next day. When hostilities stopped, this unit had ten efficient SVAs. *Ten.* Roccari received a Silver Medal and *ten.* Lordi a Bronze Medal.

On 28 November the 89ª Squadrigliat formed a SVA flight for Libya, with four pilots and four planes. In December it received pilots from many fighter squadrons, among them *ten.* Giorgio Zoli, *s.tenenti* Modesto Strazzabosco and Pietro Calcina, *serg.* Giovanni Macrì, and then more enlisted pilots. On 12 December commander *ten.* Roccari was killed, crashing on SVA 12771 at Busiago. *Cap.* Marinello Nelli then became the commander. In early 1919 the 89ª Squadriglia went to Libya with 21 pilots under the command *cap.* Nelli, and was based at Homs, participating in the operations for the reconquest of that colony.

Above: The SVAs of the 89ª Squadriglia, just arrived in Libya. (Archive Caliaro)

Above: SVA 12181 in Africa, showing an enlarged radiator. In Libya the 89ª Squadriglia adopted an insignia taken from a book by d'Annunzio that reads "*Altam supra volat ardea nubem*", the heron flies above the high cloud.

90ª Squadriglia

Above: An SVA of the 90ª Squadriglia at Busiago.

The 90ª Squadriglia was activated on14 October 1918, assigned to the new XXII Gruppo at Busiago. Its first commander was *cap.* Fourquet, when he assumed command of the XXII Gruppo, commander became *cap.* Alberto Masprone, the former removed commander of the 87ª Squadriglia. It was equipped with SVA 5s, among them 12765, 12856 and 12863 and its pilots were *tenenti* Marcello Chiappero, Paolo Silvio Palli, Giovanni Suffo, Carlo Viazzo, *serg.m.* Alfredo Algranti, *sergenti* Giovanni Cialona and Florindo Peroni, *caporali* Francesco Cicalò, Sestino Paoletti, Augusto Pandolfi, *sold.* Romolo Rossi and *carabiniere* Pietro Remotti.

Like its twin unit 89ª, the 90ª Squadriglia was heavily engaged during the final battle, with its pilots flying two or three missions each day. There were 15 sorties on 29 October, but *ten.* Palli, brother of the famous Natale Palli, flying SVA 12056, was killed by ground fire. *Cpr.* Ligi Capitani was forced down on 31 October. On 1 November cpr. Romolo Rossi was also missing in action, a shell had shot him down

at San Paolo al Tagliamento, but he was unhurt.

A few days after the armistice, on 10 November, a SVA 10 crashed in a test flight, killing *cpr.* Paoletti and motorist Vincenzo Beria. In December 1918 the 90ª Squadriglia gave many of its pilots to the 60ª, among them *cap.* Masprone, *tenenti* Suffo, Pelagatti and Chiappero, *cpr.* Cicalò, and received many other ones from disbanded fighter squadrons, including personalities such as *cap.* Antonio Riva, the new commander, *tenenti* Keller, Bacula and Eleuteri, *sergenti* Giordanino and Aliperta, assigned for deployment to Libya. Then *cap.* Attilio Viziano became the commander. The 90ª Squadriglia left Busiago and went to Mellaha, the airfield of Tripoli, Libya, in early 1919, equipped with 25 SVAs. Its pilots were *cap.* Viziano, *tenenti* Mario Frabboni, Fausto Noce and Rosario Tilesi, *sergenti* Peroni and Alberto Sprecaci, *caporali* Giuseppe Biagetti, Mario Bodini, Umberto Capati and Luigi Capitani. In 1919 *ten.* Noce flew the first direct flight from Tripoli to Benghazi, 440 km. The 90ª Squadriglia was disbanded in late 1919.

Casualties and Combat Losses of the 90ª Squadriglia

Date	Place	Aircraft	Crew	Cause
29.10.1918	?	SVA 12056	*Ten.* Palli KIA	Ground fire
31.10.1918	?	?	*Cpr.* Capitani UNH	?
1.11.1918	S. Paolo al T.	SVA	*Cpr.* Rossi UNH	Ground fire
10.11.1918	Busiago	SVA 10	*Cpr.* Paoletti KIC, *sold.* Beria KIC	Accident

91ª Squadriglia

Above: Spad 7 4691 was delivered to the 91ª Squadriglia in the spring of 1917.

The 91ª Squadriglia was formed at Santa Caterina di Udine airfield, with the best pilots of the 70ª Squadriglia on 27 April 1917 and it was assigned to the new X Gruppo. Its commander was *cap.* Guido Tacchini, with pilots *cap.* Francesco Baracca, *tenenti.* Fulco Ruffo di Calabria, Ferruccio Ranza, *s.ten.* Luigi Olivari and *serg.* Goffredo Gorini. Their fighters, coming from the 70ª, formed two flights, they were Spad 7 serials 4689, 4690, 4691, 4700, and Nieuport 17 serials 2614, 3127 and 3138.

On 7 May a flight was detached to Aiello, with *ten.* Ranza as commander, *s.ten.* Olivari and serg. Gorini, for the 10th Battle of the Isonzo. The 91ª Squadriglia scored many victories in May, for which identification of the corresponding enemy losses is easier than for the claims of other squadrons, and received ten more Spads, among them 4702 which Baracca used. The Spad could be fitted with a camera, and photographic reconnaissance missions were flown. A new pilot arrived, *ten.* Giovanni Sabelli, coming from the 71ª Squadriglia, who had flown as a volunteer for Bulgaria during the Balkans War of 1912.

On 20 May, Baracca shot down a Brandenburg; *ten.* Ruffo attacked another, but his gun jammed, his Spad was damaged, and he landed with a still engine at Bolzano, his plane was declared written off, Austrian crews claimed two Spads on that day.

On 3 June the flight detached to Aiello returned. On 6 June 1917 *cap.* Baracca became commander of the unit, which on that same day moved to Istrana with seven fighters, to support the Italian offensive in the sector of the Plateaus culminating in the battle of Ortigara, leaving two planes at Santa Caterina for *magg.* Piccio, commander of X Gruppo, and *cap.* Tacchini. Ruffo and Ranza scored victories also on the northern front, on 23 June Ranza scored his fifth confirmed victory over Armentera. The 91ª Squadriglia remained at Istrana until 2 July, and in that deployment, it flew 100 sorties and claimed three victories, and then it returned to Santa Caterina.

New pilots arrived, *ten.* Franco Di Rudinì, *ten.* Giorgio Pessi, a.k.a. Giuliano Parvis and *s.ten.* Enrico Ferreri. Flying very successfully the reliable Spad 7 fighters, the 91ª Squadriglia, operating over the Isonzo front, scored many victories in the summer of 1917. On 7 and 31 July Baracca shot down two Brandenburgs, on 2 August *magg.* Piccio shot down two Austrian airplanes in the same engagement. Sabelli claimed a victory over the leader of an Austrian patrol on 10 August. During the 11th Battle of the Isonzo, the 91ª Squadriglia flew much appreciated escort missions for the Caproni bombers.

At the end of August, Ansaldo SVA 6755 and 6757 were delivered to the 91ª Squadriglia, considered the top unit of the air force, for operational evaluation. The pilots noticed its speed and long range, but did not consider the SVA valid as a fighter, being too big, not very maneuverable and with its weapons located in a way that made intervention during jamming difficult. On 1 September 1917, the unit had at Santa Caterina 17 Spads, two SVA, one Nieuport 80 hp. Its operations never ceased, in September the pilots of the 91ª Squadriglia claimed ten victories, and later control of

Above: Baracca scored his first victories in May 1917 flying Nieuport 17 2614, showing his insignia of the black prancing horse. (Archive Lino Schifano)

Austrian data found confirmation for all of them.

On 13 October *ten.* Olivari, an ace credited with 12 victories, taking off for an escort mission, side slipped his Spad and crashed to his death. Previously, he had contributed to the design of a new fighter, the Ansaldo Balilla.

On 22 October, flying a new Spad 13 with two machine guns, *cap.* Baracca shot down two German two-seaters that were probing the Italian lines. The 91ª Squadriglia became the scourge of the German air force in Italy, shooting down at least twelve reconnaissance airplanes and one fighter. On 25 October 1917, as the Italian front collapsed, 17 war missions were flown, with six enemy airplanes destroyed, but two pilots were lost, German fighters shot down and killed *ten.* Sabelli, and *ten.* Enrico Ferreri also was shot down in flames, victim either of a German Albatros of Jasta 1 or of the Austrian ace Benno Fiala von Fernbrugg. On 26 October Baracca shot down two enemies, his Spad was hit and had to force land, but it was quickly recovered. Santa Caterina had to be abandoned, Baracca was the last one to leave, on 28 October, setting fire to eight Spads, two SVAs and a war-booty Brandenburg. The squadron retreated to La Comina, then to Arcade and on 1 November to Padua.

On 2 November *serg.* Fermo Macchi, who had joined the unit just five days before, and who had claimed a possible victory the day before, was killed in a test flight. Baracca and Parvis formed a well-trained combination, scoring a double victory on 6 November and another one the day after. On 10 November new Spads replaced the ones lost in the retreat. At the end of 1917 commander Baracca, now a Major, had pilots *cap.* Costantini, *tenenti* Guido Keller, Gastone Novelli,

Parvis, Ranza, Ruffo, *s.tenenti* Antonio Pagliari, Giovanni Bozzetto, *asp.* Amleto Degli Esposti, *sergenti* Carlo Caselli, Cesare Magistrini, Edoardo Olivero.

The 91ª Squadriglia was now flying in bigger formations, adapting to the new tactics of aerial warfare. In a series of combats on 23 November three enemies were shot down, while some Spads were damaged, including the one of Piccio, who made an emergency landing at Istrana.

On 7 and 8 December the 91ª Squadriglia was moved to Nove di Bassano to support the troops fighting in the northern sector. At the end of December Baracca went on a well-deserved leave, receiving a hero's welcome in Milan and checking the new Gamma fighter at the Pomilio factory in Turin; *cap.* Costantini replaced him at the command. By this time, the fame of the fighter aces had grown in Italy, like in the other nations at war, but the specialized press and even newspapers also reported the deeds of bomber and reconnaissance pilots and observers.

In the last day of 1917, an important photographic reconnaissance mission was tasked over the fields of Aviano and La Comina, now in enemy hands. Keller had the escort of Novelli, Ranza, Pagliari, Magistrini and Olivero, the mission was accomplished smartly in perfect weather, but by mistake the camera had no plates.

Commander Baracca returned in January. The 91ª Squadriglia received a quantity of Spad 13s, although many pilots preferred the Spad 7, and also a Nieuport 27 and a Hanriot.

On February 10, operating on the Northern sector, Ranza shot down an enemy airplane near Chiuppano, claiming a

Above: The prancing horse appeared on both sides of Nieuport 2614, here showing oil stains after a flight.

second one. On 18 February *serg.* Magistrini, dogfighting to protect an Italian two-seater, was slightly wounded by an explosive bullet.

In the night of 20/21 February German bombers struck at Padua airfield, Spad 7 5835, 6312, 6226, 6313, 6305 and Spad 13 2507 were destroyed, Spad 7 2105 and 6364, Spad 13 2499, 7206, 2442, 2443, 2444 were badly damaged and withdrawn, but unscathed were Spad 7 1710, 226, 1457, 1463, 6318, 6367, Spad 13 2426, 2429, 2445, 2503, Nieuport 27 5888 and Hanriot Hd.1 538.

On 11 March 1918 the 91ª Squadriglia moved from Padua to Quinto di Treviso, close to the front. *Serg.* Mario D'Urso, a pilot expert in night flight, was transferred from the Sezione Difesa of Padua.

In May new pilots were assigned: *tenenti* Adriano Bacula, and Mario De Bernardi, *sergenti* Gaetano Aliperta and Guido Nardini. Bad weather and a static front had curtailed activities in the spring, on 3 May Baracca scored hist 31ˢᵗ victory, and success returned to the squadron. On 17 May there was a large combat, with fighters also from other Italian squadrons, during which the Austrian ace Leut. Franz Gräser of Flik 61/J on Albatros 153.221 was shot down and killed, a victim of *serg.* Nardini who force landed near the place of his victory.

To repel the Austrian offensive of mid-June 1918, the 91ª Squadriglia was assigned to the Massa da Caccia, and on 15 June Baracca scored his last two victories. All the pilots flew to gain control of the air and to strafe enemy troops and in one such mission on the Montello, a crucial hill near the Piave where the battle was decided, *magg.* Baracca disappeared. His wingman *ten.* Franco Osnago lost him from sight. The death of Italy's top ace remained object of debate like the death of von Richthofen, the official version was that a single bulltet from an unknown soldier had struck Baracca's temple, therefore the ace had died unvanquished in the air. Something was written later about a possible suicide, Baracca shooting himself in order not to become a prisoner, while later and possibly well-grounded research claims that his death corresponds to a victory claim by the Austrian airmen Arnold Barwig and Max Kauer on Phönix C.1 121.17 of Flik 28.

Baracca's body was found a few days later next to the charred remains of his Spad. He received a *Medaglia d'oro*, and in July a royal decree officially named the 91ª "Squadriglia Baracca". As the Massa da Caccia was disbanded, the 91ª Squadriglia was assigned to the IV Gruppo, the Capronis of which it frequently escorted. *Ten.* Ruffo di Calabria became the new commander.

One Ansaldo Balilla arrived on 28 June, and two more in August, for operative evaluation, but the pilots did not like them, and preferred to fly only on Spads.

Two new pilots arrived, *serg.* Antonio De Corato and *sold.* Chiaffredo Monetti. On 12 July, returning from an escort mission, Keller and Magistrini joined a dogfight of Hanriots

Prince Ruffo progressed with a series of ever more realistic and scary skulls.

Above: *Ten*. Ruffo di Calabria in his Nieuport 17 with a macabre insignia.

and Camels against Austrian fighters, in which Scaroni was wounded, and claimed victories. *T.col*. Piccio flew with the 91ª Squadriglia, and scored six victories in July and August. On 23 August a flight was deployed at Verona airfield.

On 8 September the storm that wrecked hangars and airplanes of both belligerents all over Veneto destroyed eight hangars at Quinto, with 14 Spads and the three Balillas. Again, new supplies were plentiful, and on 23 September, when this unit was assigned to the new XVII Gruppo, with the 71ª Squadriglia, made available to the Supreme Command, it was fully efficient again. *Cap*. Ruffo was appointed commander of the XVII Gruppo, and *ten*. Ranza became commander of the 91ª Squadriglia.

On 17 October *ten*. Augusto Stobia was wounded in a strafing mission, he managed to return, landing on the race track at Treviso, but he died the next day. During the final offensive, the 91ª Squadriglia was again part of the *Massa da Caccia*, and took part in the attacks against the retreating Austrian army, suffering from the intense ground fire. *Ten*. Keller on Spad 5415 on 29 October was hit and force landed on San Fior airfield, which was still in enemy hands, the same thing happened to commander Ranza on Spad 2482 on the 30th, but that field was now abandoned, so he could fuel up and return. On 31 October *t.col*. Piccio, the commander of the Massa da Caccia, was hit and force landed his Spad 2962, and then made his escape.

On 31 October a Balilla flight was attached to the squadron, with pilots *tenenti* Antonio Brambilla, *and* Fabio

Fabi, *s.ten*. Attilio Moscadelli, *caporali* Umberto Capati, Francesco Ciabatti and Raffaele Gargiulo.

On 1 November the Italian fighters landed at La Comina airport, that they had abandoned one year before. *Ten*. Keller came back, reporting that the Austrians had treated and medicated him well

When hostilities ended, the 91ª Squadriglia was still at Quinto, with commander *cap*. Ranza and pilots *tenenti* Bacula, Arturo Bonucci, Giorgio Castelli, Carlo Alberto Conelli de Prosperi, De Bernardi, Novelli, Olivero, *s.ten*. Mario Ottolini and *sergenti* Aliperta, Guido Consonni, D'Urso. It had thirteen Spads with serials 2366, 2369, 2387, 2394, 2411, 2413, 2432, 2437, 2469, 2482, 2489, 2508, 2908 and 3001.

Piccio returned on 5 November, disheveled and wearing an Austrian overcoat: he escaped from Villach and for three days walked back 60 miles, in the general confusion.

The total activity of the 91ª Squadriglia in the war amounted to 3,412 war flights, with 117 confirmed victories. Eleven of its pilots were recognized as aces: Baracca, Piccio, Ruffo, Ranza, Olivari, Novelli, Costantini, Magistrini, Nardini, Parvis, and Sabelli. A fair number of medals were assigned: the *Medaglia d'Oro al Valor Militare* to Baracca and Piccio; three *Medaglie d'Argento* to Keller, Novelli, Olivari, Olivero and Ranza; two to Aliperta, Baracca, Bonucci, Consonni, Costantini, Ferreri, Magistrini, Pessi, Piccio and Sabelli; one to Bacula, Bozzetto, Conelli de Prosperi, De Bernardi, Degli Esposti, Di Rudinì, Nardini and Pagliari; and

Above: The Spad 7 of Francesco Baracca with the black horse insignia.

26 Bronze Medals. In the first period after the armistice, it was sent to the airfield of Zaule, Trieste.

The 91ª Squadriglia was never disbanded, and remained in service through World War 2, until modern times, its insignia, a griffon, is now part of the shield of the Italian Aeronautica Militare.

Identified Victory Claims of the 91ª Squadriglia

Date	Place	Pilots	Victim
1.5.1917	Latisana	*Cap.* Baracca	Hansa Br. C.I 229.08, Flik 12
5.5.1917	Vippacco	*Ten.* Ruffo, *s.ten.* Olivari	Hansa Br. C.I 69.20, Flik 32
10.5.1917	Biglia	*Ten.* Ruffo	Fighter OOC
10.5.1917	Vertoiba	*Cap.* Baracca	KD 28.17, Flik 41/J
12.5.1917	Podgora	*Ten.* Ruffo	Two-seater OOC
13.5.1917	Jelenik	*Ten.* Ruffo	Two-seater FTL
13.5.1917	Mount Corada	*Cap.* Baracca	Hansa Br. C.I 129.20, FlG 1
18.5.1917	Hermada	*S.ten.* Olivari	Two-seater
20.5.1917	Plava	*Cap.* Baracca	Hansa Bt. C.I 129.52, Flik 12
20.5.1917	Vodice	*Magg.* Piccio (& Baracchini, 81ª)	Hansa Br. C.I 229.10, Flik 12
24.5.1917	Grado	*S.ten.* Olivari (& Leonardi, 80ª)	Lohner L136, SFS Trieste
26.5.1917	Britof	*Ten.* Ruffo	Hansa Br. C.I 129.53, Flik 32
28.5.1917	Peuma	*Magg.* Piccio (& Olivi, 76ª)	Hansa Br. C.I 229.01, Flik 32
1.6.1917	Aisovizza	*Magg.* Piccio	Hansa Br. C.I 29.63, Flik 19?
3.6.1917	Plava	*Cap.* Baracca	Hansa Br. C.I 129.51, FlG 1
3.6.1917	Aisovizza	*S.ten.* Olivari (& Poli 70 , Novelli, 81ª)	Hansa Br. C.I 129.02, Flik 4
6.6.1917	Vodice	*S.ten.* Olivari (& Baracchini, 81ª)	Hansa Br. C.I 229.19, FlG 1
19.6.1917	Val d'Astico	*Ten.* Ruffo	Hansa Br. C.I 29.60, Flik 24?
23.6.1917	Barco	*Ten.* Ranza	Enemy aircraft FTL
26.6.1917	Val Sugana	*Ten.* Ruffo	Hansa Br. C.I 129.27, Flik 21?

Right: Luigi Olivari in front of his Spad, that had the front part of the cowling painted red.

29.6.1917	Mount S. Marco	*Magg*. Piccio	Flik 4?
29.6.1917	Vippacco valley	*Magg*. Piccio	Enemy aircraft FTL
7.7.1917	Castagnevizza	*Cap*. Baracca	Hansa Br. C.I 129.68, Flik 46/F
14.7.1917	Comen	*Ten*. Ruffo	KD 28.43, Flik 35
14.7.1917	Comen	*Cap*. Baracca	KD 28.57, Flik 41/J FTL
17.7.1917	S. Lucia di T.	*Ten*. Ruffo	Fighter?
20.7.1917	Oppachiasella	*Ten*. Ruffo	Hansa Br. C.I 69.84, Flik 23
20.7.1917	Selo	*Ten*. Ruffo	KD 28.18 or 28.58, Flik 42/J FTL
28.7.1917	Aidussina	*Magg*. Piccio	Hansa Br. C.I 129.60, Flik 19?
28.7.1917	Aidussina	*Ten*. Sabelli	KD 28.57, Flik 41/J FTL
31.7.1917	Peuma	*Cap*. Baracca	Hansa Br. C.1 69.93, Flik 46
2.8.1917	Aisovizza	*Ten*. Ranza, *ten*. Parvis	Enemy aircraft
2.8.1917	Tolmino	*Magg*. Piccio	Aviatik C.I 37.08, Flik 12
2.8.1917	Tolmino	*Magg*. Piccio	Hansa Br. C.1 129.15, Flik 12
3.8.1917	Sava Valley	*Cap*. Baracca (& Baracchini, 76ª)	Two-seater OOC
10.8.1917	Flondar	*Ten*. Ranza (& Degli Esposti, 80ª)	Hansa Br. C.I 69.92, FlG 1
10.8.1917	Mount Stol	*Ten*. Sabelli (& Allasia, 80ª)	Hansa Br. C.I 229.25, FlG 1
19.8.1917	Selo	*Cap*. Piccio	Hansa Br. C.I 229.23, Flik 35?
19.8.1917	Castagnevizza	*Cap*. Baracca	Hansa Br. C.I, Flik 28?
1.9.1917	Zagorje	*Cap*. Baracca	Hansa Br. C.I 69.10, FlG 1
6.9.1917	S. Gabriele	*Cap*. Baracca, *ten*. Sabelli	Hansa Br. C.I 129.50, Flik 34/D
7.9.1917	Bainsizza	*Magg*. Piccio	Hansa Br. C.I 29.18, Flik 32/D
10.9.1917	Biglia	*Ten*. Costantini, *ten*. Olivari	Hansa Br. C.I 329.12, Flik 23/D
14.9.1917	Avsek	*Magg*. Piccio	Hansa Br. C.I 229.31, Flik 2/D

Above: Olivari and Baracca testing one of the first SVA, a large airplane, much different from the nimble fighters that they were flying. (Archive Casirati)

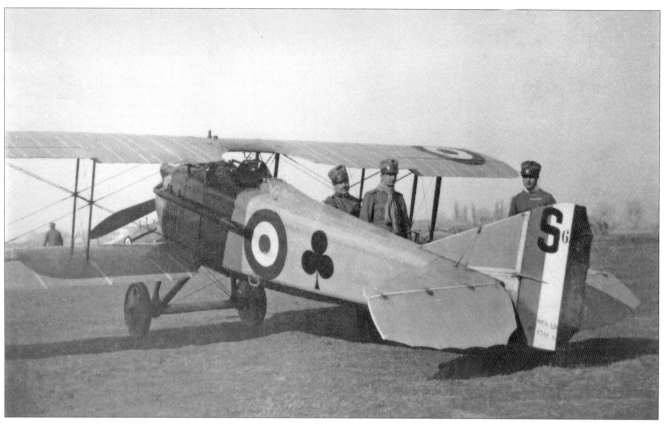

Above: Ranza, Costantini, and Novelli with the latter's Spad 7.

Date	Location	Pilot(s)	Aircraft
17.9.1917	Merna	*Ten.* Sabelli	Hansa Br. C.I, 329.17, Flik 34/D
23.9.1917	Cotici	*Ten.* Ranza, *ten.* Sabelli	Hansa Br. C.I, 129.48, Flik 35/D
23.9.1917	Chiapovano	*Magg.* Piccio	Hansa Br. C.I, 69.44, Flik 2/D
29.9.1917	Pietrarossa Lake	*Ten.* Sabelli, *ten.* Parvis (& Rizzotto, 77ª)	Hansa Br. C.I, 329.16, Flik 28
29.9.1917	Ternova	*Magg.* Piccio	Hansa Br. C.I, 129.44, Flik 12?
2.10.1917	Globokak	*Magg.* Piccio	Hansa Br. C.I, 29.02, Flik 2/D
3.10.1917	Mesnjak	*Magg.* Piccio (& Fornagiari, 78ª)	Hansa Br. C.I, 329.20, Flik 53/D
22.10.1917	Ravne	*Cap.* Baracca	DFW C.V
22.10.1917	Chiapovano	*Cap.*Baracca	DFW C.V
25.10.1917	Panovizza	*Cap.* Baracca, *t.col.* Piccio	Hansa Br. C.I 29.63, Flik 19/D
25.10.1917	Lom Tolmino	*Cap.* Ruffo	Hansa Br. C.I 129.61, Flik 4/D
25.10.1917	Lom Tolmino	*Cap.* Ruffo, *cap.* Costantini	DFW C.V, FA 17 or FA(A) 232?
25.10.1917	San Marco	*Cap.* Ruffo	Two-seater
25.10.1917	Castelmonte	*T.col.* Piccio (& Fochessati, 82ª)	DFW C.V, FA 39?
25.10.1917	Lom	*Ten.* Ranza	DFW C.V, FA 17 or FA(A) 232?
26.10.1917	Clabuzzaro	*Magg.* Baracca, *ten.* Parvis	DFW, FA 39?
26.10.1917	S. Pietro al N.	*Magg.* Baracca, *ten.* Parvis	DFW, FA 17?
26.10.1917	Castelomonte	*Cap.* Costantini	DFW
6.11.1917	Fossalta	*Magg.* Baracca, *ten.* Parvis	Albatros D.III 153.54, Flik 41/J
6.11.1917	Conegliano	*Magg.* Baracca, *ten.* Parvis	Rumpler C.IV, FA(A) 219
7.11.1917	Orsago	*Cap.* Baracca, *ten.* Parvis	DFW C.V, FA(A) 204
15.11.1917	Istrana	*Cap.* Baracca	DFW C.V, FA 14
21.11.1917	Casoni	*Ten.* Ranza	DFW C.V, FA 39
23.11.1917	M. Moncader	*Ten.* Parvis, *ten.* Keller	Two-seater FTL
23.11.1917	Cornuda	*Cap.* Costantini, *serg.* Magistrini	DFW, FA(A) 232
23.11.1917	Falzè di Piave	*Cap.* Baracca, *ten.* Novelli	Albatros D.V, Jasta 39
30.11.1917	Rivasecca	*Ten.* Costantini, *asp.* Olivero, *ten.* Bacula	DFW, FA 14
30.11.1917	Moriago	*Ten.* Ranza, *ten.* Novelli, *serg.* Magistrini	DFW, FA 14 or FA 232?

Above: A more elaborate skull on the Spad of Ruffo di Calabria.

30.11.1917	Rustignè	*Magg.* Baracca, t.col. Piccio	Kite balloon damaged
7.12.1917	Kaberlaba	*Magg.* Baracca, ten. Novelli	Hansa Br. C.I 29.20 Flik 45/D
7.12.1917	Bassano	*Ten.* Ranza, serg. Magistrini	Hansa Br. C.I 369.21 Flik 39/D
30.12.1917	Fonzaso	*Ten.* Ranza	Two-seater
1.1.1918	Comina	*Ten.* Ranza	German two-seater FTL
12.1.1918	Campo S. Pietro	*Ten.* Ranza	Rumpler, RhBZ 1
4.2.1918	Cima Mandriolo	*Ten.* Ranza	Fighter FTL
10.2.1918	Mosson	*Ten.* Ranza, *ten.* Bacula	Two-seater
10.2.1918	Chiuppano	*Ten.* Ranza	Hansa Br. C.I 29.68, Flik 17/D
3.5.1918	Grave di P.	*Magg.* Baracca, *serg.* Nardini	Hansa Br. C.I 369.28, Flik 19/D
11.5.1918	Quero	*Ten.* Novelli, *serg.* Magistrini	Hansa Br. C.I 169.07, Flik 2/D FTL
17.5.1918	San Biagio	*Serg.* Nardini (& Chiri 78ª, Reali 79ª)	Albatros D.III 153.221, Flik 61/J
19.5.1918	Fontanasecca	*Serg.* D'Urso	Fighter
20.5.1918	Volpago	*Cap.* Ruffo	Fighter
22.5.1918	Borgo Malanotte	*Magg.* Baracca, *serg.* D'Urso	Albatros D.III 153.155, Flik 51/J
26.5.1918	Spresiano	*T.col.* Piccio, *ten.* Novelli, *ten.* Keller	Albatyros D.III 153.230, Flik 42/J
9.6.1918	Moriago	*T.col.* Piccio	Hansa Br. C.I 269.62 FTL, Flik 44/D
15.6.1918	Mosnigo	*Serg.* Nardini (& Baracchini, Mazzucco 81ª)	Fighter
15.6.1918	Saletto	*Magg.* Baracca	Hansa Br. C.I 369.116, Flik 32/D
15.6.1918	San Biagio	*Magg.* Baracca, *serg.* Aliperta	Albatros D.III 153.266, Flik 51/J
15.6.1918	Fagarè	*Ten.* Ranza	Hansa Br. C.I 369.23, Flik 44
15.6.1918	Grave di P.	*Cap.* Ruffo, *serg.* D'Urso	Brandenburg
15.6.1918	Piave	*Ten.* Ranza, *s.ten.* Olivero	Two-seater
22.6.1918	Nervesa	*Ten.* Novelli, ten. De Bernardi	Two-seater
22.6.1918	Nemole	*Serg.* Nardini	Kite balloon

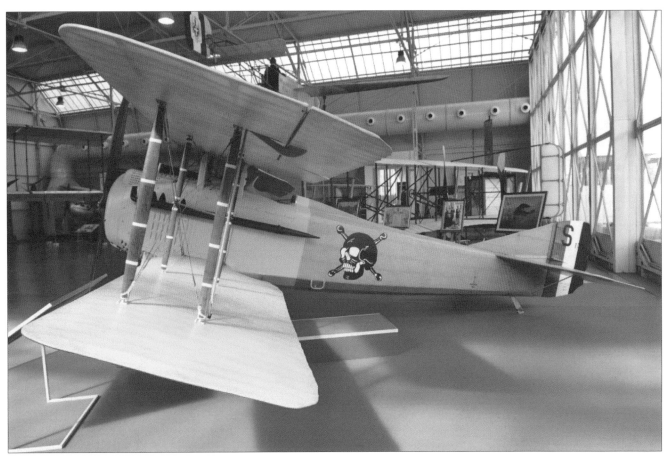

Above: The historical Museum of the Italian Air Force at Vigna di Valle shows a Spad with the colors of Ruffo. After the war, many fighters were gifted to the top aces, and many of them have survived.

12.7.1918	Monte Santo	Keller, Magistrini (& Scaroni, 76ª, RAF 45 Sqn.)	Albatros D.III 153.259, Flik 30/J
19.7.1918	San Polo	*T.col.* Piccio	Ufag C.I 161.38, Flik 47/F
29.7.1918	Motta di L.	*T.col.* Piccio	Phönix D.I 228.50, Flik 37/P
1.8.1918	Piave	*T.col.* Piccio (& McEvoy, RAF 66 Sqn.)	Albatros D.III 253.40, Flik 56/J
5.8.1918	Spresiano	*T.col.* Piccio, *ten.* Bacula	Hansa Br. C.I 369.38, Flik 57/Rb
8.8.1918	San Polo	*T.col.* Piccio	UFAG
11.8.1918	Maserada	*T.col.* Piccio, *ten.* Novelli	Phönix C.I 121.26, Flik 12/Rb
12.8.1918	Susegana	*Cap.* Costantini (& Riva, Chiri, 78ª)	Phönix D.I 128.11, Flik 40/P
16.8.1918	San Polo	*Ten.* Ranza	Two-seater
22.8.1918	Nervesa	*Cap.* Costantini	Albatros D.III 253.71, Flik 42/J
23.8.1918	Oderzo	*Serg.* Magistrini	Enemy aircraft not confirmed
1.9.1918	Fontanafredda	*Ten.* De Bernardi, *asp.* Olivero, *serg.* D'Urso	Fighter
11.9.1918	S. Lucia di Piave	*Ten.* De Bernardi	Two-seater FTL
17.9.1918	Mandra	*Ten.* De Bernardi	Fighter not confirmed
22.9.1918	Nervesa	*Ten.* Novelli, *ten.* De Bernardi	Two-seater
3.10.1918	Cimadolmo	*Ten.* De Bernardi	Aviatik D.I 238.68, Flik 74/J?
4.10.1918	Ormelle	*Ten.* Keller	Kite balloon, BK4
27.10.1918	Conegliano	*T.col.* Piccio	Albatros D.III 153.162, Flik 101/G?
29.10.1918	Oderzo	*Ten.* Ranza	Fighter
29.10.1918	Livenza	*Ten.* Ranza	Fighter OOC

Above: Ranza with a Spad 7 with the insignia of an owl; the photo is dated 2 August 1917.

Casualties and Combat Losses of the 91ª Squadriglia

Date	Place	Aircraft	Crew	Cause
20.5.1917	Bolzano VC	Spad 4703 FTL	*Ten.* Ruffo UNH	Enemy aircraft
13.10.1917	S. Caterina	Spad FTL	*Ten.* Olivari KIC	Accident
25.10.1917	Bainsizza	Spad 4699	*Ten.* Sabelli KIA	Fighters
25.10.1917	Tolmino	Spad 5411	*Serg.* Ferreri KIA	Fighters
2.11.1917	Padua	Spad	*Serg.* Macchi KIC	Accident
18.2.1918	Marcesina	Spad	*Serg.* Magistrini WIA	Fighters
19.6.1918	Montello	Spad 5382	*Magg.* Baracca KIA	?
17.10.1918	Treviso	Spad	*Ten.* Stobia DOW	Ground fire
29.10.1918	San Fior	Spad 5415	*Ten.* Keller WIA, POW	Ground fire
31.10.1918	Tagliamento	Spad 2962	*T.col.* Piccio UNH, POW	Ground fire

Above: Pilots of the 91ᵃ Squadriglia, all of them aces: from the left, Novelli, Ranza, Ruffo, Costantini and Baracca.

Above: Airplanes of the 91ᵃ Squadriglia at Padua during the retreat, November 1917. Baracca's Spad is the last of the line. Among them there are Spads, Hanriots, and Ni.27s of other units.

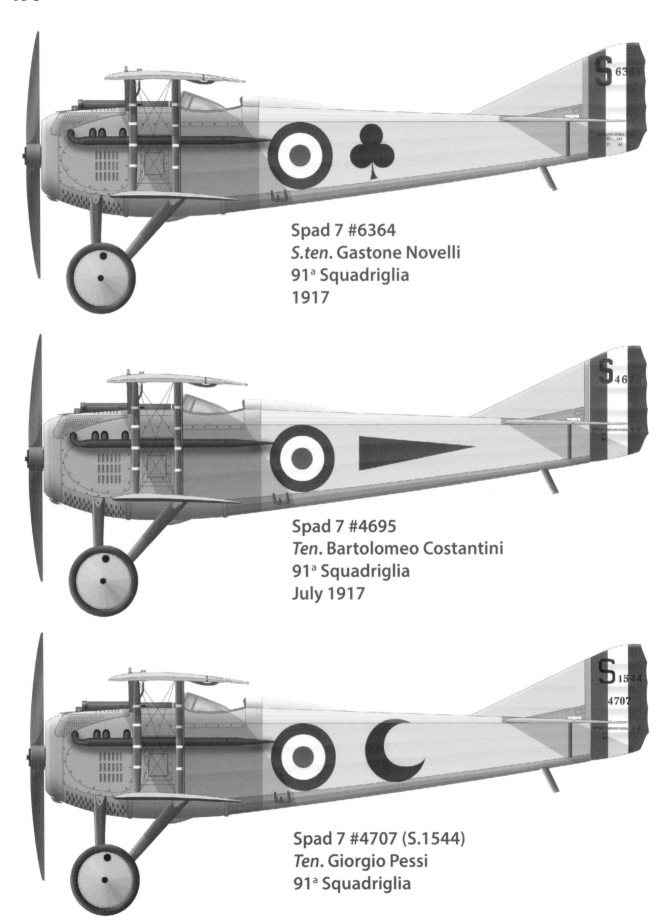

Spad 7 #6364
S.ten. Gastone Novelli
91ª Squadriglia
1917

Spad 7 #4695
Ten. Bartolomeo Costantini
91ª Squadriglia
July 1917

Spad 7 #4707 (S.1544)
Ten. Giorgio Pessi
91ª Squadriglia

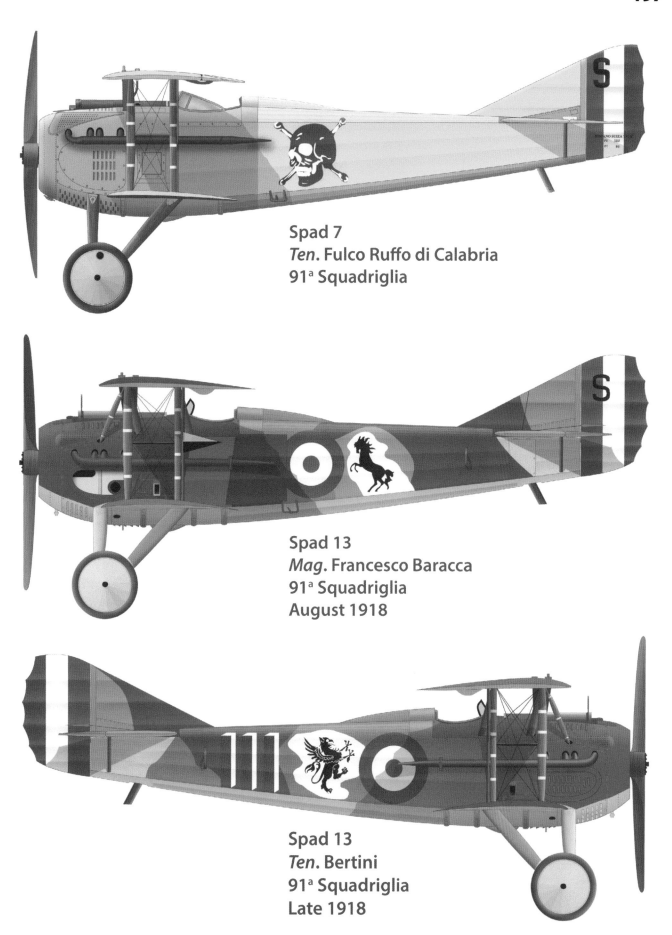

Spad 7
Ten. Fulco Ruffo di Calabria
91ª Squadriglia

Spad 13
Mag. Francesco Baracca
91ª Squadriglia
August 1918

Spad 13
Ten. Bertini
91ª Squadriglia
Late 1918

Magg. Baracca and *ten*. Ranza in front of the latter's Spad carrying the insignia of the ladder that he had taken up in memory of Sabelli.

Above: *Magg.* Baracca with his Spad 13 2445.

Above: An official photo of the pilots of the 91ª Squadriglia in the late spring of 1918. From the left: D'Urso, Aliperta, Novelli (hiding Magistrini), Costantini, Ruffo di Calabria, Piccio, Keller, Baracca, Ranza, Bernardi, Bacula, Nardini, and Olivero.

Above: The Spad of Baracca, sitting, first from the right, carrying a griffon painted on the right side.

Above: Baracca with his last victim, Albatros D.III 153.266 of Flik 51/J, shot down on 16 June 1918.

Above: *T.col.* Piccio in a Spad 7 with the griffon insignia.

Above: Pilots of the 91ª Squadriglia with the final Spad 13 of prince Ruffo, with a new form of black skull.

Above: The 91ª Squadriglia after the victory was based at Trieste. The pilot is *cpr.* Pietro Bertini.

Spad 13 "IX" of
tenente Conelli
de Prosperi.

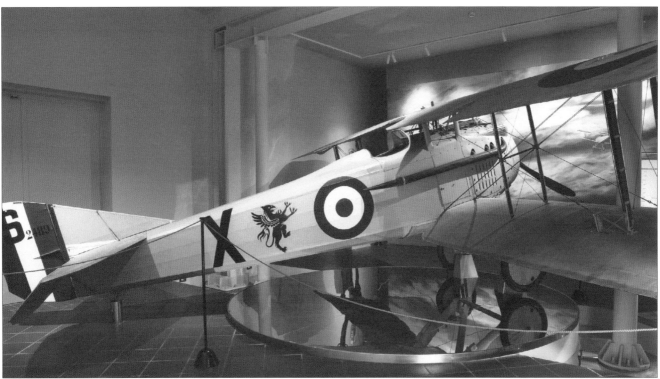

Above: Spad 7 2489 flown by the ace is preserved in the Francesco Baracca Museum in his hometown, Lugo fi Romagna.

Right: Painting of Francesco Baracca, Italy's leading ace of WWI.

92ª Squadriglia

The 92ª Squadriglia was in formation on two flights in April 1917 at Campoformido, to be equipped with Spad fighters. It never received either pilots or planes, and on 7 December 1918 its formation was officially stopped.

Part 8: Other Squadriglie from April 1916

101ª Squadriglia

Above: Farman MFC and a Nieuport 11 of the 101ª Squadriglia at Bari. The photo is dated September 1917.

This unit, prepared for the defence of Bari, the capital of Apulia, on the Adriatic coast facing Albania, was initially called 38ª Squadriglia, but very soon this number was assigned to a reconnaissance squadron, and the unit was born in September 1916 as 101ª Squadriglia Farman. During its formation a Farman crashed in the harbor of Bari on 3 July 1916, with the death of *cpr.* Emanuele Vigliani. With *cap.* Filippo Sisto as commander, the 101ª of Bari at the start of 1917 had pilots *s.tenenti* Prospero Freri and Alberto Avoglio Trotti, *sergenti* Livio Bartolomei and Pietro Pezzè, *caporali* Giovanni Taricco and Cesare Trocelli. Its equipment consisted of Farman Fiats 1710, 1712 and 1721, and Farman Colombos 1715, 1938 and 2006. In the spring of 1917, it also received Farman MFCs, among them 2662 and 2663, and a few SP.2s.

In July the airmen in service were *cap.* Sisto, *ten.* Giulio Ghislotti, *sergenti* Bartolomei, Pezzè, Taricco, Umberto Petrin and Natale Casari, *cpr.* Mario Vivaldi. The command was given to *ten.* Francesco Ferri, when Sisto, now a Major, was demoted from flying and assigned to infantry, and at the

end of 1917 the pilots serving with him were *ten.* Ghislotti, *sergenti* Antonio Fortini and Eugenio Spano, *caporali* Vivaldi and Giovanni Totti.

During May 1918, the 101ª Squadriglia formed a Sezione Idrocaccia, (seaplane fighter flight) also based at Bari, equipped with the Ansaldo Sopwith (license-built version of the Sopwith Baby) which in June became its 3ª Sezione, while the other two flights converted from the SP.2 to the SP.3. On 5 September 1918 Sopwith 5017 of *m.llo* Rolando Cheri crashed in the sea; the pilot survived. On 15 September 1918 the 101ª had 15 aircraft and nine pilots. Its service was not particularly remarkable, consisting only of patrol flights. At the end of the war, while *cap.* Ferri was still its commander, the squadron had in charge one SP.2, 4397 and eight SP.3s (3490, 4427, 4589, 4683, 6707, 6709, 6687), while its Sezione Idrocaccia besides the Sopwith 5015, 5045 and 5050 had also five Macchi M.5s (13066, 13067, 13073, 13118 and 13122). The order to disband the 101ª Squadriglia was issued on 18 January 1919.

Prospero Freri, the pioneer of parachutes in Italy and designer of the Salvador parachute used in World War 2, with Farman MFC 2663 of the 101ª Squadriglia at Bari.

Above: Farman MFC 2663: with the arrival at the front of new airplanes like the SIA 7B, many pusher biplanes became available for the defense flights.

Above: Farman Colombo MFC 2690 of the 101ª Squadriglia at Bari.

Above: The Ansaldo Sopwith, license-built Sopwith Baby, served at many seaplane bases in Italy, including Bari, but is not known to have flown any combat missions.

102ª Squadriglia

Above: SP.2 1898 of the Sezione Difesa Ancona.

This unit originated as Sezione Difesa di Ancona, formed on 1 February 1916 at Osimo, near the Adriatic city, with two pilots, *ten*. Antonio Gallotti and *cpr*. Giuseppe Sandri, and four Farmans, 822, 842, 837 and 838. Ancona had been since the first day of the war the target of repeated attacks of the Austrian naval aviation. In the spring 1916 the Sezione received also s.*ten*. Giovanni Macerandi and *cpr*. Carlo Fusar Poli. On 3 April 1916 the Austrians launched a massive attack with a raid by flying boats L66, L70, L104, L71, L69, L65, L76, L94, L74 and L90 and *ten*. Gallotti, s.*ten*. Macerandi and *serg*. Sandri took off and intercepted the attackers, trying to keep them away from the city.

The Sezione then received Farmans 773, 855, 860, 1003, 1724 and Farman Colombo 2003. It was then based at Aspio, a village near Ancona. On 9 September 1916 *serg*. Sandri took off in a Farman to challenge an enemy attack on Senigallia, and in a combat with two enemies the Italian airplane was hit. When the Sezione was to be upgraded to Squadriglia the number 39ª was initially reserved for it, then in September this was changed with 102ª. The Squadriglia was formally activated on 1 January 1917, at that time its force included *ten*. Gallotti, s.*tenenti* Silvio Natale and Cesare Salterio, *sergenti* Giuseppe Sandri and Pastormerlo. In February the unit got its first SP.2s, 1891 and 1898, together with pilots *serg*. Raffaele Franchini and *cpr*. Giuseppe Occhialini, and night flights began with the new aircraft.

On 13 June 1917 *sergenti* Salterio and Franchini took off on alarm, but in landing they smashed SP 1889 and 3548. In the summer 1917 the 102ª Squadriglia had a mixed equipment of SP.3, SP.2 and Farmans, and its pilots were *ten*. Gallotti, *ten*. Carlo Vazzoler, *ten*. Agostino Paganoni, s.*ten*. Salterio, *sergenti* Occhialini, Ugo Bullini, Giulio Pagni, Raffaele Franchini.

On 3 November 1917 *serg*. Luigi Mancini attacked an enemy seaplane and forced it to alight, but an Austrian torpedo boat came to its rescue and towed it to safety. On 15 December 1917 the 102ª Squadriglia had *ten*. Vazzoler, now its commander, s.*ten*. Salterio, *sergenti* Occhialini, Pagni and Bullini and *cpr*. Federici. The Sezione Difesa di Jesi, at the command of *ten*. Paganoni was attached for administrative tasks.

A flight of Nieuport 80 hp was then added. Its defense service went on uneventfully until 12 May 1918, when *serg*. Pacino Pacini crashed to his death at Aspio during a test flight of SP.3 6718. In August 1918 the 102ª received the SVA 3s 13955, 13968 and 13998 that replaced its old Nieuports. On 15 September this unit had fourteen aircraft, most of them SVAs (11738, 13968, 13984, 13985, 13998,

Above: The Austrian seaplane Lohner L71 from Pola was captured during a large raid on Ancona on 3 April 1916. Other seaplanes took its crew to safety.

14701, 14703, 14720, 14730) and still some SP.2s (3497, 3537, 3540, 3543) and eight pilots. In November *ten.* Sambonet briefly served in it, while s.*ten.* Salterio was moved to the 308ª. Still with *ten.* Vazzoler as commander, the unit

was ordered to disband on 18 January 1919. Two of its pilots were decorated: *serg.* Giuseppe Sandri had the *Medaglia d'Argento* and *ten.* Gallotti the *Medaglia di Bronzo.*

Right: *Serg.* Luigi Mancini flew with the 102ª Squadriglia. Here he is pictured in a post-war photo that is a puzzle, showing a Spad with an insignia, "Cacciatori del Grappa", fighters of Mount Grappa, that refers to the VI Gruppo, 76ª and 81ª Squadriglie. Behind it, a Spad of 91ª Squadriglia.

103ª Squadriglia

Above: Voisin 2087 of the 103ª Squadriglia with the crew of gunner *sold.* Dario Mazzarella and pilot *serg.* Arturo Foà.

The 103ª Squadriglia da Difesa was formed at Brindisi, an important port and naval base in the southern Adriatic Sea, in November 1916. It was based at "La Cascante" field, 3 km from San Vito dei Normanni, where now an American intelligence base is located, equipped with Voisins 1323, 1324, 1325, 2081, 2082 and 2094. Its commander was *cap. pil.* Federico Calleri di Sala. This unit operated on orders from the Regia Marina for the protection of the naval base. At the end of the year, its pilots were *ten.* Umberto Gelmetti, *sergenti* Giovanni Franco and Filippo Volontè, *caporali* Arturo Foà and Giuseppe Canonica plus several gunners. On 12 February 1917 *serg.* Giuseppe Canonica and *soldato* Mazzarella rose up to contrast a raid against Brindisi by the Austrian flying boats K178, L93, L132, L96, and L135, and were successful, as only L93 and L135 managed to drop their bombs.

In February 1917 *ten.* Giuseppe Ciuffelli also joined the 103ª. In May 1917 the SP.2 replaced the Voisins of this unit. In the summer pilots on strength were *ten.* Giovanni Macerandi, commander, *serg.m.* Ettore Cozzi, *sergenti* Carlo Moretta, Antonio Sortino and Eugenio Spano, *cpr.* Carlo Farneti. In August the squadron also got some Nieuport 11s and SP.3s that were fitted with Le Prieur rockets. In September 1917 the force of the unit consisted of pilots *ten.* Macerandi commander, *ten.* Domenico Bistolfi, *serg.m.* Cozzi, *sergenti* Natale Casari, Moretta, Umberto Petrin and Vittorio Sales with one SP.2, two SP.3s and two Ni.11s, that were used for patrol flights in the protection of Brindisi,

Taranto and Grottaglie from the raids of the Austrian seaplanes based at Kumbor.

On 16 May 1918 four aircraft took off to contrast an enemy raid (seaplanes K168 and K213 in a reconnaissance mission) but they failed to engage the enemy, on account of their obsolescence. At that time the 103ª Squadriglia had seven SP.3s and five Nieuports, for six pilots. On 9 June 1918 a large action took place: the Austrian flying boats K309, K385, K377, K372, K370, K308, K316, K376, K387, K311, K317, K378 and K384 from Durazzo attacked Brindisi, dropping 154 bombs for a total weight of 4,485 kg. *Serg.m.* Cozzi with Nieuport 2203 attacked a seaplane and followed it all the way to the enemy coast, then he attacked two more in the haze; *serg.m.* Casari on SP.3 4611 took part in the same attack and drove off the two enemies. One hour later, at 6.10 am, he spotted three more seaplanes over Brindisi and attacked them, probably hitting one of them. With good coordination, the SPs and Nieuports took off at different intervals so they were always present during all attacks, from 4.30 to 6 am. All the Italian airplanes engaged the enemy, that was constantly faster and could get away, losing only one of their number to the seaplane fighters of the Regia Marina.

On 30 June 1918 the 103ª Squadriglia had pilots *ten.* Macerandi, *sergenti* Moretta, Casari and Petrin flying SP.3 4611, 6656, 4596, 4623, 4622, 4422, 6657, 4613 and *ten.* Bistolfi, *sergenti* Cozzi and Elio Vendruscolo flying Nieuports 3274, 2203, 3296, 3225 and 2214. In early autumn, the unit received fourteen SVA 3 armed with a Fiat machine gun on

Above: The arrival by road of an SP.2 to the 103ª Squadriglia at Brindisi.

the top wing, serials 11999, 14003, 14007, 14016, 14035, 14037, 14757, 14758, 14766, 14793, 14796, 14811, 14817, 18818 and 19165 for which on 17 September four new pilots arrived: *caporali* Guido Civardi, Giovanni Ibba and Luigi Tesio and *carabiniere* Giovanni Zeppegno. The mission of the SVAs was no longer interception but the escort for the Capronis of the bomber squadrons of the Marina that were to be based in Apulia. On 15 October 1918 therefore the

103ª was formally assigned to the Regia Marina. At the armistice the 103ª Squadriglia was at San Vito dei Normanni with detachments at Valona, with pilots *cap.* Armando Giua, commander, *tenenti* Bistolfi and Macerandi, *serg.m.* Cozzi, *sergenti* Casari, Moretta, Petrin, Vendruscolo, *caporali* Civardi, Luigi Etesio, Ibba, *carab.* Zeppegno, and soon after it was disbanded.

Above: A Nieuport 11, possibly 3286, at Brindisi.

Above: A minor accident for SP.2 2761 of the 103ª Squadriglia. (Archive De Antoni)

Above: A line-up of the airplanes of the 103ª Squadriglia, first an SP.2 armed with no less than ten Le Prieur rockets, then six more Savoia Pomilios and four Nieuports. The importance of the naval base at Brindisi justified these strong defenses. (Archive De Antoni)

Above: An SVA 3 (the short span version of the SVA) crashed at Brindisi on 13 October 1918. Its pilot, *brig*. Zeppegno, later died in a crash flying for d'Annunzio in the occupied city of Fiume in 1919. (Archive De Antoni)

Nieuport 11 3248 of the 103ª Squadriglia.

104ª Squadriglia

Above: An accident on 18 November 1915 to the Farman of *capitani* Degan and Parvopassu in the surroundings of Tripoli.

After the retirement in 1914 of the 17ª Squadriglia Farman, the Italian colony of Libya remained without any aviation force. In September 1915 a small detachment of three Farmans arrived, at the command of *cap.* Jacopo Degan, with *cap. oss.* Giuseppe Parvopassu, that got the name Squadriglia di Tripoli, and that on 5 October flew its first reconnaissance mission. Arab rebels, led by Turkish officers, had wrestled control of most of the territory from the Italians. On 18 October a Farman for the first time dropped bombs on a rebel camp, and many similar missions followed against the lines of trenches of the rebels who were to all effects besieging Tripoli. In early 1916 the Farman flight had a force of three pilots and two observers, one being *ten.* Massimo Adolfo Vitale, for only one efficient airplane, but then five more aircraft arrived from Italy. In the first three months of 1916 that unit took many photographs of the enemy positions. In May the Farmans took part in the conquest of Zuara, some 70 miles east of Tripoli, where the first airplane landed on the 18th, even before the troops got there. A battle developed on the 21st, and the airplanes took part in it with many bombing missions.

Air support was often the determining factor, and activity was very intense. In August 1916 the airplanes directed a naval bombardment against Sorman, that caused the subjugation of the local chiefs. In August 1916, 21 bombing missions were flown, 29 in September, all of them with long flights.

An advanced airfield was set up at Zuara. The unit now had two flights, and in Tripoli the aircraft moved to a new airfield, Mellaha, where also the 12ª Squadriglia Caproni that came from Italy was based. On 10 October 1916 the unit got the name 104ª Squadriglia Farman da Difesa at the command of *cap. pil.* Cesare Suglia.

The 104ª Squadriglia operated in support of the garrison of Zeffren, besieged by Arab rebels and Turks, and bombed Azizia. On 25 October 1916 a Farman was lost for an engine failure and *ten. oss.* Ermanno Bartolini and *serg. pil.* Raul Moore were captured and kept as prisoners in Azizia. They returned 38 days later, thanks to a dramatic escape on 1 December, during the first bombing of Azizia by Caproni three engined bombers. In October the 104ª flew 70 hours and dropped 1,500 kg of bombs. 14 more bombings took place in November.

On 22 December 1916 the Squadriglia formed its 3ª Sezione Farman at Tripoli, while its main force was at Benghazi, Cyrenaica. The unit operated from Tripoli, Zuara, Homs and Benghazi. It whittled down to two airplanes, then in March 1917 it received six new Farmans and one Savoia Pomilio. In May 1917 the 104ª moved a flight of SP.3s to Tobruk. Besides ground attack missions, it began to operate escorting ships and hunting for German submarines, that were present in the area, sailing from the Libyan port

Left: Farman 883 of the 104ᵃ Squadriglia.

of Misurata. On 23 August 1917 an airplane attacked a U-Boat with bombs north of Tripoli, and another German submarine was bombed on 1 December off Bu Chemmasc. In September the rebels attacked with cannon fire the airfield of Homs damaging the two airplanes in the hangar. On 1 September 1917 its flight at Tripoli became a new unit, the 106ᵃ Squadriglia.

On 15 December 1917 the 104ᵃ Squadriglia had in force *cap. pil.* Giuseppe Rizzoli, *tenenti* Alberto Savoini and Vittorio Valenti Gonzaga, *s.ten.* Giuseppe Camarda, *sergenti* Italo Berretta, Carlo Marchiaro, Stefano Mazzini, Raul Moore, Giovanni Poli and *ten. oss.* Mario Cottran.

The 104ᵃ at Benghazi, on 13 September 1918 lost a Farman that crashed at sea, *cpr.* Silvio Sartori was killed, *ten.* Fiori was rescued, and finally in December 1918 it was known as *Squadriglia Mista Farman di Bengasi*, with a flight at Zuara and one at Tobruk. It remained in active service in the post-war years in the operations for the garrison and reconquest of Libya.

During the war its airmen earned a good recognition in medals: *Medaglie d'Argento* for *ten.* Bartolini and *serg.* Moore, *Bronzo* for *ten.* Athos Barchi, *serg.* Camarda (who in just one year, between 1915 and 1916, flew 70 offensive missions) and *s.ten. oss.* Antonio Vittorio Zanelli. Unfortunately, the gaps in the archives don't allow to bring justice to a unit of intense and admirable activity, in a very difficult environment and using obsolete aircraft.

Right: A four-leaf clover for Farman 4754.

Above: Farman 887 of the 104ᵃ Squadriglia used to carry the mail; during the war there was no connection by land among the Italian-held cities in Libya.

Below: Late-production Farman 4730 of the flight of the 104ᵃ Squadriglia at Tobruk. (MSAM)

Above: A postcard of the airfield at Tobruk with variations of individual insignia of the Farman 883 of the 104ª Squadriglia, two devil's heads and a moon.

Above: This Farman has landed near the border with Egypt; a moon's face is painted on its nose.

Right: No serial number, but a very apparent devil's head on this Farman of the 104ª Squadriglia. (Zattoni via Miles)

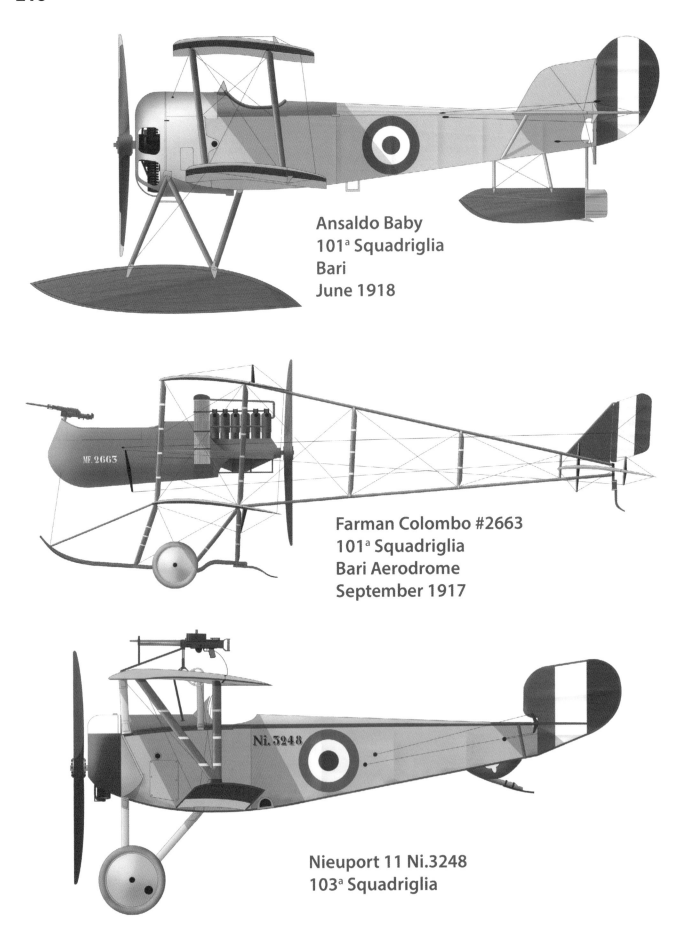

Ansaldo Baby
101ª Squadriglia
Bari
June 1918

Farman Colombo #2663
101ª Squadriglia
Bari Aerodrome
September 1917

Nieuport 11 Ni.3248
103ª Squadriglia

Savoia-Pomilio SP.2
103ª Squadriglia
Brindisi
Summer 1917

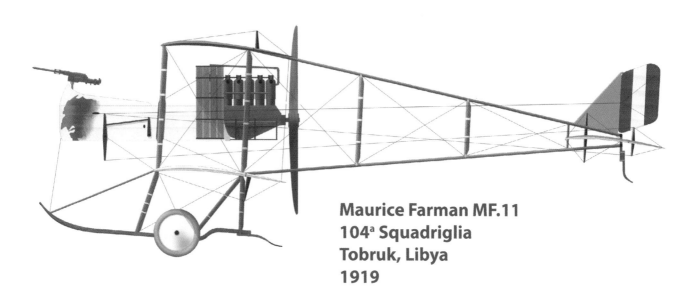

Maurice Farman MF.11
104ª Squadriglia
Tobruk, Libya
1919

SAML S.2 S2961
111ª Squadriglia

105ª Squadriglia

Left: Voisin 1322 of the 105ª Squadriglia, here pictured on a visit to the flying school of San Giusto, Pisa.

Below: *Serg.m.* Franco Macchi, with the Canton Unnè engine of a Voisin, in a photo for his friend Felice Trojani. Due to a bureaucratic mix-up, he was assigned the honor and prizes of the deceased Fermo Macchi.

This Squadriglia da Difesa too was conceived with a number, 40ª, that was instead assigned to a reconnaissance squadron, so when it was born, in September 1916, it was as 105ª Squadriglia. Armed with Voisins, it was tasked with the defence of Florence, operating from the parade ground "Campo di Marte" in the city (where the football stadium now is) at the command of *cap. pil.* prince Ferdinando Rospigliosi. On 25 November 1916 Voisin 1329 crashed in an accident wounding *ten. pil.* Enrico Jamone and killing *soldato* Bracco. *Sold.* Felice Trojani, future engineer and polar explorer on the airship "Italia", and designer of the AUT.18 fighter, also served in this unit, which he described as something like a country club. On 1 January 1917 the 105ª Squadriglia had pilots *ten.* Cesare Tomassetti, commander, *serg.* Franco Macchi, *caporali* Massimiliano Gallotti and Amedeo Peragio, with Voisins 1322, 1327, 2096, 2097, 2099. It then received pilots *sergenti* Sante Bazzoli and Gian Giacomo Chiesi and *s.ten.* Salvatore Scarantino.

In the second half of 1917 the 105ª had as commander *ten.* Armando Deidier with pilots *sergenti* Chiesi and Bazzoli, Oscar Prochet, Giovanni Cielo, Gianni Mangiante and *cpr.* Emilio Del Piero.

There were no remarkable events in the activity of this Squadriglia, that flew with nine Voisins. On 1 January 1918 its commander was *cap. pil.* Emilio Maiocchi with pilots *ten.* Umberto Sansone and Armando Deidier, *serg. maggiori* Mangiante and Bazzoli, *cpr.* Del Piero and *soldato* Domenico Stefanini.

It then received *ten. pil.* Camillo Silva, later a designer of sailplanes, who became commander, while the unit began conversion on the Savoia Pomilio. On 29 June 1918 Voisin 2099 crashed while flying above the Cascine park for a

Above: A minor accident to an SP.3 of the 105ª Squadriglia.

patriotic meeting, its crew, *serg.m.* Sante Bazzoli and *cap.* Umberto Sansone, was killed. On 18 July 1918 SP.3 6741 also crashed and the commander Camillo Silva and *cpr.* Domenico Cipriani were seriously wounded, the latter dying of his wounds.

On 15 September 1918 the 105ª Squadriglia had eight SP.2 and SVA 5 and seven pilots. At the end of the war, it had on charge SP.2 2764, 2790, 2807 and 2837 and SVA 3 13979 and 13989. It passed under the command of *cap. pil.* Luigi Giovanardi and it was disbanded on 18 January 1919.

Casualties and Combat Losses of the 105ª Squadriglia

Date	Place	Aircraft	Crew	Cause
25.11.1916	Florence	Voisin 1329	*Ten.* Jamone WIC, *sold.* Bracco KIC	Accident
29.6.1918	Florence	Voisin 2099	*Cap.* Sansone KIC, *serg.m.* Bazzoli KIC	Accident
18.7.1918	Florence	SP.3 6741	*Ten.* Silva WIC, *cpr.* Cipriani DOW	Accident

Above: The unarmed SVA 3 13979 most likely of the 105ª Squadriglia in Florence.

A Voisin of the 105ª Squadriglia. Four
soldiers are showing their empty pockets.

106ª Squadriglia

Above: Farman 1944 of the 106ª Squadriglia being loaded up with bombs in Zuara. (Archive Longhi)

The 106ª Squadriglia was formed on 1 September 1917 out of the *Sezione Autonoma Farman da Difesa* at Tripoli, coming from the 104ª Squadriglia, also called *Sezione da Ricognizione della 12ª Squadriglia Caproni*. Its commander was *cap. pil.* Cesare Suglia, and by the end of the year its pilots were *tenenti* Athos Barchi and Antonio Lupi, *s.tenenti* Enrico Castello and Baldassarre Vasile, *sergenti* Mario Comparini, Epifanio Del Ponte and Francesco Patti, *soldato* Giuseppe Gianna and observers *tenenti* Salvatore Chiara, Vincenzo G. De Meo, Felice Fiorentini, Sandro Gaetani and Armando Orlando. Known serials of its Farmans are 777 and 1944. In September 1917 the 106ª participated in a big operation toward Zanzur, flying 43 reconnaissance and 29 bombing missions, for a total of 163 flight hours in seven days.

Besides operations against Libyan rebels, the 106ª Squadriglia was also active in anti-submarine patrols. On 7 October 1917 after a mission against a submarine that had shelled an Italian coastal position, the Farman of *cap.* Rizzoli and *cap. oss.* Domenico Lorusso crashed on landing at Tripoli, Lorusso was killed while *cap.* Rizzoli was seriously wounded. Seven more Farmans were delivered in late 1917.

In July 1918 the 106ª had the following personnel: *cap. pil.* Giuseppe Rizzoli, commander, pilots *tenenti* Vittorio Valenti Gonzaga, Arturo Gioseffi and Giuseppe Camarda, *serg.m.* Stefano Mazzini, *sergenti* Italo Beretta and Giovanni

Poli, *caporali* Antonio Pasta and Giuseppe Gianna, observers *tenenti* Paolo Maggi, Secondo Cassini, Giacomo Mannone and *s.ten.* Eraldo Rossetti.

On 25 July 1918 a flight of the squadron detached from Tripoli to Homs began a series of attacks against Misurata, that was an important base of German submarines in the Mediterranean. Farmans 4734, 4739 and 4777 with the crews *ten.* Maramaldo della Minerva and *ten.* Maggi, *serg.* Mazzini and *ten.* Levis, *serg.* Berretta and *all. uff.* Calascibetta operated together with the seaplanes of the local Sezione FBA. Another important bombing took place on 25 August against Ben Aden together with the Capronis of the 12ª Squadriglia. On 8 September 1918, six Farmans attacked Misurata together with three Italian FBAs and two Felixtowe F.5 flying-boats of the Royal Navy detached from Malta. The joint air offensive of the British and Italians against Misurata and Ben Zliten had good results, as all German radio stations were destroyed.

On 28 September 1918 bombs accidentally exploded on a Farman. *Serg. pil.* Italo Beretta was killed, despite the efforts to save him of the observer *ten. oss.* Paolo Maggi, who was decorated with a *Medaglia di Bronzo* for his bravery. Other decorations assigned to the men of this unit during the war were the Cross of *Cavaliere dell'O.M.S.* and the *Medaglia d'Argento* to *cap.* Rizzoli, Silver Medal to *cap.* Lorusso and

Above: Farman 1944 at Zuara, on the left there are two Ascari, the gallant Eritrean colonial troops. (Archive Longhi)

Bronze to *ten.* Simone Levis, *ten. pil.* Valenti Gonzaga, *ten. oss.* Eraldo Rossetti.

In December 1918 the 106ª moved to Benghazi but in early 1919 it was back in Tripoli, with four efficient Farman*s*.

Thus it most likely was the last operational unit in the world equipped with the ancient Farman "Shorthorn". In the second half of 1919 this Squadriglia was disbanded.

Above: A Farman, probably serial 4978, of the 106ª Squadriglia. On its rudder there is an inscription "Ali + ?", wings plus… (Nannarelli via Ballista)

Above: A camouflaged Farman. The photo is dated Tobruch 15 September 1918. (Nannarelli via Ballista)

Above: The British Felixstowe flying boats from Malta cooperated with the Italians in Libya in the fight against German submarines in the Mediterranean.

107ª Squadriglia

Above: An Ansaldo A.5, six SVAs, and two Hanriots of the Gruppo Comunicazioni Aeree at Centocelle in 1919.

The Sezione Difesa di Centocelle, Rome, was formed in August 1916 with Farmans, tasked with the defense of the capital of Italy. It became the 107ª Squadriglia on 22 November 1916. In February 1917 it had four pilots, two SP.2s and five Farmans. On 12 July 1917 the pilot *sold.* Giuseppe Resegotti and *s.ten.* Giulio Cerioli were killed in a crash of SP.2 1826, and on 24 July *cpr.* Salvatore Conti was killed in another accident with SP.3 4554.

On 27 July 1917 a storm destroyed all the aircraft of this unit, that could not return to fly until September, when some more Farmans and SP.3s arrived. At that time the pilots were *ten.* Mario Ponis, *ten.* A. Biava, *serg.* Alfredo Veronesi and *cpr.* Giulio Federici. On 23 September *ten.* Biava was killed as his SP.3 crashed at Centocelle. *Cap.* Oreste Salomone, who had earned the first *Medaglia d'Oro* of aviation was attached to the 107ª together with *sergenti* Tito Menna and Luigi Milanese. In October the unit received a flight of SP.2s armed with 25-mm cannon, with *ten.* Andrea Sani. By 15 December 1917 the commander of the 107ª Squadriglia was *cap.* Mario Ponis, pilots were *tenenti* Giuseppe Brancati and Sani, *sergenti* Menna, Raffaele Franchini, Veronesi, Milanese, Carlo Farneti and *cpr.* Ottaviano Nobile. In 1918 it had also *ten.* Guerra, *s.ten.* Luigi Corona and *soldato* Giovanni Ressent. In March also a Caproni armed with 25-mm cannon was supplied with pilots *s.ten.* Giovanni Castiglioni and *cpr.* Michele Pallotta.

In the late spring of 1918, the 107ª converted to the SVA, receiving SVA 2 11790, 11794, 11825, 11826, 11808 and 11831 that also caused accidents. On 7 July 1918 *soldato pilota* Ressent was killed in the fall of a SVA at Centocelle. On 21 July SVA 11826 crashed on landing and *serg.* Livio Bartolomei was wounded. On 11 August 1918 *s.ten.* Giulio Pecile was killed in the crash of SVA 13954, and on 31 August SVA 13938 turned over in landing, wounding *ten.* Emilio Reina.

At the end of the war the 107ª Squadriglia had on strength *cap.* Vincenzo Giovanardi, commander, *ten.* Mario Zoppola, *s.ten.* Renato Naldi, *sergenti* Giuseppe Del Curto and Giuseppe Regazzi, *caporali* Ercole Bertoli and Emilio Saletta, *soldati* Angelo Rolla and Lorenzo Zambelli. On 26 November 1918 it was assigned to the new Gruppo Speciale Comunicazioni Aeree, a special unit that was to pave the way for the introduction of civil aviation in Italy, and it was used to carry the mail during strikes of railroads in the turbulent postwar period. Thus, this unit, together with the 110ª, 307ª, 309ª, 310ª and 311ª Squadriglie, no longer reported to the military Comando Generale di Aeronautica but to the civil Commissariato Generale per l'Aeronautica.

It was then reinforced, growing by January 1919 to a strength of 24 aircraft and 16 pilots. Based at Pisa, it flew the mail during the railroad strike of 1920 and was disbanded in May 1920.

Above: A SVA showing the Roman Eagle insignia of the Gruppo Comunicazioni Aeree getting ready for a mail flight during the strikes in 1919. The panel reads "Air mail – route Rome – Pisa – Genoa".

Above: At Centocelle, Rome's airport, a SVA of the Gruppo Comunicazioni Aeree.

108ª Squadriglia

Above: Ten. Giovanni Fasoli of the 108ª Squadriglia.

Above: Ten. Francesco Carabelli with a Nieuport 11.

The 108ª Squadriglia Nieuport was formed on 18 January 1918, assigned to the defense of Milan together with the 122ª SAML and based at Trenno, a suburb of the city. Its commander was *cap.* Arnaldo Bevagna, with the pilots *tenenti* Pier Fausto Barelli, Arturo Capobianchi, Giovanni Fasoli, Giovanni Gisci, Giovanni Gobbi, *s.tenenti* Arturo Ferrarin, Antonio Pagliari and Eolo Restelli, *serg.*m. Annibale Granese, *sergenti* Bruno Albertazzi and Bruno Valenti, and

soldati Vincenzo Bonanni and Angelo Colombo. Initially it was equipped with twelve Nieuport 11s that were soon passed to the 122ª while the 108ª re-equipped with Nieuport 17s. This unit trained much in night flying and progressively it re-equipped with Nieuport 27s and Hanriots, having four of the former and five of the latter at the war's end.

In September, with *cap.* Bevagna the pilots were *tenenti* Vittorio Bonomi, Francesco Carabelli, Fasoli, Gisci, Pagliari and Restelli and *serg.* Valenti. The unit was to convert on the SVA, but armistice came first and the 108ª Squadriglia was disbanded on 30 November 1918.

109ª Squadriglia

Above: Caproni 2346 of the 109ª Squadriglia, here possibly after its assignment to the training airfield at Capua.

A first Sezione of Capronis armed with cannon, to be used in defense against airships and for ground attack was formed in August 1917, based at Pozzuolo del Friuli at the command of *ten.* Giuseppe Buttafava. This Sezione after the Caporetto retreat was based at Padua, then it was ordered to move back. The 109ª Squadriglia was formed at Taliedo on 18 January 1918 for the night defense of Milan, and it was based at Trenno, a suburb of the city. It began operations on 1 March 1918, its commander was *ten. pil.* Manrico Zelioli. It was equipped with eight SP.3s (serials 6673, 6674, 6720, 6721, 6727, 6730, 6753) for pilots *s.ten.* Romeo Massagli and *sergenti* Licinio Bornacin and Marino Morganti, and with Caproni Ca.3 2346 and 4196 assigned to pilots *s.ten.* Alfredo Alderighi, *m.llo* Luigi Monnier, *s.ten.* Antonio Ferrari and

serg. Pietro Nave. There were also twelve gunenrs.

The 109ª received in the spring some SP.2 with *serg.* Luigi Piticco and *serg.* Angelo Bianco, but it gave away its two Capronis. On 18 May 1918 it lost SP.3 6730 with the death of *serg.* Filiberto Boccacci and *cpr.* Santo Carlaschelli, remaining with just two SP.3s.

This unit operated from Trenno throughout the war without remarkable events: there were no combats, and no decorations. At the end of the war its force consisted of *ten.* Zelioli with *sergenti* Bianco, Bornacin, Morganti and Piticco. Its total activity consisted in 29 patrol flights, 374 training and test flights, 50 night flights, 13 launches of leaflets. It was deactivated on 30 November 1918.

110ª Squadriglia

Above: SP.3 4561 of the 110ª Squadriglia, armed with a 25-mm cannon and equipped with a searchlight.

The 110ª Squadriglia was formed in March 1918 for the defense of Naples where, at Capodichino, a flight of two SP.2 armed with cannon, 3514 and 3474, and a flight of two Nieuport 110 hp were based in March 1918. The reason for this presence was the bombing of Naples in the night of 10/11 March 1918 by Zeppelin LZ 104 (L 59) that, coming from Bulgaria, dropped 6,400 kgs of bombs badly damaging the Cantieri Pattison yards, hitting also the center of the city and the ILVA steel plant at Bagnoli and killing about thirty people. This unit soon received four Nieuport 11s, 1451, 3228, 1675 and 2123, (the first one of them had been Francesco Baracca's personal fighter two years before). The 110ª Squadriglia was formally born on 30 April 1918 at the command of *cap.* Cesare Bertoletti. It then received more SPs, serials 3507, 3523, 3675, 4509, 4521, 4585 and 4561 and

Farman 4737. On July 28, 1918, in a large ceremony presided by Commissioner Eugenio Chiesa, the unit received two SVAs, which were christened "*Città di Napoli*", 11885, and "*Banco di Napoli*". In the summer also SVA 3s were provided, the first ones being 11887 and 11889.

On 1 August 1918 Farman 1926 crashed and *ten.* Giuseppe Moneta was wounded. By 15 September the 110ª had ten aircraft and six pilots, one of them *ten.* Giovanni Ranucci, and *cap.* Bertoletti remained as commander until the end of the war. After the war this unit was used for air mail services and for the first experiments of air lines, with the Gruppo Sperimentale Comunicazioni Aeree, to which it was assigned on 1 December 1918, having on strength 18 aircraft and 12 pilots, and a full complement of personnel, until it was disbanded in May 1920.

Above: SP.3 4509 of the 110ª Squadriglia. Above the searchlight is written *"Trasformato"*, modified, with the logo of the company that did the work. (Archives Caliaro)

Above: SVA 6823 at Naples' Capodichino airfield.

Ten. Giovanni Ranucci, a veteran of the valiant 25ª Squadriglia, flew also with the 110ª Squadriglia. Here he is with a SVA in a photo dedicated to Francesco Brach Papa.

111ª Squadriglia

Above: The first flights of the SAML S.1 of the 111ª Squadriglia at Campoformido, 5 July 1917.

The order to create the 111ª Squadriglia SAML was issued on 3 March 1917 and the unit was born at the Centro Formazione Squadriglie of Arcade. In April it received its aircraft at the La Comina airfield, in mid-April it moved to Campoformido and on 21 April 1917 it began operations, assigned to the X Gruppo where it replaced the disbanded 33ª. From the latter Squadriglia came its commander, *cap.* Mario Ajmone Cat. Initially there were six SAMLs, including serials 1585, 1685, 2428, 2838 and 2839, in two flights with nine pilots: *ten.* Enrico Talli, *s.tenenti* Eugenio Benaglio, Ugo Benfante, Luigi Guerci, Enrico Jamone and Mario Marinoni, *serg.* Sante Rocco and *cpr.* Cesare Cattani, two observers, *ten.* Ambrogio Comi and *s.ten.* Dino Bacci and five gunners, many coming from the 33ª. The third flight was formed at Aviano on 5 May, for the day and night defense of Udine with SP.2s 2775, 2767, 2776, 2771 and 2667, that also took up Farmans 850, 973 and 1589 formerly of the 33ª.

The first war flight of the 111ª was on 2 May 1917. On 10 May the SAML of *ten.* Benfante and *ten. oss.* Giuseppe Bortolotti over the Carso had a long combat with an enemy fighter that finally gave up. In support of the offensive at the Hermada and then in June, the 111ª flew many bombing and reconnaissance missions, and the valor of *ten. oss.* Paolo Bodojra was remarked. In June the 111ª had SAMLs 1583,

2139, 2420, 2431, 2589, 2835, 2837, 2845, 2846, 2848, 2895, 2947, 2951, 2953, 2959, 2976 and 2968. On 31 July all its equipment was turned over to the 114ª Squadriglia together with observers *ten.* Emilio Benini and Agostino Ancillotto. Then the 111ª Squadriglia moved to Taliedo to re-equip, as it was destined to deploy in Macedonia, where the allied Armée d'Orient, including the 35ª Divisione di Fanteria from Italy was fighting against the Bulgarians and their German allies.

On 13 September 1917 the 111ª Squadriglia sailed from Taranto with a force of eight officers and 97 troopers, arriving at Santi Quaranta, Albania. On 5 October its 1ª Sezione reached Dudular, near Thessaloniki, where it replaced the disbanded 47ª Squadriglia Farman. Pilots had asked to fly to the Balkans, but they were not allowed to. On 8 October the first aircraft arrived at Sakulevo. On 20 October commander *cap.* Ajmone Cat flew to all the Allied airfields to show the shape of the SAML. The 111ª had in charge SAML 2479, 2865, 2931, 2932, 2936, 2943, 2944, 2965, 2979, 2980, 2990, 2998 and pilots *cap.* Ercole Guadagni, *tenenti* Benaglio, Benfanti, Guerci and Jamone, *sergenti* Luigi Angeleri and Rocco, observers *ten.* Attilio Abbriata, Manlio Barichello, G. Emanuele Bariè, Andrea Ferraris, Silvestro Martinelli, Salvatore Scandariato, Nino Tuzi, and *s.tenenti* Tommaso Debbia and Pompilio Giannini.

Above: *Cap*. Ajmone Cat with a SAML of the 111ª Squadriglia. He later became commander of the Regia Aeronautica in the war in Ethiopia and of the Italian Air Force after World War 2.

By 26 October already two thirds of the personnel were down with malaria. The first operational flight was on 27 October with Ajmone Cat and *ten. oss.* Tuzi. On 28 October two German fighters attacked the airplane of Guadagni and Ferraris, who just the same managed to drop their bombs on Budakovo and leaflets in Bulgarian. German fighters were very active in the region of Monastir, but the 111ª sent up at least four missions each day. Again, four fighters on 30 October attacked the SAML of *ten.* Benaglio and *ten. oss.* Bariè near Nospal, wounding the observer, but with the help of *ten. pil.* Benfante and *ten.* Ferraris, who took part in the combat, one was claimed shot down, as it was seen going down spinning north of Budakovo. The SAML returned with 23 bullet holes. Also *cap.* Guadagni in October had combats with fighters and drove off one of them.

On 7 November anti-aircraft guns damaged the SAML of Ajmone Cat and *ten.* Martinelli. On 15 November the 111ª attacked the airfield at Kanatraci with its five efficient airplanes, with crews Ajmone Cat and Tuzi, Ugo Benfante and Manlio Barichello, Benaglio and Abbriata, Jamone and Ferraris, Angeleri and Emanuele Bariè, while *serg.* Rocco and *cap.* Guadagni reconnoitered the results. They dropped 15 90-mm bombs on the enemy base, and four fighters rose up in challenge. They damaged the SAMLs of *ten.* Jamone and of *serg.* Rocco and mauled the SAML of Benaglio wounding *ten.* Abbriata with three bullets. Firing just with his left hand Abbriata shot down a fighter over Vlaklar, then they crash

landed just within the allied lines. 150 bullets had hit the SAML and *ten.* Abbriata received the *Medaglia d'Argento* on the field. Benaglio had scored his second victory in 15 days.

On 4 December Ajmone Cat and Giannini went out for a reconnaissance and strafing of trenches, but it was so cold that their gun froze and the observer was frostbitten. On 15 December two enemy fighters attacked and damaged the SAML of *serg.* Angeleri and *ten.* Tuzi over Dorbusovo, that returned carrying a badly wounded observer.

For the operations during 1917, *Medaglie d'Argento* were tributed to *tenenti* Abbriata, Bariè, Benaglio, (two, for his two air victories) Benfante, Ferraris and Tuzi, and a Bronze to *s.tenente* Debbia, while *cpr.* Angeleri was promoted to *sergente* for war merits.

On 7 January 1918, during a low-level attack, ground fire killed *ten. oss.* Silvestro Martinelli, his pilot *cap.* Guadagni brought back the damaged airplane with the dead observer. Ajmone Cat and Bariè took part in this action. In January the squadron started using wireless telegraphy for communication with the artillery. In mid-March, with the return of good weather, reconnaissance and spotting missions increased. On 21 March again an enemy fighter attacked without success the aircraft of Ajmone Cat and *s.ten.* Enrico Romanelli. On 1 April *s.ten* Guerci and Barichello had a take-off accident and wrecked a SAML. On 5 April there were eight missions: aircraft usually operated in pairs, one charged with the reconnaissance and the other one acting

Above: SAML S.2 2943 in Macedonia with the unit's insignia, a star with the three colors of the national roundel.

as escort. On 4 May 1918 the engine of the SAML of *ten.* Pietro Ogna and *ten. oss.* Michele Atlante backfired and the plane burned. The pilot, his clothes on fire, crash landed and the two airmen jumped out, but Ogna was seriously burned.

On 25 May the 111ª Squadriglia joined the new XXI Gruppo, of which Ajmone Cat became commander, thus in 1 June *cap.* Guadagni became commander of the squadron. The usual missions went on, and the Italian air force deserved merit in those faraway skies. Once more on 11 July an enemy fighter attacked the SAML of *cap.* Guadagni and Ferraris but it was driven off by accurate fire, and a similar event happened on 2 August to Guadagni and *ten.* Giovanni Peruzzini. On 28 July the airplane of *tenenti* Renato Ciucci and Romanelli was destroyed on take-off.

On 13 August, the 111ª Squadriglia moved from Kumian to the new advanced airfield at Bac, and there on 7 September Ajmone Cat ferried from Dudular 13783, the first of the new Pomilio PEs that came to replace the worn-out SAMLs, now down to just four efficient aircraft. The other PEs, that were shipped from Mirafiori in late May were 7812, 7834, 13729, 13736, 13779, 13782, 13784, 13788, 13841, 13846.

On 13 September also the first two SVAs arrived, 13879 and 13882, but the one piloted by *serg.* Guido Cenni had an engine failure and landed at the field of the French 504éme Escadrille. Other Pomilios were 13842, 13790 and 13881. In total the unit received 14 PEs, two double controls PDs, (3993 and 3995) and seven SVAs, (among them 11876, 11882, 13881, and 11850) but another shipment of no less than 26 Pomilios is documented.

In September the final offensive of Allied troops in

Macedonia began. On 18 September, there was a large joint bombing and strafing raid over Hill 1900: in action were Ajmone Cat with Romanelli, Jamone with *cpr.* Romano, *ten.* Guercio and *ten.* Debbia, *cap.* Guadagni and *cap.* Andrea Ferraris, *ten.* Pani and *ten.* Ciucci, with the escort of a SVA of *serg.* Cenni. The following day, 19 September, was tragic for the 111ª Squadriglia, that lost Pomilio 13783 of *ten.* Ciucci and *ten.* Salvatore Scandariato shot down by three fighters. They had flown together with Guerci and Debbia to drop bombs and leaflets. The latter crew, after landing discovered that there were no nuts fixing the propeller to the hub bolts. The same day SAML 2991 of *cap. pil.* Ercole Guadagni and *s.ten. oss.* Enrico Romanelli went into a spin right after take-off, the squadron leader and his observer were killed.

After the death of Guadagni *cap.* Andrea Ferraris became commander. The next day, to raise up the morale of the unit, Ajmone Cat went out on a mission with Abbriata. On 26 September *ten.* Pani and *cap.* Ferraris spotted a large column of enemy infantry resting along a road and strafed it. There were still many more missions, then at the end of September Bulgaria laid down its arms, so in October the 111ª Squadriglia made only training flights.

The 111ª remained at Bac. The last day of 1918 Pomilio PE 13736 crashed killing *serg.* Massimo Casciani and *cap. oss.* Andrea Ferraris. *Ten.* Abbriata then became commander. In May 1919 the squadron welcomed the Capronis and SVAs of the Gruppo Sperimentale Comunicazioni Aeree lead by Mercanti flying from Rome to Costantinople. On 27 June 1919 an explosion destroyed all the aircraft at Dudular, but on 1 July Ajmone Cat was flying again with SVA 12151. The 111ª Squadriglia returned to Italy in August 1919 and

Above: Line-up of SAMLs of the 111ª Squadriglia in Macedonia.

was disbanded.

For the operations of 1918 the *Medaglia d'Argento* was assigned to *cap.* Ajmone Cat, *cap.* Guadagni (two), *tenenti* Ciucci, Guerci, Jamone, Martinelli, Romanelli and Scandariato and *serg.* Rocco, the *Medaglia di Bronzo* to *ten.* Barichello. The final log of the 111ª Squadriglia is remarkable: 600 war flights, including 257 reconnaissance missions in Macedonia, over 3,000 photographs, 90 artillery spottings, 145 bombings, two enemy fighters shot down, one airplane lost behind the lines and four badly hit and forced down, seven killed, including two commanders, three seriously wounded, sixteen *Medaglie d'Argento* and two *di Bronzo*.

Casualties and Combat Losses of the 111ª Squadriglia

Date	Place	Aircraft	Crew	Cause
30.10.1917	Nospal	SAML	*Ten.* Benaglio UNH, *ten.* Bariè WIA	Fighters
15.11.1917	Kanatraci	SAML	*Serg.* Benagli UNH, *ten.* Abbriata WIA	Fighters
15.12.1918	Dorbusovo	SAML	*Serg.* Angeleri UNH, *ten.* Tuzi WIA	Fighters
7.1.1918	Macedonia	SAML	*Cap.* Guadagni UNH, *Ten.* Martinelli KIA	Ground fire
4.5.1918	Macedonia	SAML	*Ten.* Ogna WIC, *ten.* Atlante UNH	Accident
19.9.1918	Macedonia	PE 13783	*Ten.* Ciucci KIA, *ten.* Scandariato KIA	Fighters
19.9.1918	Bac	SAML 2991	*Cap.* Guadagni KIC, *s.ten.* Romanelli KIC	Accident
31.12.1918	Macedonia	PE 13736	*Serg.* Casciani KIC, *cap.* Ferraris KIC	Accident

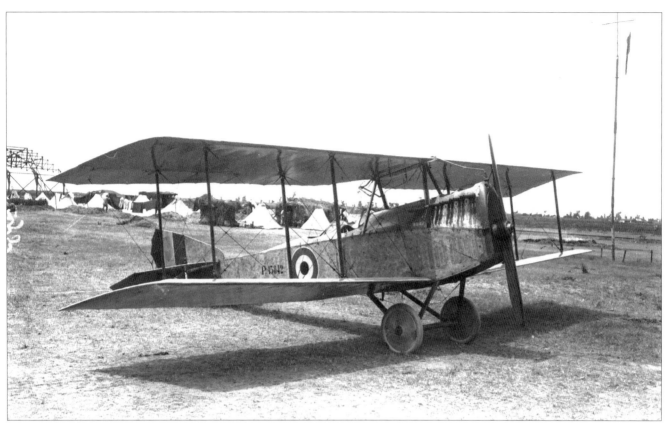

Above & Below: Pomilio PE 13842 of the 111ᵃ Squadriglia.

Above: Six Pomilios and three SVAs of the 111ª Squadriglia.

Above: A Pomilio PE and an SVA in Macedonia.

112ª Squadriglia

Above: SAML S.1 2436 of the 112ª Squadriglia shot down on 5 June 1917.

Formed in April 1917 in Turin with "six struts" SAML, the 112ª Squadriglia was assembled at the Centro Formazione Squadriglie of Arcade and then it was based at Villaverla. Commander was *cap.* Arnaldo Bevagna, pilots were *tenenti* Diego Galli and Stefano Pucci, *s.ten.* Carlo Scavini, *serg.m.* Carlo Balbo, *sergenti* Giuseppe Bin, Eugenio Boccasavia, Guido Brusorio and *cpr.* Francesco Montesi, the observers were *tenenti* Innocente Alè, Lorenzo Bellei, Pietro Ripamonti, Carlo Ronzoni, Spartaco Rossi and *s.ten.* Walter Blasi. Its first SAML, 2427, flew in and *cap.* Bevagna tested it on 24 April, the other ones came by rail.

The unit was assigned to the new IX Gruppo, on the 1ª Armata's northern front. Its first aircraft were SAML 2427, 2429, 2430, 2436, 2852 and 2853 and from the 74ª Squadriglia came gunners Alemagna, Marchi and Riccardo Mella. On 12 May SAML 2429 crashed in landing, its pilot *ten.* Galli and *ten. oss.* Stefano Bonino were slightly injured.

The first two war flights were made on 18 May and on 23 May 1917, a reconnaissance over the Pasubio by Bellei and Bevagna, taking 25 photos. On 24 May SAML 2430 of *serg.m.* Balbo got lost and had to force land at Ronco d'Adige getting smashed, gunner Mario Alemagna was wounded. On 4 June *ten.* Pucci and Rossi were sent on a reconnaissance to Caldonazzo, but they got lost and returned after two hours

of aimless flight: commander Bevagna ordered them to take off again immediately. The second time they found an Austrian fighter that shot up their SAML. The Diary of the unit reports: «*They were praised by the squadron commander and criticized by the group commander*». The next day, June 5, it was the turn of *serg.m.* Balbo with *s.ten.* Blasi but the Austrians were waiting for them and shot them down over Levico. The two Italian airmen were taken prisoners and their SAML 2436, turned over but not badly damaged, was repaired by the Austrians and flown with serial 00.45.

On 10 June the Squadriglia was mobilized for a big action on the plateau that failed due to bad weather and *ten.* Galli in a test flight crashed and was badly hurt, while his gunner Alessandro Rossi was bruised. On 19 June six SAMLs of the 112ª took off to strafe enemy troops on the Asiago plateau, together with other aircraft of the IX Gruppo, the SAML of *serg.* Bin with gunner Benasciulli had a duel with an enemy fighter. Two new observers arrived, *ten.* Umberto Benvegnù Pasini from 42ª Squadriglia and *ten.* Vincenzo Mesina from 43ª, who remained until 10 July, and then returned to their squadrons.

At the end of June 1917, *cap.* Bevagna went to Turin to test gun synchronization on the SAML and *ten.* Ripamonti was acting commander until 9 July. On 10 July there was

Above: The Austrians patched up SAML 2436 and flew it with the registration 00.45.

the order to stop all SAML flights so that fighters could attack a SAML with Italian colours flown by the Austrians (obviously the captured 2436), there were two missions on 12 July, then flights were again stopped.

On 20 July 1917 the 112ª Squadriglia flew to Lavariano (Chiasiellis) where it was re-equipped with four-struts SAML S.2, and was attached to the I Gruppo serving for the 3ª Armata. The squadron was assigned the tough sector from the Vippacco River to the sea. Its officer pilots then were *cap.* Bevagna, *ten.* Diego Galli, Stefano Pucci and *s.ten.* Carlo Scavini, its observers *tenenti* Innocente Alè, Lorenzo Bellei, Pietro Ripamonti, Carlo Ronzoni, Spartaco Rossi. On 21 July the American mission of Major Raynal C. Bolling came on a visit. In 22 July there was the first mission, with two planes dropping leaflets. *Ten.* Vincenzo Lioy, a new observer, arrived.

On 28 July the SAML of *serg.* Brusorio with the gunner Oscar Rota in a mission over the Vippacco lost its propeller in flight, the airmen were scolded by boiling water but they managed to bring back to base the airplane.

On 2 August 1917 anti-aircraft artillery hit the airplane of *serg.* Montesi and *ten.* Lioy engaged in a photo mission in the area of Komen-Grabovica, the SAML crash landed, but the two airmen survived. On 14 August SAML 2427 of Boccasavia and Ronzoni was smashed in take-off. In the second half of August the 112ª flew thirty bombing missions

supporting the Bainsizza offensive with its new SAMLs 2940, 2969, 2974, 2985, 2993 and 3001, for a total of 90 offensive missions in August including bombing raids in formation of six planes. On 20 August SAML 2940 of *cap.* Bevagna and *ten.* Lioy was hit by flak, it force-landed at S. Maria la Longa but hit a building and was smashed. The unit got a new pilot, *ten.* Adolfo Abrial.

There were intensive actions also in the first week of September. On 15 September *cap.* Bevagna flew on a test flight "for acoustic experiences". On 29 September the unit received two SIA 7B but bad weather precluded most flights.

On 14 October the 112ª was passed from the I to the V Gruppo as a "*squadriglia per il servizio di artiglieria d'armata*" (army artillery unit) and ordered to move to Bolzano del Friuli. Instead, because of Caporetto, it retreated to La Comina on 29 October. From there it sent five aircraft on 30 October to bomb and strafe the road from Udine to Cormons, finally on 3 November it moved to Padua, where it started to re-equip on the Pomilio P.

On 12 November 1917 *ten.* Stefano Pucci became acting commander, as *cap.* Bevagna went to the I Gruppo, to which the 112ª still belonged. On 20 November, *tenenti* Pucci and Rossi faced five enemy fighters but managed to escape them. On 29 November, three Austrian fighters of Flik 42/J shot down over the Piave SAML 2495 of *ten.* Vincenzo Lioy and *serg.* Francesco Montesi, and the two airmen were captured,

Above: The accident to SAML 2853 at Villaverla on 10 June 1917.

the Austrian airmen warmly welcomed their prisoners.

In December 1917 the 112ª Squadriglia lacked efficient airplanes, it received a few SAMLs, it flew its last missions over Asiago with *cap.* Sella, commander of the I Gruppo. On 28 December *cap.* Luigi Coniglio was appointed commander. The 112ª received the Pomilio PE, but a raid of enemy bombers on Padua on 30 December destroyed at a stroke twelve PEs and Nieuports. During 1917 this unit put up 266 combat flights. *Ten.* Lioy and *serg.* Montesi were decorated both with the Silver and Bronze medals, gunner Rota had the *Argento, tenenti* Pucci, Ripamonti and Spartaco Rossi the *Bronzo*.

On 1 January 1918 the 112ª Squadriglia of the I Gruppo, with commander Coniglio, had pilots *ten.* Abrial and Pucci, *sottotenenti* Barbiroglio and Scavini, *asp.* Boccasavia, *sergenti* Bin, Brusorio, Giuseppe Foresto, Enrico Proietti, *cpr.* Carlo Ballesio, and observers *tenenti* Alè, Coraglia, Gasparinetti, Ottaviani and Spartaco Rossi, *s.tenenti* Borsani and Cherubini. It moved from Padua to Fossalunga, close to Itsrana, on 4 February 1918 with two PEs and a SAML and went on converting on the Pomilio PE, but like so many other units it suffered heavily on account of the bad flying characteristics of this airplane. On 20 February a flight accident at Fossalunga killed *s.ten. oss.* Riccardo Borsani and wounded *ten.* Giuseppe Calaresi when their Pomilio 6991

went down in a flat spin.

In March 1918 the 112ª Squadriglia of the I Gruppo - that operationally reported to the V Gruppo - began flying reconnaissance missions again. On 19 March it was moved to Castenedolo, in the IX Gruppo, operating for the 7ª Armata. On 1 April it received PE 6976, 6994 and 7026, the last one immediately written off on 3 April by *ten.* Barbieri. The same Barbieri, despite his name Fortunato (lucky), had an engine failure on 23 April and brought PE 7032 to a crash landing at S.Zeno, surviving with observer Cherubini.

The 112ª Squadriglia operated with the escort of the Nieuport 27s of the 83ª Squadrglia, at that time also in the IX Gruppo. On 2 May the engine of PE 6993 caught fire and in the ensuing crash *serg.* Robiglio and *ten. oss.* Beretta were wounded, while anti-aircraft guns hit PE 6976 of *sold.* Secondo Marconi and *ten. oss.* Giuseppe L'Abbadessa. On 3 May the squadron commander *cap.* Coniglio had a landing accident while test flying SAML 3098 of the 120ª Squadriglia, his passenger *ten.* Paracchi was wounded. Another accident on a ferry flight brought serious injuries to *cpr.* Francesco Serra on 8 May. Meanwhile the 112ª was lending its observers to the new 136ª, while its Pomilios practically turned every landing into a prang.

On 13 May *cpr.* Adolfo Vajra and *ten.* L'Abbadessa on Pomilio 6938 managed to keep two fighters at bay in Val

Above: SAML S.2 2965 with cap. Bevagna, standing, commander of the 112ᵃ Squadriglia, and *ten*. Ripamonti in the cockpit. The 7 of Diamonds is the winning card in the Italian card games scopa and scopone.

Daone, in that same mission *sold*. Marconi and *ten*. Basilio Tramontano got lost in the fog and landed at Ponte San Pietro. On 2 June two fighters attacked and riddled with bullets the aircraft of *ten. oss*. Armando Passamonti and *cpr*. Agostino Biondi, one bullet going through the flying suit of the observer.

During the summer of 1918 the 112ᵃ dropped leaflets and converted on the Pomilio the crews of the 120ᵃ. Still based at Castenedolo, the 112ᵃ had Pomilios 3980, 3695, 6994, 7836, 6938, then got 7020, 13799, 18416. A flight was moved to Medole at the command of *ten*. Edoardo Barbiroglio to train the pilots of the 120ᵃ Squadriglia in the conversion to the PE. On 22 June, probably due to the growing mistruts of the Pomilio, *col*. Gaviglio, commander of Aeronautics of the 7ᵃ Armata, flew with *ten*. Barbiroglio in a reconnaissance and inspection mission.

On 4 July, fighters attacked the airplane of *ten*. Giandomenico Cherubini. On 31 July *serg*. Vajra and *ten*. Passamonti after a reconnaissance attacked the Austrian airfield at Campo Maggia and hit a hangar with two bombs. During July the 112ᵃ flew 34 missions shooting 408 photographs and dropping 200.000 leaflets. On 13 August the unit flew a mass bombing and strafing attack,

and repeated this action on August 31. During the month it took 465 photographs. On 28 August 1918 anti-aircraft guns shot down Pomilio PE 13799 of *ten*. Barbiroglio and *ten*. Paracchi, the plane hit the ground at Mirano Superiore but the crew was unharmed.

At the end of the summer its force consisted of pilots *capitani* Coniglio, commander, and Giovanni Casalicchio, *ten*. Barbiroglio, *sergenti* Biondi, Gilli, Robiglio and Vajra, *caporali* Marconi, Micò and Serra, *soldato* Cappelli, observers *cap*. Paracchi, *tenenti* Berretta, Cherubini, Cignetti, Del Vita, Fabbri, L'Abbadessa, Maso, Perris, Rapisarda, Soreca, Tramontano, and *s.ten*. De Toma and Di Piramo. On 18 September *cap*. Casalicchio became commander. The 112ᵃ received new production PEs 18389, 18420, 18534, 19050, 19067, 19069, 19099, 22074. In September there were 17 missions, with 174 photographs.

In October, like other reconnaissance Squadriglie, the 112ᵃ received for test one Fiat R.2, serial 8506 which had its share of teething troubles, and was soon inefficient. During the final offensive that began on 24 October this unit was practically inactive and it flew just two reconnaissance missions, on the 31ˢᵗ, with the crews *serg*. Galli and *s.ten*. De Pirano and *serg*. Robiglio and *cpr*. Tagliaboschi. On armistice

Right, & Below: The accident to Pomilio PE 13686 of *cpr.* Serra at Castenedolo on 8 May 1918.

Below: Major Raynal C. Bolling, chief of the American aviation mission to Italy in July 1917. Much appreciated in Italy for his commitment and integrity, he died in action in France in March 1918, Bolling Field, DC, was named after him.

Above: A black panther over the roundel of this Pomilio of the 112ª Squadriglia, first from the right is *ten.* Edoardo Barbiroglio.

day this unit was at Castenedolo in the IX Gruppo with three efficient Pomilios and its flying personnel was pilots *cap.* Casalicchio, *ten.* Barbiroglio, *asp.* Robiglio, *sergenti* Biondi, Gilli, Marconi, Micò, Vajra, and observers *cap.* Amerigo Manzini and Paracchi, *tenenti* Cherubini, Cignetti, Fabbri, L'Abbadessa, Maso, Passamonti, Peris, Rapisarda, Tramontano, *s.tenenti* De Toma, Di Piramo and Marone.

During 1918 it had flown a modest total of 172 war flights. For the operations in 1918 *ten.* Alè, *ten.* Barbiroglio, *s.ten.* Borsani, *cpr.* Vajra and *ten. oss.* Armando Passamonti got the *Medaglia d'Argento, ten.* Cherubini and *serg.* Gilli got the Bronze. The 112ª Squadriglia was disbanded on 18 January 1919, its forces merging with the 136ª.

Above: A souvenir photo for the fitters and mechanics of the 112ª Squadriglia; *ten*. Barbiroglio is the first from the left.

Above: An original piece of canvas with the black panther of the 112ª Squadriglia is preserved by a reputed aviation historian. (Collection William Rabito)

Casualties and Combat Losses of the 112ª Squadriglia

Date	Place	Aircraft	Crew	Cause
24.5.1917	Ronco d'Adige	SAML 2430	*Serg.* Balbo, *sold.* Alemagna WIC	Accident
5.6.1917	Dellach	SAML 2436	*Serg.* Balbo POW, *ten.* Blasi POW	Fighters
10.6.1917	Villaverla	SAML 2853	*Ten.* Galli WIC, *sold.* Rossi	Accident
2.8.1917	Komen	SAML 2425	*Serg.* Montesi, *ten.* Lioy	Ground fire
20.8.1917	S.Maria la Longa	SAML 2940	*Cap.* Bevagna UNH, *ten.* Lioy UNH	Ground fire
29.11.1917	Grisolera	SAML 2495	*Serg.* Montesi POW, *ten.* Lioy POW	Fighters
20.2.1918	Fossalunga	PE 6991	*Ten.* Calaresi WIC, *ten.* Borsani KIC	Accident
2.5.1918	Ponte S.Marco	PE 6993	*Serg.* Robiglio WIC, *ten.* Beretta WIC	Accident
8.5.1918	Castenedolo	PE 13686	*Cpr.* Serra WIC	Accident
28.8.1918	Tirano	PE 13799	*Ten.* Barbiroglio UNH, *ten.* Paracchi UNH	Ground fire

Above: Pomilio PE 13686 of the 112ª Squadriglia after an accident.

113ª Squadriglia

Above: SAML S.1 3-bay two-seaters 1592 and 2884 of the 113ª Squadriglia.

The 113ª Squadriglia was formed on 18 March 1917 in Turin. Its personnel was then shifted to Arcade and on 28 April began flight training at Campoformido. Meanwhile the observers of the 40ª Squadriglia *s.tenenti* Bodojra and Bortolotti had flown with aircraft of the 113ª Sqadriglia in training, and faced a tough combat on 4 April that ended with the airplane of Bortolotti crash landing in the bed of a river.

Another Sezione was formed in April at Aviano. The 113ª Squadriglia was activated on 10 May 1917, at the command of *cap. pil.* Mario Van Axel Castelli, with the pilots *ten.* Alberto Iacopini, *asp.* Filppo Rossi, *cpr.* Mario Doria and *serg.* Giovanni Monzardo and the observers *ten.* Ubaldo Chiara, Roberto Lordi and Antonio Tassinari, with two Sezioni equipped with SAML S.1, of Fratelli Frattini construction, and called "Condor". The squadron was assigned to the new XII Gruppo of the Aeronautica della 4ª Armata, northern sector of the front. Initially its two flights operated separatedly, the 1ª Sezione at Feltre, at the command first of *ten.* Rino Corso Fougier in April, then *ten.* Chiara, while the 2ª Sezione remained at Campoformido and reported to the II Gruppo, (Aeronautica della 2ª Armata) until 24 May, when it was assigned to the VI Gruppo. The 1ª Sezione at Feltre went immediately into action and it had its first air combat on 3 May, involving *ten.* Fougier over Ternova. On 20 May Fougier had a tough combat with three Austrian fighters and was wounded twice, bullets also hit his observer *ten.* Ubaldo Chiara without wounding him. Their aircraft was written off, 8th victory of the Austrian ace Brumowski who, unfamiliar with the SAML, claimed a

Spad two-seater. The flight very soon left Feltre, in order to allow for some works, like covering a ditch, to make it more amenable to unexperienced pilots, and moved to Belluno, returning to Feltre on July 2.

The 2ª Sezione of Campoformido had *s.ten. pil.* Innocenzo Paroli, *ten. oss.* Raul Bambini and on 26 May it moved to Cavazzo Carnico, where it was assigned to the VI Gruppo that had formed a *Sottogruppo* (sub-group) Cavazzo. In the first month the two flights of the 113ª flew 12 war missions.

On 14 June the Hungarian ace Kiss shot down in Val d'Assa, Asiago, the SAML of *aspirante* Filippo Rossi and *ten. oss.* Ugo Negro. Negro was wounded, the two Italians managed to sabotage the aircraft before their capture.

In mid-July the commander of the Comando d'Aeronautica 4ª e 6ª Armata, *magg.* De Masellis, complained that Van Axel Castelli had crashed three aircraft in forty days, two at Belluno and one at S. Giustina. By that time, the 1ª Sezione had only one efficient airplane, SAML 2884.

In August the 113ª Squadriglia had its 2ª Sezione at Cavazzo Carnico and its 1ª Sezione at Villaverla, in the XII Gruppo, to which was added the 3ª Sezione, with *ten.* Serafino Battaini, commander, *ten.* Iacopini, *asp.* Stefano Achenza, *serg.* Ubaldo Lenzi and *ten.* De Claricini. This last flight on 28 August was gave birth to the new 115ª Squadriglia SAML. On 1 September the Sezione at Cavazzo Carnico got two more flights, one new and one coming from the 115ª, and the 113ª Squadriglia was now complete, formed by its commander *magg.* Renato Pascale, the pilots *ten.* Innocenzo Paroli, *s.ten.* Giovanni Monzardo,

Above: The Minister of War General Morrone visiting the 113ᵃ Squadriglia with *cap.* Paroli. (Archive Franco Ragni)

sergenti Ruggero Ceredi, Mario Doria, Germano Riccetti, *carabiniere* Giuseppe Castra, and the observers *cap.* Giuffrè, acting commander, *tenenti* Dario Armanino, Duilio Bartoli, Giuseppe Del Vivo, Carlo Guerritore, Arcibaldo Trevisan, *s.tenenti* Roberto Lordi and Giovanni Toldi.

The mountain front of the Carnia was not an easy one. On 1 September an enemy airplane had a combat with the SAML of *serg. pil.* Doria, and his observer was wounded. On 4 September again Doria had a combat above Ternova, his adversary was forced down but the Italian pilot was wounded. On 7 September *ten. oss.* Livio Palazzi was killed on SAML 2892 with *ten.* Paroli as pilot, during a photo reconnaissance mission to the cableway of Mount Koderohohe (or Zellon Kofel) hit by the Austrian ace Stojvaslievic of Flik 16.

After the Caporetto retreat the 113ᵃ Squadriglia went to S. Giustina Bellunese on 28 October, to Nove di Bassano on 3 November and to Casoni on 11 November. There it was assigned to the II Gruppo but operationally it reported to the XII. At the end of the retreat, there were *cap.* Pascale with pilots *tenenti* Dario Armanino and Innocenzo Paroli, *s.tenenti* Damiano Miari Fulcis and Giovanni Monzardo, *sergenti* Mario Doria, Ruggero Ceredi, Germano Riccetti, *cpr.* Peirano and *carab.* Giuseppe Cantù, and observers Ugo Giuffrè and Roberto Lordi, *allievi osservatori* (observer trainees) *tenenti* Lucio Albani, Duilio Bartoli and Arcibaldo Trevisan. As the commander of the XII Gruppo, Porro, was just a captain, *magg.* Pascale was shifted and command of the 113ᵃ was given to *cap.* Giuffrè, then since 11 November to Innocenzo Paroli, who was now a *capitano pilota*.

From its base at Casoni the 113ᵃ Squadriglia was intensively engaged in the operations for the defense of Mount Grappa and in December it flew 56 war flights. At the end of 1917 with *cap.* Paroli there were the pilots *s.ten.* Monzardo, *asp.* Rodolfo Zamboni, *sergenti* Ceredi, Doria and Riccetti, *carab.* Cantù and the observers *capitani* Leonida Bernardi and Giuffrè, *tenenti* Albani, Bartoli, Luigi Del Vivo, Carlo Guerritore, Giovanni Toldi, Trevisan and *s.ten.* Lordi. Decorations assigned in 1917 were *Medaglia d'Argento* to *serg.* Doria and to *tenenti* Lordi, Palazzi and Toldi, *Medaglia di Bronzo* to *cap.* Giuffrè, *cap.* Paroli and *asp.* Filippo Rossi.

In early 1918 the 113ᵃ Squadriglia received new SAMLs. It lost its observers Bernardi, Giuffrè, Bartoli, Toldi and Lordi (the last one went to flying school, in the Thirties he was chief of the Italian Air Mission to China and he died shot by the SS in the Fosse Ardeatine massacre in 1944) and received *ten.* Adriano Monti and *ten.* Celeste Pecchini.

On 1 January 1918 three fighters attacked the SAML of *asp.* Zamboni carrying *ten.* Negroni of the 22ᵃ Squadriglia but one of them was shot down above Foza. On 5 January enemy bombers successfully attacked Casoni and damaged

Above: A SAML S.2 of the 113ª Squadriglia with individual number on the tail.

seven SAMLs.

On 28 February 1918 the 113ª Squadriglia moved away from the front to Medole, Mantua, operating as a training unit, teaching troops of the 5ª and 7ª Armata signals and cooperation with the air force. In the new base it reported to the IX Gruppo. On 23 May 1918 *serg.* Germano Riccetti and *ten. oss.* Franco Italo crashed on Medole airfield with SAML 3048 and were killed.

In June the 113ª sent six of its aircraft to reinforce the 39ª Squadriglia, that was the only efficient sqiuadron of the V Gruppo, in view of the coming Austrian offensive. Then in June the 113ª moved from the IX to the XX Gruppo while remaining at Medole. During the Battle of the Piave its airplanes flew 120 combat missions in 40 days. In one of these, on 19 June, a gaggle of Austrian fighters attacked the airplane of *ten.* Monzardo who held his own, and returned with 30 bullet holes.

In June the order was issued to convert the 113ª on the Pomilio, but it managed to keep the SAML until the end of the war. On 17 July it moved to Cividate Camuno replacing the disbanded 40ª Squadriglia, and received also a flight of Hanriots detached from the 72ª and 74ª Squadriglie. There it took part in the offensive on the Adamello and to the action on the Tonale, both high Alpine peaks. On 28 August *ten.* Baldo Viglino was wounded in a test flight accident.

In early autumn 1918 the personnel of the 113ª consisted of commander *cap.* Paroli with pilots *cap.* Ugo Rolli, *s.tenenti*

Giacinto Arvigo, Alcide Gatti, Monzardo and Zamboni, *m.llo* Federico Spagnolo, *serg.* Ceredi, *cpr.* Cesare Gavardi, *carab.* Cantù and *sold.* Alfredo Bersotti, with the observers *tenenti* Dante Cavazzini, Luigi Cecchini, Mario Cuccioli, Mario Da Pozzo, Salvatore Landolina, Riccardo Maldonato, Vincenzo Meucci, Manlio Molfese, Ezio Padovani, Febo Rege Gianas, Mario Santagostino *s.ten.* Nicola Simoni. On 26 October 1918 *sold. pil.* Alfredo Bersotti died at Boca di Chiampo in an accident during the delivery flight of a SAML.

On 4 November 1918, Victory Day, the 113ª Squadriglia was in the XX Gruppo for the VII Armata at Cividate Camuno with three efficient SAMLs. Its decorations were the *Medaglia d'Argento* to *ten.* Ruggero Ceredi, *serg.* Riccetti, *asp.* Zamboni and *ten.* Trevisan, *Bronzo* to *carab.* Cantù, *s.ten.* Monzardo, *ten.* Enzo Padovani, *cap.* Paroli and *asp.* Zamboni, most of these medals for the flights in June, when operating with the 39ª.

In total, 458 war flights are recorded for this unit. It was not disbanded in the post-war period, remaining in service at Campoformido. In December 1919, still equipped with SAMLs, it had as commander *ten.* Adriano Monti and was part of the Gruppo da Ricognizione Tattica and Strategica. The 113ª Squadriglia remained in active service until World War 2, re-equipped the the Fiat R.2 in 1922 and then progressively with new reconnaissance aircraft.

Above: SAML 2958 of the 113ª Squadriglia at Cavazzo Carnico showing an insignia with the eagle and the shield of Savoy, and non-standard large roundels over the top wings.

Casualties and Combat Losses of the 113ª Squadriglia

Date	Place	Aircraft	Crew	Cause
4.4.1917	Carso	SAML	?, *ten.* Bortolotti UNH	Fighters
20.5.1917	Isonzo front	SAML	*Ten.* Fougier WIA, *ten.* Chiara WIA	Fighters
14.6.1917	Roana	SAML	*Asp.* Rossi POW, *ten.* Negro WIA POW	Fighters
1.9.1917	Carnia	SAML	*Serg.* Doria UNH, unk. observer WIA	Fighters
4.9.1917	Ternova	SAML	*Serg.* Doria WIA	Fighters
7.9.1917	Koderkohe	SAML 2892	*Ten.* Paroli UNH, *ten.* Palazzi KIA	Fighters
23.5.1918	Medole	SAML 3048	*Serg.* Riccetti KIC *ten.* Italo KIC	Accident
26.10.1918	Boca di Chiampo	SAML	*Sold.* Bersotti KIC	Accident

Facing Page, Below: The pilots and observers of the 113ª Squadriglia; first is *cap.* Paroli, with their SAMLs that are now carrying roundels on the fuselage.

Above: SAML 4439 of a rare production batch, possibly 4439–4488, of which very little data or photos are known.

Aspirante Zamboni in a picture celebrating his victory claim over Foza on 1 January 1918. (Archive Franco Ragni)

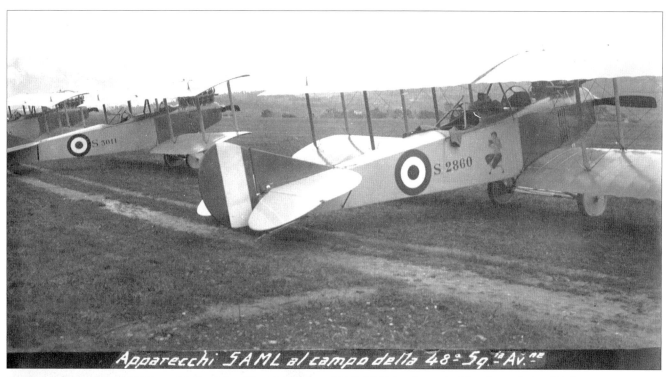

Above: SAMLs of the 113ª Squadriglia at San Piero in Campo, SAML 2860 is adorned with a faun playing his flute.

Above: Close-up of a SAML showing the eagle insignia on the fuselage and the Italian colors of green, white, and red on the nose. (Archives Zoltàn Cz.iròk)

Above: The 113ª Squadriglia at Cividate Camuno in the summer of 1918 with three Hanriots of the fighter flight from the XXIV Gruppo (72ª and 74ª Squadriglia) attached to it.

Above: SAML 3092 of the 113ª Squadriglia with an individual insignia, a diamond on a card with a running fox.

Above: The SAMLs of the 113ª Squadriglia, some of them showing camouflage on the wings, top fuselages and tails, applied in different fashions.

Above: The SAMLs of the 113ª Squadriglia at Villaverla. (Archive Caliaro)

SAML S.2 #2965
112ª Squadriglia
Autumn 1917

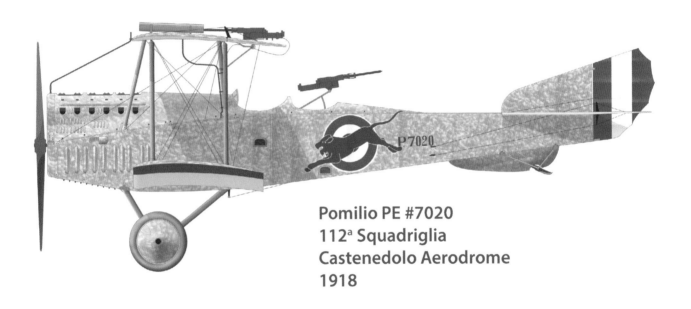

Pomilio PE #7020
112ª Squadriglia
Castenedolo Aerodrome
1918

SAML S.2 #2958
113ª Squadriglia

SAML S.2 '6'
113ᵃ Squadriglia

SAML S.2 S.2522
114ᵃ Squadriglia

Pomilio PE P.22039
114ᵃ Squadriglia
Summer 1918

114ª Squadriglia

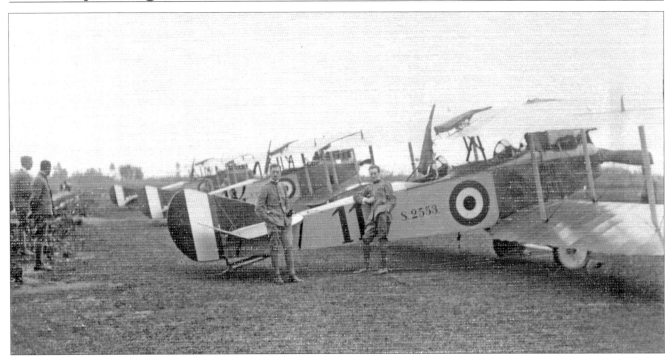

Above: SAML aircraft of the 114ª Squadriglia; the first one is serial 2553.

The order to form the 114ª Squadriglia, fourth of the new SAML squadrons, was issued on 12 March 1917 but this unit was born at Campoformido only on 1 July. It was equipped with SAML S.2, at the command of *cap.* Giuseppe Parvo Passu, and initially it was assigned to the X Gruppo, for reconnaissance and for the defense of Udine, directly reporting to the Comando Supremo. The 114ª replaced the 111ª shifted to the Balkans and it took over the latter's equipment. The pilots were *tenenti* Mario Oltolini, Mario Vannuccini, Arturo Freddi Cavalletti, *s.ten.* Angelo Brondolo, *serg.* Cesare Cattani. They were soon joined by *m.llo* Pietro Rovera, *ten.* Dario Armanino, *cpr.* Enrico Fiore and *serg.* Marino Campolmi and observers *ten.* Emilio Benini and Agostino Ancillotto.

The first combat flight was on 9 July, with the crew of *cap.* Parvo Passu and *ten.* Benini. The 114ª was employed for the protection of Udine, so it also received a night defense flight formed on 31 July 1917 with SP and Farman, and manned by pilots *ten.* Pietro Piras, *s.ten.* Antonio Cesa, *serg.*m. Giuseppe Sandri, *serg.* Licinio Bornacin.

The 114ª was active in August during the battle of the Bainsizza. On 25 August 1917 an enemy fighter above Lokve repeatedly attacked the SAML of Freddi Cavalletti, with pilot *ten.* Piras who had volunteered to fly as observer. The fighter riddled with its bullets the SAML, Piras was repeatedly wounded but he returned fire. Freddi Cavalletti, targeted also by artillery, managed to crash land saving both his companion and the notes from their reconnaissance. Author of the attack was the Austrian ace Brumowski on KD 28.69 but this certain victory was not confirmed to him.

Four aircraft of the 114ª bombed the forest of Panovizza on 28 August, and seven aircraft went to the Podgora on 4 September, four to bomb and three to observe, but during this mission the SAML of *serg.* Mario Doria and *ten.* Antonio Mangano met an enemy airplane, probably of Flik 2/D, and had a long duel. A bullet slightly wounded Doria, going through his helmet, engine and radiator were hit and the SAML force landed at Medeol.

On 14 September 1917 the 114ª Squadriglia was assigned to the II Gruppo, although remaining at Campoformido. On 10 October 1917 *cpr.* Enrico Fiore and *ten. oss.* Agostino Ancillotto out on a reconnaissance went missing in the area of Tolmino. Their SAML was shot down in unknown circumstances, Ancillotto was killed and Fiore was taken prisoner.

On 16 October *cap.* Francesco Forquet became commander, replacing *cap.* Parvo Passu. On 22 October the 114ª sent out four aircraft for a long-range reconnaissance, one of the many that failed to discover the preparation of the Austro-German offensive. In the confused combats that developed on 25 October, fighters shot down the SAML of *serg. pil.* Marino Campolmi, who died of wounds on 28 November, while his observer *s.ten.* Angelo Federici was wounded. Seven aircraft went up on 26 October to strafe and bomb the advancing enemy troops. The next day the 114ª Squadriglia retreated to Aviano, then to Nove di Bassano on 1 November, but it was a fighting retreat. With *cap.* Forquet there were the pilots *tenenti* Brondolo, Freddi Cavalletti, Oltolini and Vannuccini, *m.llo* Rovera and *serg.* Cattani, observers *cap.* Benini, *tenenti* Federico Forti and Camillo

Above: SAML 2522 with an unusual disposition of the national colors on the rudder. (Archive De Antoni)

Livi, observer trainees *tenenti* Sante Di Cuzzo, Gino Santoni, Urbano Fauci and Antonio Mangano, *s.ten.* Liuzzo.

From Nove the unit went to Casoni on 10 November, still assigned to the II Gruppo. On 15 November two aircraft with the crews *ten.* Oltolini and *ten. oss.* Di Cuzzo, and *ten.* Vannuccini and *s.ten. oss.* Vincenzo Volo during an escort mission to another two-seater engaged a duel with enemy fighters and managed to drive them away. On 21 November 1917, SAML 2999 of *ten. pil.* Mario Vannuccini and *ten. oss.* Mangano was shot down during an escort flight over Feltre. This was the 10th victory of the Austrian ace Stojvasljevic of Flik 16, flying Albatros 153.66. Mangano at the time was reported dead, actually he survived and he was killed in a flight accident at Mirafiori in 1920. During the period of the retreat the 114ª Squadriglia flew 26 photo reconnaissance and 12 bombing missions.

When the front settled along the Piave, the 114ª Squadriglia was assigned to the 4ª Armata, like all squadrons of the II Gruppo. On 15 December 1917 with *cap.* Francesco Fourquet there were pilots *cap.* Vittorio Fossombroni and Umberto Re, *tenenti* Freddi and Oltolini, *m.llo* Rovera, *serg.* Cattani and observers *cap.* Amerigo Fontana, *tenenti* Volo, Di Cuzzo, Forti, Brondolo, Giuseppe Cioni, *s.ten.* Federici, they flew several SAMLs, among them 2522, 2527 and 3025. At the end of the year Di Cuzzo, Oltolini and Forti left the unit.

In 1917 the 114ª Squadriglia had flown 279 missions, and no less than nine *Medaglie d'Argento* and one *Bronzo* were earned: Silver for *cap.* Parvo Passu, *tenenti* Ancillotto, Benini, Freddi Cavalletti, Mangano, Oltolini, Piras, Vannuccini, and *serg.* Campolmi, Bronze for *cpr.* Fiore.

In January 1918 the 114ª Squadriglia at Casoni was active over the Grappa and the Asiago plateau. In this period, it operated without escort. From 17 to 26 February 1918, it was based at Isola di Carturo (today Isola Mantegna), from 26 February to 30 March at San Pelagio, where it was used to provide cooperation training for the infantry. On 1 March *cap.* Vittorio Fossombroni became commander.

In March la 114ª Squadriglia was assigned to the 2ª Armata, and on the 30th it moved from San Pelagio to Istrana entering the new XIX Gruppo together with the 118ª. On 5 April 1918 SAML 2547 was lost in a crash, and another accident on 19 May wrote off SAML 2551. At this time the 114ª Squadriglia was in a deep crisis, for lack of personnel, it had a single observer, *ten.* Celeste Pecchini, who managed to give the necessary support to artillery. With its forces rebuilt, the 114ª took part in the Battle of the Piave, taking important photographs of the bridge at Villa Jacur, among else. In the Battle of Mid-June this unit took 254 photographs, dropped 150 bombs and shot 2,750 rounds, and all its aircraft returned more or less hit. On 21 June SAML 2553 went into a flat spin and crashed wounding its pilot *soldato* Ruggero Magro and the observer *ten.* Luigi Colecchia.

On 1 July the 114ª Squadriglia had *cap.* Fossombroni, commander, *cap.* Re, *m.llo* Rovera, *sergenti* Luigi Barella, Cesare Cattani, Francesco Cerrato, Vittorio Ferraro, Enrico Pozzi, *cpr.* Alfredo Villa, *soldati* Ruggero Magro, Liberato Pilloni, G.Battista Rabellotti, Mario Maresca and Guido Granelli, and observers *tenenti* Cioni, Colecchia, Armando Ferroni, Pecchini, Sorrentino, and *s.ten.* Catullo Soldati, with SAML 2553, 2558, 2569, 3083, 19043 and Pomilio PD 3908. In July in fact the 114ª began conversion on the

Above: A closer view of SAML 2522, the pilot is *ten*. Umberto Re, an important pioneer of aviation. (Archive De Antoni)

Pomilio, using three of them, a PE, a double controls PE and a double controls PD, formerly of the 115ᵃ (the latter unit didn't want the Pomilio so it took over the SAMLs of the 114ᵃ).

The 114ᵃ Squadriglia was passed over to the 8ᵃ Armata as artillery squadron, assigned to the XXVII Corpo d'Armata. The pilots who converted on the Pomilio were Fossombroni, Re, *ten*. Angelo Brondolo, *m.llo* Rovera, *sergenti* Luigi Casati, Cerrato, Ferraro, Cristoforo Manenti, Anselmo Montagna, Pilloni, Pozzi, Rabellotti, Ugo Santini, *sold*. Guido Granelli, Ruggero Magro.

Passage on the Pomilio was particularly troublesome and many troop pilots were rejected from flying. The 114ᵃ Squadriglia managed to fly only two war missions in August, seven in September when conversion was completed. Meanwhile its observers flew with aircraft of the 23ᵃ and 115ᵃ Squadriglia, because the 114ᵃ still had very few airplanes.

In October it was efficient again and ready for the final offensive. During the preparation it flew 14 artillery spotting flights, a remarkable mission was on Cison di Valmarino, spotting for 381-mm naval cannons (built for the *Caracciolo*

class battleships that were never completed). Together with Pomilios 7812, 13722, 18421, 18496, 18505, 18520, 18538, 19059, 19074, 19081 and 21993, the 114ᵃ received its first Fiat R.2. Its observers now were *tenenti* Colecchia, Ferroni, Mario Melano, Luigi Pane, Pecchini, Soldati, Sorrentino, and *s.tenenti* Ernesto Luzzato and Efrem Cantoni. During the Battle of Vittorio Veneto, the 114ᵃ shot 102 photographs, dropped 241 bombs and strafed enemy troops. On 30 October 1918 the new Fiat R.2 8509 of the veteran and expert pilot *maresciallo* Pietro Rovera and *ten. oss.* Giuseppe Cioni was lost. The two airmen were considered missing after a strafing mission at Sacile, victims of enemy ground fire.

The 114ᵃ Squadriglia flew 195 war missions in 1918, for a total of 474 in the war, including 349 visual observations, 46 artillery spottings, 7 escort flights. It had shot 2,070 photographs, dropped 480 bombs and 94.000 leaflets and shot 9,540 rounds. It had combat losses, but not a single fatal accident. During the last year of war decorations of this unit were *Argento* to *cap*. Forquet, *tenenti* Giuseppe Cioni and Camillo Livi, *m.llo* Rovera, and to *serg*. Cattani, *s.ten*. Ferroni, *ten*. Celeste Pecchini and *ten. oss.* Catullo Soldati. The 114ᵃ Squadriglia was disbanded on 6 February 1919.

Above: A concentration of Pomilios and SAMLs of different squadrons, including the 114ª, at Casoni airfield, possibly for the large mission of 7 December 1917.

Casualties and Combat Losses of the 114ª Squadriglia

Date	Place	Aircraft	Crew	Cause
25.8.1917	?	SAML	*Ten.* Freddi UNH, *ten.* Piras WIA	Fighters
4.9.1917	Liga/Kisa	SAML	*Serg.* Doria WIA, *ten.* Mangano UNH	Fighters
10.10.1917	Plezzo	SAML	*Cpr.* Fiore POW, *ten.* Ancillotto KIA	Unknown
25.10.1917	Sabotino	SAML	*Serg.* Campolmi DOW, *ten.* Federici WIA	Fighters
21.11.1917	Feltre	SAML 2999	*Ten.*Vannuccini KIA *ten.* Mangano POW	Fighters
21.6.1918	?	SAML 2553	*Sold.* Magro WIC, *ten.* Colecchia WIC	Accident?
30.10.1918	Sacile	R.2 8509	*M.llo* Rovera KIA, *ten.* Cioni KIA	Ground fire

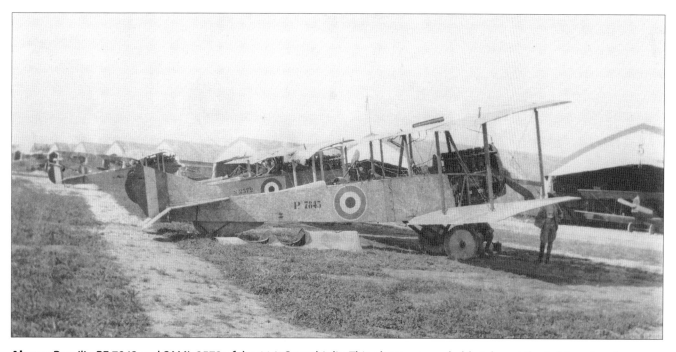

Above: Pomilio PE 7843 and SAML 2572 of the 114ª Squadriglia. This photo was probably taken at the Rubiera depot.

Above: Pomilio PE 22039 of the 114ª Squadriglia. The airman is *cap*. Napoleone Del Duca, commander of the XIX Gruppo to which the 114ª Squadriglia belonged.

115ª Squadriglia

Above: SAML S.1 of the 115ª Squadriglia at Nove di Bassano.

The 115ª Squadriglia was activated at the Centro Formazione Squadriglie of Arcade airfield on 17 August 1917 at the command of the gallant *cap. pil.* Luigi Sella (formerly an observer of the 3ª Aviatik and 31ª Farman, who in the first semester of 1917 had got his pilot brevet at Cascina Costa). The 115ª was equipped with SAMLs with Fiat A12 200 hp engine, and on 23 August it went to Nove di Bassano as part of the VII Gruppo. Its pilots were *cap.* Renato Pascale, *ten.* Ludovico Castiglioni, *s.ten.* Severo Milani, *serg.m.* Matteo Fabbian, *sergenti* Ubaldo Lenzi, Martinelli and Pilade Nebbia, and its observers were *tenenti* Umberto Benvegnù Pasini and Orazio Giannini and *sottotenenti* Leonida Bernardi, Andrea Ferraris and Ennio Silenzi.

Initially it deployed two Sezioni at Nove di Bassano with the VII Gruppo and a third one at Cavazzo Carnico, which was later taken away to complete the strength of the 113ª Squadriglia. On 30 August its Sezioni moved from Nove to Villaverla and took over the local 1ª Sezione of the 113ª, (pilots *cap.* Van Axel Castelli, *ten.* Alberto Iacopini and *asp.* Filippo Rossi, observer *ten.* Antonio Tassinari) and then the 115ª joined the XII Gruppo. In September however the squadron split up again like before: two Sezioni returned to Nove and operated with the VII Gruppo, leaving the 3ª Sezione at Villaverla for the XII Gruppo.

On 15 October *cap.* Sella became acting commander of the I Gruppo. On 20 October finally the 115ª Squadriglia reunited all its flights at Villaverla. On 11 November three Austrian fighters attacked *serg.* Nebbia, in a reconnaissance over Cima Vezzena with *ten.* Benvegnù Pasini, but the Italians managed to return to base.

On 17 November 1917 the fighters of Flik 55/J met a formation of three SAML with the escort of two Ni.27 of the 79ª Squadriglia and shot down SAML 2935 of *cap. pil.* Ludovico Castiglioni and *ten.* Umberto Benvegnù Pasini on SAML 2935. The two airmen were killed, 19th victory for ace Julius Arigi and 4th for Jószef Maier. The next day, 18 November, *ten. oss.* Enrico Silenzi was killed flying on the airplane of Sella, SAML 2941, that returned bringing the dead observer. Their adversaries were again Arigi, Josef Kiss and Maier. But the crucible of the 115ª went on: SAML 2952 of *ten.* Tullio Lowy and *ten. pil.* Severo Milani was shot down on 27 November by fighters of Flik 55/J, 13th victory for József Kiss and 3rd for Georg Kenzian. *Ten.* Battaini and *s.ten.* Achenza, who were with them on an S.1, dueled for 20 minutes with an enemy fighter and survived, complaining that their escort, two Spads of 71ª Squadriglia, had deserted them.

On 8 December 1917 the whole squadron moved to San Pietro in Gu where it joined the new XV Gruppo, tasked with *ricognizione d'Armata*, that is, strategical reconnaissance. *Cap. pil.* Renato Pascale became the new commander, replacing Sella who was now commander of the I Gruppo. Pascale was considered a daring pilot and a good commander.

On 16 December 1917 four SAMLs set off to bomb and attack the enemy in Val Goccia; the SAML of *serg.m. pil.* Matteo Fabbian and *s.ten. oss.* Orazio Giannini was lost over Arsiè, shot down in flames during a strafing in Valle Goccia by Julius Arigi, of Flik 55/J, his 25th victory, by Kiss, his 17th and by Franz Lahner, his 3rd victory.

Above & Below: The dramatic view of SAML 2941 returned from combat on 18 November 1917 with its fuselage stained by the blood of *s.ten*. Silenzi.

Above: SAML 2567 of *cap*. Reboa with his personal insignia, the flag of Elba Island, where he was born, with Napoleon's three gold bees on a red band.

By the end of the year, the personnel of the 115ª Squadriglia consisted of commander *cap*. Renato Pascale, pilots *cap*. Alberto Iacopini, *cap*. Amedeo De Sanctis (just nominally, as he was commander of the VII Gruppo) *ten*. Serafino Battaini, *sergenti* Lenzi, Nebbia, Guido Borghi, *cpr*. Vincelli and observers *ten*. Bernardi and *sottotenenti* Stefano Achenza, Carmelo Di Bella, Andrea Ferraris, Mario Guida, Arnaldo Molaschi, Gino Santoni and Donato Sardi. In the period of the defensive battle, 2 November to 16 December, the 115ª Squadriglia flew 20 bombing and 43 reconnaissance and strafing missions and had seven casualties. Five *Medaglie d'Argento* rewarded these sacrifices, to Benvegnù Pasini, Castiglioni, Milani, Silenzi and *cap*. Sella.

On 18 January 1918, five fighters attacked the SAML of *serg. pil*. Lenzi and *ten*. Achenza, the Italians managed to damage one of them and to escape the other ones, returning to base with a badly damaged aircraft. Their adversaries were the Phönix of Flik 60/J lead by Frank Linke-Crawford who claimed his 14th victory. A similar adventure befell on 26 January the SAML of *cap. pil*. Ludovico Andreuzzi who, bounced by six fighters, managed to get away and returned badly damaged. These were the Albatros of Flik 55/J again, and Kiss claimed his 19th victory. In this period, during the offensive of Mount Valbella, the 115ª Squadriglia had only

one efficient airplane, but managed to fly twelve combat missions. On 28 January five German fighters attacked above Gallio the SAML of *serg*. Nebbia and *cap*. Enrico Branchi, without success. The SAML of Nebbia and *ten*. Molaschi was attacked again on 20 February in Val Campomulo.

On 1 March 1918 the 115ª, assigned to the Comando Truppe Altipiani (Command of the troops of the plateaus) had three airplanes, four pilots and four observers: *cap*. Pascale and *cap*. Andreuzzi, *serg*. Lenzi, *serg*. Nebbia, *cap. oss*. Silvio Morelli, *tenenti* Sebastiano Cardiel, Achenza and Molaschi. On 18 March 1918 the 115ª left the field of San Pietro in Gu to the squadrons of the VII Gruppo and moved to San Luca (Treviso) tasked for the *ricognizione d'Armata* for the 8ª Armata.

On 27 April SAML 3075 crashed for an engine failure, killing *cap*. Ludovico Andreuzzi who had taken off to drop leaflets on the troops on Saint Mark's Day, while *ten*. Molaschi was wounded.

In June 1918, during the Battle of the Piave the 115ª made its three SAMLs available to other squadrons. On 1 July with *magg*. Pascale there were the pilots *cap*. Pietro Botta and Mario Reboa, *tenenti* M. Celleri, Dario Trabucco, Felice Ragno, Luigi Monti, *sergenti* Lenzi, Nebbia, Cristoforo Manenti, *caporali* Roberto Alba and Giuseppe Bocconi,

Above: *Ten.* Angelo Vassalli in a SAML with an insignia on the deck of the fuselage. (Collection Mirko Sernaglia)

soldato Ugo Santini, and the observers *cap.* Morelli, *tenenti* Achenza, Giuseppe Cioni, Molaschi and Guido Sampietro, later joined by pilots *cpr.* Anselmo Montagna and Giuseppe Guglielmotta, *sold.* Luigi Casati, observers *tenenti* Augusto Millozza and Angelo Vassalli, *s.ten.* Giuseppe Mazzesi from the disbanded 139ª Squadriglia; observers *tenenti* Sante Di Cuzzo, Gino Santoni and Vincenzo Volo from the 114ª Squadriglia.

Since 4 June the 115ª Squadriglia started conversion on the Pomilio, having received Pomilio PD 3923 and 3954 and Pomilio PE 7848, 13602, 13803 and 13828. but the unit fell in a deep crisis of equipment and morale. It could not participate in the battle of mid-June, but it leased its three remaining SAMLs with their crews to other squadrons. In the first two weeks of July, it had to be reorganized, so it received all the SAMLs of the 114ª and 118ª Squadriglia and gave away its much-disliked Pomilios. Without the Pomilio it couldn't do strategic reconnaissance, so it was tasked with infantry service for the VIII and XXVIII Corpo d'Armata of the 8ª Armata, and it trained in co-operation with the troops.

On 4 August 1918 *serg.* Lenzi was badly wounded when his SAML S.2 19043 went into a spin. On 5 August the 115ª moved from San Luca to Fossalunga, with its SAML, its ten pilots and twelve observers and it was tasked with liaison with the infantry. On 28 August enemy ground fire seriously

damaged the SAML of *serg.* Nebbia and *ten.* Quercia near Moriago but they flew on and completed their mission. It spent the summer doing exercises training the units of the VIII and XXVII Army Corps in cooperation with airplanes.

On 14 September 1918 *cap.* Pietro Botta became the commander. Sixteen SAMLs were in service in September for the pilots *cap.* Reboa, *tenenti* Luigi Monti and Filippo Palange, *sergenti* Dositeo Meazza, Nebbia, Gian Battista Trucco and Filippo Veronesi, and *cpr.* Mario Maresca, the seven observers were *tenenti* Vincenzo Balsamo, Ernesto Faggi, Fusconi, Alfredo Knight, Gaetano Leonesi, Nicola Tedesco and *s.ten.* Vito Rastelli.

Ten. Tedesco was discovered having lied when on two missions, Oct. 7 and 12, he did not drop leaflets over Sernaglia but within the Italian lines, and he was sent back to infantry.

The 115ª Squadriglia was active flying reconnaissance and ground attack missions in the final phase of the war. From August to October, it flew 180 photo reconnaissance, 15 bombing and 16 visual observation missions, often carrying observers of the other Squadriglie of the XIX Gruppo (114ª and 118ª) that had not completed their conversion on the Pomilio PE. Three more SAMLs arrived from the 121ª, serials 2524, 3008 and 3116 with their pilots *sergenti* Giuseppe Negri, Claudio Mazzanti and Lorenzo Mercati.

Above: A SAML of the 115ª Squadriglia at Nove di Bassano; the tall steeples of the churches of every town in Veneto allow identification of the locality.

On 28 October the unit flew special missions to drop 25,600 bullets to the Brigata Cuneo isolated at Molin Ripetto and four other flights to drop food and clothing to a platoon of *arditi* (assault troops) surrounded on the banks of the Piave in front of Nervesa. During the final offensive the 115ª Squadriglia provided 15 infantry liaison, 50 reconnaissance, 15 bombing and 15 air supply flights.

At the end of the war the 115ª Squadriglia had at Fossalunga nineteen SAMLs (including serials 2989, 2985, 3008, 3091, 3096, 20356, 20572, 20576, 20575, 20582) and one Fiat R.2, 8502, delivered on 22 October. Operations in 1918 brought decorations: *Medaglia d'Arg*ento for cap. oss. Enrico Branchi, *tenenti* Achenza, Di Cuzzo, Lenzi and *serg.* Pilade Nebbia, and *Medaglie di Bronzo* for *magg.* Renato Pascale, *capitani* Morelli, Andreuzzi, Botta, *tenenti* Mazzesi, Millozza, Molaschi, *s.ten.* Filippo Veronesi. *sergenti* Cattani, Meazza, *cpr.* Filippo Rosati, and Alfredo Villa. The scoreboard of the 115ª Squadriglia reports 1.038 reconnaissance and spotting sorties, 186 bombings, 193 strafing and supply dropping sorties.

Casualties and Combat Losses of the 115ª Squadriglia

Date	Place	Aircraft	Crew	Cause
17.11.1917	Cima Ecker	SAML 2935	*Cap.* Castiglioni KIA, *ten.* Benvegnù KIA	Fighters
18.11.1917	Trentino	SAML 2941	*Cap.* Sella UNH, *s.ten.* Silenzi KIA	Fighters
27.11.1917	Trentino	SAML 2952	*Ten.* Milani KIA, *ten.* Lowy KIA	Fighters
16.12.1917	Valle Goccia	SAML	*Serg.* Fabbian KIA, *ten.* Giannini KIA	Fighters
18.1.1918	Valstagna	SAML	*Serg.* Lenzi UNH, *ten.* Achenza UNH	Fighters
26.1.1918	Monte Alagna	SAML	*Ten.* Andreuzzi UNH, *ten.* Molaschi UNH	Fighters
27.4.1918	San Luca	SAML 3075	*Cap.* Andreuzzi KIC, *ten.* Molaschi WIC	Accident
4.8.1918	San Luca	SAML 19043	*Serg.* Lenzi WIC	Accident

From 30 November 1918 the 115ª belonged to the XIX Gruppo. In March 1919 it moved to Campoformido going to the XX Gruppo. At the end of 1919, when commander was *ten.* Giuseppe Gennari, it was part of the Gruppo da Ricognizione Tattica and Strategica, together with the 58ª, 59ª, 87ª, 113ª and 121ª Squadriglia. On 1 April 1921 it moved to "Fausto Pesci" airport of Bologna, where it remained until World War 2, except for a one-year period at Ferrara, progressively equipped with Ansaldo A.300, Romeo Ro.1, Fiat A.120, and Romeo Ro.37.

Above: SAML of the 115ª Squadriglia with camouflaged top wings at Fossalunga.

Above: The 115ª Squadriglia received in October 1918 from the 112ª Squadriglia this SAML, 2524, with a unique camouflage.

Above: The gallant *serg.* Pilade Nebbia in a camouflaged SAML, which unusually is equipped with a Scarff TO.3 ring for the defensive gun.

The 115ᵃ Squadriglia received some Pomilios, but did not like them, and remained equipped with SAMLs until the early '20s.

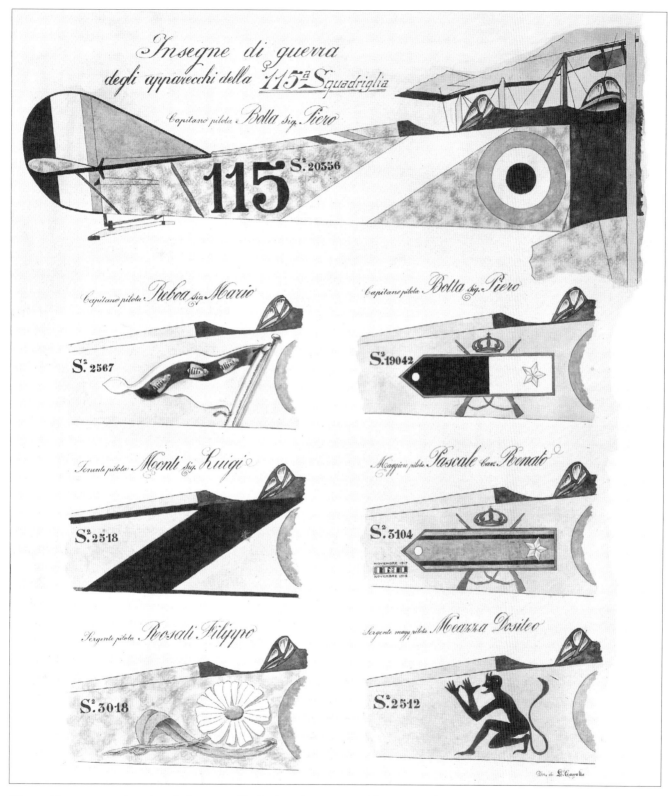

Above: The commands ordered all personal insignia to be presented for approval; some drawings have survived, like these ones for the 115ᵃ Squadriglia.

SAML S.2 S.2542
Serg. **Dositeo Meazza**
115ª Squadriglia

SAML S.2 S.2548
Ten. **Luigi Monti**
115ª Squadriglia

SAML S.2 S.2567
Cap. **Mario Reboa**
115ª Squadriglia
July 1918

SAML S.2 S.3018
Serg. Filippo Rosati
115ª Squadriglia

SAML S.2 S.3014
Mag. Renato Pascale
115ª Squadriglia

SAML S.2 S.19042
Cap. Piero Bolla
115ª Squadriglia

Above: A SAML of the 115ª Squadriglia with a personal insignia, the collar tabs of an infantry brigade, possibly the Brigata Lucca, in amaranth and white. The original caption locates the picture at Porcellengo, a village halfway between Istrana and Quinto di Treviso, where no airfield is known to be located.

Below: A camouflaged SAML of the 115ª Squadriglia with a monkey painted on its fuselage. The airplane is unarmed, and the photo may be post-war. (Archive Emiliani)

Printed in Great Britain
by Amazon